D0455703

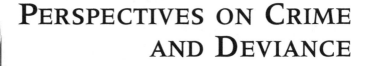

PERSPECTIVES ON CRIME AND DEVIANCE

THIRD EDITION

Allen E. Liska
University at Albany, State University of New York

Steven F. Messner
University at Albany, State University of New York

PRENTICE HALL, UPPER SADDLE RIVER, NEW JERSEY 07458

Library of Congress Cataloging-in-Publication Data

LISKA, ALLEN E.
    Perspectives on crime and deviance/Allen E. Liska, Steven F. Messner.—3rd ed.
        p.   cm.
    Rev. ed. of: Perspectives on deviance/Allen E. Liska. 2nd ed. © 1987
    Includes bibliographical references and index.
    ISBN 0-13-235771-2
    1. Deviant behavior.   2. Crime—Sociological aspects.
    I. Messner, Steven F.   II. Liska, Allen E. Perspectives on deviance.   III. Title.
    HM291.L553   1999
    302.5'42—dc21   98-6254
                                                                                 CIP

Editorial director: Charlyce Jones Owen
Editor in chief: Nancy Roberts
Acquisitions editor: John Chillingworth
Managing editor: Sharon Chambliss
Marketing manager: Christopher DeJohn
Editorial/production supervision
    and electronic page makeup: Kari Callaghan Mazzola
Interior design and electronic art creation: John P. Mazzola
Cover director: Jayne Conte
Cover designer: Bruce Kenselaar
Buyer: Mary Ann Gloriande

This book was set in 10/12 Meridien by Big Sky Composition
and was printed and bound by Courier Companies, Inc.
The cover was printed by Phoenix Color Corp.

Prentice Hall

© 1999, 1987, 1981 by Prentice-Hall, Inc.
Upper Saddle River, New Jersey 07458

Previously published under the title of *Perspectives on Deviance*.

Printed in the United States of America
10   9   8   7   6   5   4

ISBN 0-13-235771-2

PRENTICE-HALL INTERNATIONAL (UK) LIMITED, *London*
PRENTICE-HALL OF AUSTRALIA PTY. LIMITED, *Sydney*
PRENTICE-HALL CANADA INC., *Toronto*
PRENTICE-HALL HISPANOAMERICANA, S.A., *Mexico*
PRENTICE-HALL OF INDIA PRIVATE LIMITED, *New Delhi*
PRENTICE-HALL OF JAPAN, INC., *Tokyo*
PRENTICE-HALL ASIA PTE. LTD., *Singapore*
EDITORA PRENTICE-HALL DO BRASIL, LTDA., *Rio de Janeiro*

CONTENTS

PREFACE

Our basic purpose in preparing a third edition of *Perspectives on Crime and Deviance* (previously entitled *Perspectives on Deviance*) has been to bring the material up-to-date, while retaining those features of earlier editions that have given the book its distinctive character. The underlying structure of the book remains unchanged—that is, the book is organized theoretically. Each of the main chapters explicates a major perspective on crime and deviance that has its roots in general sociological theory. In addition, the respective chapters illustrate how theory informs research and how both theory and research stimulate public policies to reduce crime and deviance.

Also consistent with earlier editions, we do not attempt to provide encyclopedic reviews of the literature but rather focus on selected studies that serve as examples of efforts to apply the respective theories. We have become ever more convinced, on the basis of our previous experience in using the book in the classroom, that it is less important for students to know the details of the research literature (i.e., "who said and did what") than it is for them to understand the logic underlying theories and the kinds of research strategies that have evolved to test these theories. We use "serial cites" in the text to provide a springboard for more extensive searches of the literature. These references are likely to be particularly useful for graduate students.

There are, nevertheless, a few general changes introduced in the third edition. As reflected on the title page, the book is now co-authored. While Allen E. Liska authored the first two editions, Steven F. Messner has taken the lead in updating the third edition while retaining the book's unique organization. And, as implied by the change in title, greater emphasis is placed on "crime" as a specific form of deviance. This change has been prompted by the increased prominence of theory and research on crime within the sociology of deviance, reflected at the institutional level in the emergence and expansion of programs in criminology and criminal justice. Despite this change in emphasis, we continue to call attention to the generality of most theories that have been applied to crime and to draw upon selected illustrations pertaining to other forms of deviance (e.g., suicide, mental disorders).

In addition, we have updated examples and statistics and have incorporated new material on topics of special importance today. In particular, we have expanded the use of comparative and historical illustrations, and given greater attention to issues pertaining to race and gender (e.g., differential social control, family violence).

Each chapter has undergone some major updating. With respect to more specific changes, the principal revision in Chapter 1 is a thorough updating of the material on biological and psychological theories. Given the sociological focus of the book, this discussion continues to be brief, but the revised text reflects contemporary work in these areas.

An important change in Chapter 2, "The Structural/Functional Perspective," is the introduction of new material reflecting the revived interest in the anomie/strain perspective that has occurred over the past decade. Topics include Agnew's "general strain theory" and various efforts to elaborate the basic Mertonian anomie framework (e.g., applications to white-collar and organizational crime, efforts to recapture the macrolevel character of traditional anomie theory).

The title of Chapter 3 has been changed from "The Chicago Perspective" to "Ecological Perspectives: Social Disorganization, Control, and Learning Processes." Consistent with the earlier editions, the chapter covers theories that deal with community social organization and social control. The more general conceptualization of the perspective, however, allows us to deal with a broader range of topics that fall within the ecological tradition (in both its micro and macrolevel variants) but that are not necessarily part of the classical Chicago school. Such topics include "routine activities" theory, "life course" theory, "power-control" theory, and "self-control" theory. The policy section gives greater attention to neighborhood decline and community crime prevention, and strategies for "designing out" crime.

Chapter 4 has also been reconceptualized in a broader manner, as reflected in a title change from "The Deterrence Perspective" to "The Rational Choice/Deterrence Perspective." The chapter incorporates selected work by economists on crime to complement the traditional deterrence approach. Recent research on capital punishment and on arrests for domestic violence has been added, along with an extended discussion of imprisonment and incapacitation.

Chapter 5, "The Labeling Perspective," incorporates recent theoretical developments, such as Link, Cullen, and colleagues' "modified labeling theory" of mental disorders, and Braithwaite's work on "reintegrative shaming." The research section has been extended to cover recent studies that attempt to integrate labeling processes with more conventional etiological approaches and that apply the labeling perspective to nonwestern societies.

The title of Chapter 6 has been changed from "The Ethnomethodology Perspective" to "The Constructionist Perspective," reflecting changes in the field. The theory section of this chapter now includes discussions of the experiential understanding of deviance, the construction of social rules, and the construction of social problems. This shift in emphasis is reflected in the research section, which includes contemporary illustrations of the constructionist approach.

Chapter 7, "The Conflict Perspective," retains the basic structure of previous editions. The major change is to give greater emphasis to race and gender stratification as bases of social conflict. This is reflected in the theory section and in the review of research on the differential application of law by class, race, and gender. Also, new case studies on interest groups and law creation have been added.

Chapter 8, the concluding chapter, has been completely redone. It is now composed of two main sections: a discussion of the rise and fall of theoretical perspectives and a commentary on the prospects for integrating perspectives, a contemporary concern. The chapter concludes with some speculative remarks about future directions in the study of crime and deviance.

Our hope is that this third edition will expose students to the classic insights and key contemporary works on crime and deviance, and will communicate to them the excitement and vitality of this field of social scientific inquiry.

ACKNOWLEDGMENTS

We would like to thank colleagues who used earlier editions of the textbook, many of whom have told us what they liked and disliked about the book. We are also grateful to the reviewers of our prospectus and of the first draft of this edition. Numerous students over the years have offered comments on the book and have provided valuable ideas for revisions. We are grateful to Nancy Roberts at Prentice Hall for her sustained encouragement for a third edition. We also wish to acknowledge that the discussion of theoretical integration in Chapter 8 draws upon an essay written in collaboration with our colleague here at Albany, Marvin D. Krohn. Finally, we thank our spouses for their much-needed support during the long ordeal of revising the book.

INTRODUCTION

SUBJECT MATTER OF STUDY

The subject matter of "deviance" encompasses an incredibly wide range of behavior. Textbooks and readers on deviance cover topics as diverse as street crime, alcohol and drug abuse, deranged behavior, prostitution, suicide, homosexual acts, and police lying (Kelly 1996; Little 1995). Although the commonality underlying these behaviors is difficult to identify, sociologists have attempted to formally demarcate an area of study that captures their common meaning. One basic approach to this definitional task is reflected in the following quotes:

> According to any standard dictionary—still the best source of clearly stated nominal definitions—to deviate is to stray as from a path or standard. (Matza 1969, 10)

> [D]eviant behavior refers to conduct that departs significantly from the norms set for people in their social statuses. (Merton 1971, 824)

While different in some respects, the common theme underlying these definitions is the notion that deviance involves norm or rule violation.

Another approach to the conceptualization of deviance gained prominence in the 1960s and 70s and remains influential today. According to this perspective, deviance is best understood as a social definition:

> The deviant is one to whom that label has successfully been applied; deviant behavior is behavior that people so label. (Becker 1963, 9)

> What deviance *is* does not depend on the inner, intrinsic, or inherent properties an act (or, less often, a condition) might have—that is objec-

tive characteristics. Instead, what makes an act deviant is what certain
people (or audiences) make of that act—what they think and how they
react to it.... What makes an action (or condition) deviant is the actual
or potential condemnation that it would attract from observers or 'audiences.' (Goode 1996, 8)

These latter definitions shift attention from deviance as a pattern of behavior to deviance as a social definition or label that some people use to
describe the behavior of others. The study of deviance as a norm violation
and as a social definition constitutes the sociology of deviance.

DEVIANCE AS NORM VIOLATION

To be a bit more precise, the study of norm violations refers to the study of
behavior that violates social rules and the study of the individuals who violate these rules. In principle, the violation of all rules of social behavior is
the subject of study: rules against socially harmful behavior, such as homicide, as well as rules against relatively innocuous behavior, such as spitting
in public; and rules adhered to by most members of society as well as rules
adhered to by small groups or single organizations, such as the rules of
classroom etiquette or the work rules at the Ford Corporation. In practice,
however, research has focused on rules adhered to by most members of
society, particularly by the middle and upper classes.

The study of norm violations can be divided into norm-violation rates
and individual norm violations. The former refers to norm violations for
sociopolitical units (neighborhoods, cities, counties, states, and nations) and
is usually expressed as the number of violations standardized by population
size (e.g., the number per thousand or hundred thousand population).
Various questions about norm violation rates are asked: (1) What are the
rates? Are they higher in some areas than others? Are they increasing or
decreasing? (2) What are the social correlates of high and low rates and of
increasing and decreasing rates? Do norm-violation rates, for example, correlate with the age structure or the racial, ethnic, and social class composition of a city, state, or nation? (3) What are the consequences of high and
low norm-violation rates on community life? Can a high crime rate, for
example, disrupt community life by creating fear in people, or can it build
community solidarity by posing a common problem to which community
action can be directed? (4) Finally, why are rates higher in one city, state,
or nation than in another? Why, for example, is the homicide rate generally higher in southern than in northern U.S. cities? Why is it higher in the
United States than in Canada or Japan? Why is it increasing in some
nations and decreasing in others?

The second major area of study concerns individual norm violations.
Essentially, the same types of questions are asked. Who are the norm violators? What characterizes people who violate norms (alcoholics, drug
addicts, child molesters, tax evaders)? Are they male or female, old or

young, black or white, rich or poor? Most significantly, why do people violate social norms? Why do different people violate different norms to varying degrees? Why do some people violate a norm only once or sporadically while others engage in regular and systematic violations?

Courses on norm violations in the social sciences are related and frequently overlap. It is difficult for students, and in some cases for professors, to clearly differentiate between courses entitled "deviance," "social problems," "criminology," and "sociology of mental disorders." This section further demarcates the study of norm violations by distinguishing it from the study of social problems, crime, and psychological abnormality.

Social problems are social conditions that citizens or governmental officials evaluate negatively and wish to change. While numerous norm violations are regarded as social problems, such as delinquency, drug addiction, prostitution, and robbery, norm violations and social problems are not equivalent. On the one hand, many social problems do not involve norm violations. For example, traffic congestion, water and air pollution, residential slums, disease, migration, economic depression, and war are certainly social problems, but they do not involve norm violations. On the other hand, many norm violations are not considered serious enough to be social problems, such as conversational discourtesy, jaywalking, and profanity.

Crime refers to behavior that violates the law. In a literal sense, all crime constitutes norm violation because crime is defined with reference to the formal law, which is a codified body of rules or norms. However, given the processes by which laws are formulated in most legal entities, the laws "on the books" do not necessarily reflect the day-to-day social norms. The relationship between the technical legal rules and prevailing social norms is thus a subject of study. In the United States many crimes, such as gambling, driving over the speed limit on highways, and various sexual practices prohibited by broadly defined sodomy statutes, are not norm violations (Siegel 1995, 399). The potential discrepancy between crime and social norm violation is clearly illustrated by alcohol prohibition during the 1930s. Buying and selling alcohol was illegal, although drinking approximated a national norm, especially in urban areas. A similar situation may exist today for underage drinking, following the raising of the legal drinking age to twenty-one. On the other hand, many norm violations are not law violations, such as the expelling of air through the mouth (belching) while in the presence of others, the use of profane language, consuming alcoholic beverages at breakfast, and marriage between people of widely different ages, especially when the male is younger.

Definitions of psychological abnormality are shaped by general theoretical frameworks. Psychoanalysts define abnormality in terms of emotionality; cognitive theorists define abnormality in terms of distorted thinking and nonrational decision making; and behaviorists discuss abnormality in terms of nonproductive or maladaptive behavior. Whatever the exact definition, psychological abnormality is not equivalent to norm-violating behavior. One can suffer from emotional problems and make nonrational decisions but still conform to social norms of behavior. In fact, some psychiatrists talk of compulsive conformity. On the other hand, one can violate social norms without being psychologically abnormal. Many sociologists argue that the vast bulk of norm violations are a result not of emotional problems, cognitive distortions, or faulty decision making, but of rational decisions by emotionally healthy people, frequently for political, social, and economic gains (robbery, burglary, tax evasion, false advertising, insider trading).

To summarize, deviance as a norm violation refers to actions that can be studied in other social science courses and under other conceptual rubrics. Some norm violations are law violations; some are social problems; and some reflect psychological abnormalities. Conceptual overlap, however, is not equivalence. Many norm violations are not law violations, and many law violations are not socially meaningful norm violations; many social problems are not norm violations, and many norm violations are not social problems; and while psychological abnormality may be reflected in norm violations, not all norm violators are psychologically abnormal.

DEVIANCE AS SOCIAL DEFINITION

The study of deviance as a social definition centers on two questions: *What* is labeled deviance, and *who* is labeled deviant? The former refers to the study of the emergence and development of social norms and social labels for describing norm violations and violators, and the latter refers to the study of how such labels are used in specific cases and situations.

What is labeled deviance? While the norm-violations approach to deviance assumes that norms vary and change, it does not conceptualize normative change as an object of study. Norms simply constitute a reference point according to which behavior is judged to be deviant or nondeviant. When the norms of the different segments of society conflict (lower class versus middle class, black versus white, young versus old), the norms of the more powerful segments tend to be used as the reference point.

Sociologists who orient their research to deviance as a social definition have emphasized the emerging, changing, and conflicting character of norms. Some have focused on the historical emergence of general societal norms, asking, for example, why the norms of alcohol consumption in Italy are different from those in the United States, or why the norms of sexual behavior in Mexico are different from those in Sweden. Other sociologists have been concerned with the situational emergence of norms, arguing that general norms of behavior are frequently very ambiguous as behavioral directives in specific situations. For example, norms governing alcohol consumption vary not only from country to country and from region to region within a country but from situation to situation. The norms of proper drinking depend on the day of the week (weekend, weekday), the time of day (morning, evening), and even the amount of time elapsed at a party. Greater freedom is typically permitted as a party goes on. The same is true of sexual behavior. Flirting with someone else's spouse may be permissible at 1:00 A.M. at a party but not during the morning while grocery shopping.

Sociologists have also examined the historical emergence of social labels used to describe norm violations and violators. This is not just a quarrel over semantics but a question of how norm violations and violators are socially treated. The category "mental illness" is instructive. Today people who experience emotional problems and cognitive distortions are treated in many ways like people with a physical illness (Conrad and Schneider 1992). They are treated by experts trained in medicine (psychiatrists), quite often in a hospital setting. A similar "medicalization" can be observed for other forms of deviant behavior, such as alcohol abuse, childhood behavioral disorders, and even crime. This type of social response has not always been the case in the United States and is not now the case in all parts of the world. In the United States, at one time or another, such people have been labeled as evil, lazy, or possessed by the devil and, accordingly, have experienced a very different social response.

A special case of the question—What is labeled deviance?—is the study of legal norms (laws) and the categories used to describe law violations and violators. Special attention has focused on studying how some norms are transformed into laws, thus making some norm violators criminals (Coltrane and Hickman 1992; Michalowski and Kramer 1987; Quinney 1970). For example, marijuana smoking is illegal, but cigarette smoking and alcohol use are not. Why? Prostitution is illegal in most but not all states and cities. Why? The emergence of categories to describe law violations and violators has also been a fruitful area for study. For example, juvenile norm violators constitute a formal legal category in the United States. They are treated under a special set of legal procedures (juvenile court) and are subject to a special set of court dispositions. Why?

Who is labeled deviant? This question refers to the study of how existing categories for describing norm violators and violations are applied in specific situations (Dixon, Gordon, and Khomusi 1995; Lemert 1967; Schur 1979). Of all individuals who violate norms only some are socially identified and labeled by their families, friends, colleagues, the public, and organizational authorities. Others somehow escape the social label. Their norm violations remain socially unnoticed. Why? Under what circumstances are people identified as norm violators (delinquents, drug addicts, witches, mentally ill)? On the other hand, some conformists are falsely identified as norm violators. Why? Under what circumstances are people falsely labeled as norm violators?

These concerns are important because of the psychological and social consequences of being publicly identified—correctly or falsely—as a norm violator (drug addict, drunken driver, tax evader, embezzler). A considerable amount of study has been directed toward discovering the extent to which such public labels affect people's social relationships (family relations, friendship patterns, economic opportunities) and the extent to which this in turn influences future norm violations.

As a special case, attention has been directed toward the study of how existing legal categories are applied to individuals and the consequences of such applications. Like norm violators more generally, only some law violators are publicly identified; of those who violate laws, only some are arrested; of those arrested, only some are prosecuted; and of those prosecuted, only some are legally sanctioned. What affects the degree to which law violators become involved in the legal process and are officially labeled, and what are the psychological and social consequences of different degrees of involvement? To what extent, for example, does imprisonment or prosecution affect psychological dispositions and social relationships, and to what extent do changes in these dispositions and relationships affect future law violations?

Generally, the social definitional approach to the sociology of deviance focuses on the following questions:

I. What is labeled deviance?
   A. What are the general and situational social norms, and how have they emerged?
   B. What are the social categories and labels for describing norm violators and norm violations, and how have they emerged?
   C. As a special case of the above, what are the legal norms (laws) and legal categories for describing law violators and violations, and how have they emerged?
II. Who is labeled deviant?
   A. To whom is the label of deviant likely to be applied?
   B. What are the consequences of being labeled a deviant?
   C. As a special case of the above, who is likely to be labeled a deviant, and what are the consequences of being so labeled?

LEVELS OF EXPLANATION

Now that the subject matter of the sociology of deviance has been defined, this section presents a brief examination of biological, psychological, and social levels of explanation.

BIOLOGICAL THEORIES

Biological theories ignore the study of deviance as a social definition and focus on norm violations. In one manner or another they assert that social behavior can be explained by certain biological structures or processes. The early efforts along these lines tended to be rather simplistic, postulating highly deterministic explanations for deviance. Contemporary work in this area is much more sophisticated and is rooted in a variety of scientific disciplines including genetics, biochemistry, endocrinology, and neurophysiology (Fishbein 1990).

Much of the early work on biology and deviance was characterized by an extreme position on the age-old "nature" versus "nurture" debate. Many of these theorists assumed that the causes of deviance are essentially "programmed" into the basic structure of the individual at birth. Later deviant behavior is simply an expression of the innate, biological raw material (see Wolfgang 1960; Wilson and Herrnstein 1985; and Bartol 1995 for reviews). Contemporary biological perspectives, in contrast, emphasize the interaction between biological features of the organism and the larger environment. As one advocate of biological theories puts it, contemporary work is built upon the notion of "nature plus nurture" rather than "nature versus nurture" (Fishbein 1990, 29). The term *biosocial* is often used to refer to perspectives that incorporate an important role for both biological and socioenvironmental factors.

Contemporary biological and biosocial approaches adopt an analytic framework that gives primacy to the brain as the "controller of all behavior" (Ellis 1990, 13). Individuals basically do what their brains tell them to do. Brain functioning reflects genetic factors in interaction with both social and nonsocial environmental factors (see Figure 1.1). Consistent with this general orientation, biological and biosocial theorists employ a distinctive view of *learning* and its causal role in human behavior. Learning entails a change in the neural structure and biochemical composition of the brain (Fishbein 1990). From this perspective, then, the key to understanding deviance (or any other form of human behavior) is to identify those factors that affect brain functioning either directly or indirectly (see Jeffrey 1990, 188–210).

Much recent biological research on deviance can be organized into three areas of study: genetic predispositions, psychophysiological correlates, and biochemical correlates (Fishbein 1990). The genetic studies attempt to estimate the role of heredity in explaining deviant behavior. To do so, researchers typically study the resemblance between family members who differ in genetic makeup to varying degrees. One major type of family study

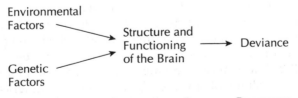

FIGURE 1.1   CAUSAL LOGIC OF THE BIOSOCIAL PERSPECTIVE

involves the comparison of identical (monozygotic, or MZ) and fraternal (dizygotic, or DZ) twins. MZ twins share 100 percent of their genes, while DZ twins share 50 percent of their genes. If a trait has an appreciable hereditary component, then the degree of similarity or "concordance" in that trait should be greater for MZ than for DZ twins, reflecting the greater genetic similarity of the former. Numerous twin studies have, in fact, reported higher concordance for MZ twins across a range of deviant behaviors, such as schizophrenia, neuroses, alcoholism, and crime (Bartol 1995, 34).

Another technique for estimating heritability is to study adoptees who are raised by unrelated, adoptive parents rather than by their biological parents. Similarity between adoptees and their adoptive parents indicates environmental factors, while similarity between adoptees and their biological parents suggests hereditary influences. Although there are limitations associated with conventional adoption designs, the results of a number of these studies are consistent with the inference of a genetic factor in crime and various psychopathologies (Fishbein 1990).

The twin and adoption studies try to establish the extent to which deviant behavior is generally attributable to biological inheritance, but they usually do not identify the specific genetic conditions that lead to such behavior. During the mid-1960s and 1970s, interest emerged in a specific genetic correlate of crime: the XYY chromosomal abnormality. The normal male complement is forty-six XY chromosomes, while the normal female complement is forty-six XX chromosomes. However, in a rare number of cases (about 1.3 per 1,000), an additional Y chromosome appears. Reports in the mid- and late 1960s noted that XYY males are tall, aggressive, and have criminal histories (Shah and Roth 1974). Additional studies reported that males with an extra Y are more prone to psychopathology and are convicted of crimes at a young age. These findings led some investigators to conclude that having an extra Y chromosome predisposes males to engage in antisocial behavior, perhaps due to excessive aggressiveness associated with the extra "maleness."

Subsequent research suggests the need for cautious conclusions about the role of the XYY chromosomal anomaly in explaining crime. The most extensive study was done in Denmark by Witkin et al. (1977). These researchers found that XYYs were more likely than controls to have records of criminal convictions. This difference, however, occurred for property crimes, not violent crimes, which is contrary to the notion of enhanced aggressiveness. The researchers did observe lower levels of measured intelligence for the XYYs. This could conceivably lead to higher involvement in property crimes, but it could also produce a greater likelihood of apprehension and hence a record of a criminal conviction. In any event, given the rarity of the XYY abnormality, it could, in principle, account for only a small proportion of the volume of deviance in contemporary America.

Genes provide the genetic blueprint for observed traits, or what geneticists call *phenotypes*. The most direct way for genes to affect behavior is through the manifestation of the genetic blueprint in the central nervous system, and in particular, in the brain—the "controller of all behavior." Genes do not completely determine the nature of the brain and central nervous system. As noted earlier, contemporary biological theorists assume that all observed biological traits reflect the interaction between genes and the environment.

A second area of study, a logical extension of the work on genetics, is to examine the actual structure and functioning of the brain and nervous system. These psychophysiological studies focus on indices of nervous system functioning such as heart rate, blood pressure, arousal levels, skin conductance, and brain waves (Fishbein 1990).

Much of the work on psychophysiology has focused on electrical brain wave activity, as measured by electroencephalograms (EEGs). The EEG reflects the activity of neuronal groups located in the cerebral cortex; it represents a signal composed of rhythms and transient charges. The EEG is described in terms of the amplitude and frequency of waves. The frequency range is categorized into bands described by Greek letters: delta, theta, alpha, and beta.

Studies have reported differences in brain wave activity for persons diagnosed as psychopaths in comparison with people diagnosed as normal. One such difference is a slow-wave pattern that is characteristic of children and that suggests an immature nervous system. There is also evidence to suggest that psychopaths have low levels of arousal in the cerebral cortex, which leads to stimulation-seeking. Research further suggests that psychopaths differ from others in levels of arousal in the autonomic nervous system, which makes them relatively resistant to training or conditioning (Bartol 1995).

A third area of interest in contemporary biological perspectives is that of biochemical correlates of deviance. Researchers have examined the potential role of hormones, neurotransmitters, metabolic processes, and environmental toxins on deviant behavior (Fishbein 1990). The link between biochemical factors and aggression has received particularly close attention. One such factor is serotonin. Serotonin is a neurotransmitter that inhibits behavioral responses to stimuli. Researchers theorize that low levels of serotonin disinhibit an individual and increase the likelihood of aggressive behavior. Several studies report the predicted differences in serotonin levels between controls and persons categorized as violent (Fishbein 1990).

Another important area of biochemical research is the relationship between aggression and sex hormones. Given the general tendency for males to be more aggressive than females, researchers have speculated that levels of the male sex hormone *testosterone* might be related to aggression. Animal studies support this hypothesis, and several studies of human populations suggest a similar relationship. There is also some support for the hypothesis that imbalances in female sex hormones are associated with aggression for women. Although the evidence on the role of hormones in explaining human aggression is somewhat ambiguous, there is a growing consensus that hormones may interact with external stimuli and indirectly affect aggressive behavior (see Tedeschi and Felson 1994, 25–30).

The methodological quality of contemporary biological and biosocial studies is far superior to that of the pioneering studies in this field. Moreover, contemporary researchers have devoted much more systematic attention than did earlier theories to explicating the processes that could link biological conditions with complex behavioral outcomes. Some of the basic criticisms of the past research nevertheless remain relevant today.

One limitation of the biological research is that the findings are often inconsistent. A large number of studies purport to identify a biological factor that differentiates deviants from nondeviants, yet the specific biological factor frequently differs across studies. Also, in those areas of research with reasonably consistent findings (e.g., the twin and adoption studies), the magnitude of the biological effect tends to be modest (Walters 1992).

Another limitation of biological theories is that they typically focus on biological abnormality, thereby restricting their application to a limited portion of the population (for an exception, see Rowe and Osgood 1984). Yet official records and self-report surveys show that norm and law violations are widespread throughout the society. Hence, the relevance of these theories for explaining the bulk of norm violations is open to question.

Finally, biological theories have a difficult time accommodating the relativity of social definitions of deviance. The common approach to this issue is to assume some universal category of behavior that presumably can be explained with reference to biological processes, irrespective of whether or not that behavior happens to be defined as deviant in a given culture (e.g., Ellis 1990). Thus, for example, Fishbein cautions that biocriminological theories will not apply globally to "crime" but only to "maladaptive behaviors ... that are detrimental to individuals so affected or their milieu" (1990, 32). But who decides whether or not a given pattern of behavior is detrimental to individuals or to the larger milieu? Will there necessarily be consensus about such judgements? Shifting the focus from crime to maladaptive behavior does not really offer a satisfactory solution to the definitional problem of demarcating the subject matter of interest to criminologists. More generally, biological theories are simply not well-suited to address the important questions surrounding deviance as a social definition.

PSYCHOLOGICAL THEORIES

Psychological theories also ignore the study of deviance as a social definition and focus on norm violations. They explain these norm violations in terms of processes and structures of the individual psyche. The common premise underlying most psychological explanations of deviance is that, on the basis of past social experiences, individuals develop relatively stable dispositions to respond in certain ways to situations and environmental stimuli. The general causal logic of this approach is described in Figure 1.2. The major differences between the various theories center around the nature of the psychological dispositions and the mechanisms through which they are acquired.

One of the more distinctive approaches to the explanation of deviant psychological dispositions is the psychoanalytic perspective, which derives from the writings of Sigmund Freud. Psychoanalytic theory distinguishes three components of the mind: the id, the ego, and the superego. The id is the reservoir of unconscious, instinctual drives; the superego is the internalized voice of moral authority, or the individual's conscience; and the ego is the set of conscious beliefs about the world. According to psychoanalytic theory, the ego must adjudicate between the often conflicting demands coming from the id and the superego. The way in which the ego executes this function depends on the past experiences of the individual and, in particular, on early childhood experiences.

Psychoanalytic theory enumerates several key stages of psychosexual development (oral, anal, and phallic) during which the individual confronts distinctive psychic conflicts. If these conflicts are not satisfactorily resolved, the individual is prone to develop an abnormal or pathological personality. Deviant behavior later on in life is, then, the result of this personality disorder.

A sophisticated example of the general psychoanalytic approach is provided by William and Joan McCord's (1960) classic theory of alcoholism. Consistent with psychoanalytic theory, they argued that all people have dependency needs, which are particularly acute during early childhood. In some cases these needs are not adequately satisfied. The failure to meet these needs then leads to psychological problems at later stages in life. This is particularly true for males in the United States because masculine gender roles dictate that adolescent boys and adult men be independent. The personality need for dependence thus clashes with the social demands for independence, creating intense psychic conflict. Alcoholism relieves the associated guilt and anxiety and relaxes social inhibitions, thereby permitting the satisfaction of dependency needs.

The psychoanalytic approach has been subjected to severe criticisms over the years and its scientific integrity has been challenged repeatedly. Indeed, the psychoanalytic perspective has never been looked upon very

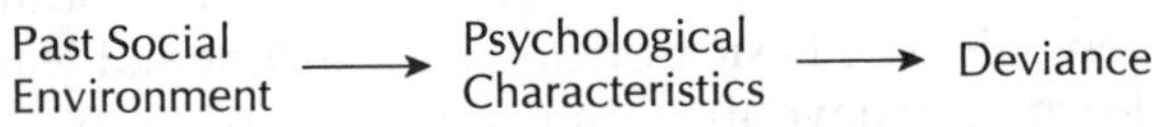

Past Social Environment $\longrightarrow$ Psychological Characteristics $\longrightarrow$ Deviance

FIGURE 1.2   CAUSAL LOGIC UNDERLYING PSYCHOLOGICAL THEORIES OF DEVIANCE

favorably by academic psychology. This perspective has nevertheless had a major influence on traditional psychiatry (Bartol 1995, 17), and efforts to revise and expand the original framework appear periodically in the literature on deviance (see, for example, Goldman 1987).

More mainstream research in the psychological study of deviance has focused on efforts to develop inventories of personality traits that reliably differentiate between deviants and nondeviants. The two most important of these inventories are the Minnesota Multiphasic Personality Inventory (MMPI) and the California Psychological Inventory (CPI). The MMPI is divided into subscales reflecting selected psychopathologies (e.g., depression, schizophrenia, anxiety). The items for these subscales were selected based on their capacity to discriminate between presumably normal populations and populations diagnosed as suffering from the various psychopathological conditions. Researchers have used the MMPI to predict various forms of deviant behavior, with mixed success (Goldstein 1986, 69; Wilson and Herrnstein 1985, 186–190).

The psychologist Hans Eysenck has developed a multidimensional approach to the study of personality and antisocial behavior. According to Eysenck's theory, there are three major dimensions of personality—extraversion, neuroticism, and psychoticism—that are correlated with criminality. Research offers some support for Eysenck's predictions, although the observed correlations vary by age. Extraversion appears to be more important than neuroticism for juvenile offenders, while the reverse is true for adult offenders. Psychoticism correlates with offending at all ages (Eysenck 1989).

In addition to the work on personality and antisocial behavior, psychological research has examined the role of basic learning processes. There are three major learning theories in contemporary psychology, each of which calls attention to a distinctive kind of learning process: associative learning theory, instrumental learning theory, and cognitive learning theory (Jeffrey 1990; Tedeschi and Felson 1994). Associative learning theory emphasizes the process of classical conditioning. In classical conditioning, a neutral stimulus is presented along with a stimulus that elicits a behavioral response. After repeated conditioning trials, the organism begins to respond to the previously neutral stimulus. The famous example of this process is Pavlov's dogs, who were conditioned to salivate at the sound of a bell by repeated association of the bell with the provision of food (Goldstein 1986, 32).

Instrumental learning theory, in contrast, emphasizes the process of operant conditioning. Operant conditioning entails training based on the consequences of one's behavior. Some behaviors lead to punishment and others lead to rewards. The basic principle of instrumental learning theory is that people learn to behave in certain ways as a result of the reinforcement and punishment schedules to which they have been exposed.

Cognitive learning places primary emphasis on the complex thinking capabilities of humans (i.e., their cognitions). People learn not only through the direct experience of rewards and punishments but by observing others and by anticipating the likely consequences of their behavior. Cognitive learning theories thus direct attention to the critical importance of imitation or modeling as the cause of behavior.

These learning theories have been applied in a variety of ways to account for deviant forms of behavior. For example, a prominent role has been assigned to classical conditioning in the emergence of psychopathy. Several theories have suggested that the psychopath is someone who is comparatively resistant to classical conditioning (Wilson and Herrnstein 1985, 202–204). Hence, to the extent that socialization requires such conditioning, it is not surprising that psychopaths should be prone to engage in antisocial behaviors. These theories typically attribute poor conditionability to features of the central nervous system and are thus biopsychological in nature.

The instrumental and cognitive learning theories have been applied most commonly to the explanation of aggressive acts of deviance. A fairly large body of literature has accumulated on the effects of reinforcement and modeling. This literature strongly suggests that the reinforcement of aggression can increase its frequency and intensity (Tedeschi and Felson 1994, 100) and that exposure to aggressive models elevates levels of aggression, at least under certain circumstances (Goldstein 1986, 39–65).

Modern psychology has clearly made major strides toward advancing our understanding of the psychological processes underlying behavior. Nevertheless, there are also limitations associated with this approach to the study of deviance. Efforts to explain norm violations in terms of reasonably stable psychological dispositions of individuals have met with only limited success to date. To be sure, relationships between norm violations and personality characteristics have been reported frequently in the literature (see Andrews and Wormith 1989). These reports, however, are not very compelling because in many of the studies the differences are quite minor, and in most cases it is not clear whether the personality characteristics caused the violations or the violations caused the characteristics. For example, being publicly identified and convicted as a regular drug user may cause a good deal of anxiety and stress, thereby producing a relationship between psychological disorder and drug use. Finally, some psychological theories have been criticized for the tendency to emphasize rare or abnormal personalities in explaining norm violations, for ignoring or at least deemphasizing the present social situation in explaining norm violations, and for ignoring the study of deviance as a social definition.

This discussion does not thoroughly review biological and psychological theories and research. Some theories are more sophisticated than others, and some incorporate social variables in addition to biological and psychological factors. This review is intended to describe the general logic of biological and psychological theories of norm violations and to serve as a point of departure and comparison for the discussion of social theories.

SOCIAL THEORIES

The theories discussed thus far emphasize biological and psychological process and structures in explaining deviance as norm violations, with a primary focus on individual norm violations rather than on rates of violations. Social theories, in contrast, direct attention to social processes and structures in explaining deviance both as norm violations (individual violations and group rates) and as social definitions (group definitions and individual applications).

Social theories of norm violations can be classified into those that emphasize structure and those that emphasize process. Social structure refers to repetitive, stable patterns of social interaction. A good example of a theory of deviance that assigns central importance to the concept of structure is Merton's (1938) theory of anomie. Merton argued that norm violations are a direct result of disjuncture between the cultural goals into which people are socialized and the structural opportunities to achieve these goals; cultural-structural disjuncture creates pressures for norm violations. Societies with acute disjuncture show high rates of norm violations; and those individuals most exposed to the structurally induced pressures exhibit the greatest involvement in norm violations. Durkheim's ([1897] 1966) theory of suicide is another structural theory. He argued that social cohesion (the strength of social ties or relationships) offers protection against suicidal impulses; hence, as social cohesion decreases, suicide rates increase.

Social process refers to a continuing change or development of social interaction over time. Processual theories explain norm violations in terms of a sequence of stages by which the violations develop. Becker's (1963) theory of regular marijuana use is a classic example of a social process theory of deviance. Becker explicated how people actually become regular users, arguing that the smoker must first learn to inhale the drug correctly, then identify its effects, and finally, define these effects as pleasurable. In one sense, the final stage (defining the physiological effect as pleasurable) is the proximate "cause" of regular marijuana use. Processual theories, however, emphasize the sequence of steps by which people become involved in deviance.

Theories of deviance as a social definition can also be classified as structural or processual. Similar to structural theories of norm violations, structural theories of deviance as a social definition refer to repetitive, stable patterns of interaction. Quinney (1977), for example, argued that economic structures strongly influence the patterns of behavior that become defined as crime in a society. Capitalist economies lead to a certain kind of behavior being defined as criminal, whereas socialist economies give rise to different definitions of crime. Quinney further asserted that position within a capitalist society (being a capitalist or a worker) strongly affects the likelihood of being defined or labeled a criminal.

Processual theories have come to be particularly significant in explaining deviance as a social definition. At the social level, research has traced the development of various social definitions of deviance, such as mental illness and alcoholism, over decades and even centuries, and has examined the stages through which social definitions are transformed into medical definitions. At the individual level, research has examined the sequences or stages through which a person's social identity is transformed from that of a nondeviant to that of a deviant. Sandstrom (1990), for example, recently described the processes through which people acquire and personalize an AIDS-related identity.

Social theories, like biological and psychological theories, are also subject to criticism. The arguments are sometimes unclear; the concepts can be vague and difficult to measure; and the supporting research is often weak. These criticisms will be discussed in the chapters to follow.

In sum, theories differ with respect to the basic kinds of structures and processes that are given primacy in the explanation of deviance. These differences, however, should not be exaggerated. It is not always easy to distinguish theories by the level of explanation. Many theories are actually hybrids. Biopsychological theories include both biological and psychological conditions in their explanation, and many theories are social-psychological, including both social and psychological factors in their explanation. For the most part, biological and psychological theories, and biopsychological hybrids, restrict their attention to norm violations; questions of social definition tend to be ignored. Social theories address both norm violations and social definitions. Given their emphasis on social structure and social process, these theories usually ignore individual variation in "constitutional factors" (i.e., factors present at or soon after birth) (Wilson and Herrnstein 1985, 69).

A Theoretical Perspective

A theoretical perspective is a conceptual scheme that does the following:

1. defines some part of the social world as problematic, that is, deserving of study, and specifies certain questions for study (subject matter)
2. provides answers to these questions (theory)
3. includes empirical tests of the theory (research)
4. based on theory and research, suggests directions for social policy

This book, then, while organized around theoretical perspectives, is not just theoretical; it emphasizes the integration of subject matter, theory, research, and social policy.

SUBJECT MATTER

Previous sections have described the subject matter of the sociology of deviance as the study of norm violations and social definitions. This discussion need not be repeated here, except to note that each perspective specifies and highlights different aspects of these two general areas of study. The structural/functional, human ecological, and rational choice perspectives focus on norm violations, each posing somewhat different questions for examination; and the labeling, constructionist, and conflict perspectives focus on social definitions, each also posing different questions for examination.

THEORY

Of the four components of a perspective, *theory* is the most difficult to define, as the concept is used in different ways by different sociologists (Cohen 1989; Turner 1989). Here the term means an interrelated set of statements or propositions used to explain the events or things that constitute the subject matter of a perspective. Explanation is the key word in the definition, but like the term *theory* it too is vaguely and loosely used in the social sciences.

Many scholars subscribe to the deductive interpretation or meaning of explanation. An event is said to be explained when it is deducible from a set of statements or propositions. Consider the following:

> For countries, if unemployment increases, norm violations increase.
> In country A, unemployment increased from 1980 to 1990.
> Therefore, in country A norm violations should have also increased from 1980 to 1990.

If norm violations did, in fact, increase in country A between 1980 and 1990, that event is regarded as having been explained because it is deducible from a set of propositions (major and minor premises in a deduction system). The major premise (if unemployment increases, norm violation increases), then, may itself become the subject of explanation. It, too, is said to be explained when it can be deduced from an even more general set of propositions.

> For countries, if status changes increase, norm violations increase.
> Unemployment is a status.
> Therefore, if unemployment increases, norm violations should increase.

This logical process is continued until all the events and things defined as the subject matter of the perspective are deduced and until all the major premises are accepted as needing no further explanation.

While explanation as logical deduction is accepted by some social scientists, others are concerned less with the logical form of an interrelated set of statements and more with the substance of what is asserted. These scholars argue that statements must assert something about the values or motives of people to constitute an explanation, while others argue that statements must assert something about causality to count as an explanation. The latter is particularly important as many—if not most—social scientists adhere to it in their everyday work. In effect, they argue that an event or thing is explained when its cause has been identified. "Cause," however, is a vaguely defined concept.

While the debate over the properties—logical and substantive—of an explanation is interesting and worthy of consideration, it is not the focus of this book. For present purposes, explanation will be defined as an answer to the question, Why do the events occur and the things exist that constitute the subject matter of a perspective? A theory, then, is defined as an interrelated set of statements used to answer this question. By using a broad definition, the theory of each perspective can be described and evaluated in its own terms. Some perspectives attempt to answer the "why" question by deducing the events and things in questions; some attempt to answer the "why" question with assertions about causality; and others employ still different criteria in answering the "why" question.

In describing a set of interrelated assertions, which comprise a theory, it is worthwhile to distinguish between those assertions that are testable (subject to empirical observation) and those that are not. (The former will be discussed in the research section.) The latter are frequently referred to as theoretical assumptions; some are explicitly stated, and some are unstated but implicit assertions of the theory.

One of the more important untestable assumptions for theoretical perspectives on deviance concerns the degree of order in society. All six theoretical perspectives discussed in this book make assumptions about the extent to which society is orderly. Some theoretical perspectives assume—implicitly or explicitly—that society is essentially orderly, that is, the norms of behavior are reasonably clear, consistent, and stable. Other perspectives assume that society is essentially disorderly; that is, the norms of behavior are vague, inconsistent, and unstable. These assumptions are important because they affect the subject matter of study and the nature of the testable propositions. Perspectives that assume an essentially orderly society tend to define norm violations as the proper subject matter of study. However, if norms are assumed to be vague, inconsistent, and unstable, norm violations are difficult—if not impossible—to define and, consequently, to use as a reference point. Perspectives that view society as essentially disorderly tend to study the emergence of norms and social definitions of deviance.

All six perspectives also make assumptions about the link between the individual and society. Some perspectives assume that individuals are basically passive in their interaction with society, implying that individuals are acted upon by the social environment and come to reflect the objective characteristics of that environment. Other perspectives assume that individuals act upon the social environment. Individuals select environments in which to behave; they select aspects of the environment toward which to direct their attention; they interpret the environment; and they attempt to change it. The perspectives that focus on norm violations (structural/functional, human ecology, and rational choice) tend to view individuals as more passive than active. They generally explain norm violations in terms of the influence of social environments. Social definitional perspectives are more difficult to characterize as active or passive. The constructionist perspective typically takes an active conceptualization of individuals, leading to the study of how people and organizations construct social norms and categories of norm violators (Best 1987; Cicourel 1968). The conflict perspective (particularly orthodox Marxism) and the labeling perspective adopt a somewhat more passive conceptualization, leading to the study of how the economic and political order of society affects social definitions of deviance and how the application of these definitions affects behavior.

Untestable assumptions about the nature of society (orderly or disorderly) and the nature of the relationship between individuals and society (active or passive) influence the testable assertions and even the subject matter of study; and the latter, in turn, influences these assumptions. It is not necessary to disentangle the degree of mutual influence here; it is important, however, to appreciate the significance of untestable and sometimes implicit assumptions of a theory.

RESEARCH

Social scientists generally define research as the systematic observation of the social world. They disagree, however, over the techniques for making valid observations and the types of observations necessary to validate theories.

Observing Norm Violations Considerable debate has ensued as to the most valid way to measure norm violations. The three most common approaches are: (1) to rely on official records, (2) to collect information from self-report surveys, and (3) to make direct observations.

Records of socially problematic norm violations, such as alcoholism, drug use, suicide, mental illness, and crime are maintained by various public and private agencies. Crime statistics, for example, are compiled by criminal justice agencies (police, prosecutors, correctional facilities) at the municipal, county, state, and national levels. Since the 1930s the FBI has organized the police statistics on crime into reasonably comparable categories and published them as the *Uniform Crime Reports*. These records have been used to estimate the volume of crime, including the degree to which it is increasing or decreasing; to describe the distribution of crime in geographical and social space; and to test various theories.

Are official statistics of norm violations valid? In answering this question one must critically review the components in their construction. Official statistics include only those norm violations known to and recorded by the authorities. Violations become known to authorities by two routes: Either the public observes and reports them or authorities detect them. These processes suggest two possible sources of error. Official statistics will be inaccurate if the public is unwilling to report violations and/or if official agencies are unable to detect them. It is widely assumed that official records tend to underestimate the actual levels of norm violations because many of them are neither reported to the recording agency by the public nor detected by that agency.

Another possible source of error occurs at the recording stage. Even if norm violations come to the attention of official agencies, these violations might not be recorded properly, or they might not be recorded at all. The official recording of norm violations is likely to be affected by factors such as the professionalism of agency personnel, organizational pressures to show high or low levels of norm violations, and the nature of the interactions between citizen reporters and official recorders (O'Brien 1995, 61).

The presence of some error in officials records of crime would not be particularly troubling to researchers if the error could be assumed to be random. However, there are often plausible reasons for anticipating systematic error. Consider the finding that many types of norm violations are higher in urban than rural areas. Does this variation reflect differences in real rates, reportability, detectability, or recording propensity of officials? As to reportability, research suggests that, because informal social control is considerably lower in urban than in rural areas, urbanites are prone to rely on formal social control agencies. Detectability and recording propensity may also be higher in urban than in rural areas. Studies suggest that urban social control agencies are better equipped, more professional, and considerably larger per capita than are rural social control agencies. Hence, it is reasonable to expect that official records would show higher levels of norm violations in urban than in rural areas even if the true levels were similar.

Comparisons of official records over time are also problematic. Official statistics frequently show that norm violations have increased over recent decades. For example, the official data reveal the following trend in rates of violent crime (murder, forcible rape, and aggravated assault) per 100,000 population in the United States over the 1960–95 period (Maguire and Pastore 1995, 305; Federal Bureau of Investigation 1996, 19):

1960	160.9
1970	363.5
1980	596.6
1990	731.8
1995	713.6

These figures seem to suggest a dramatic increase in levels of criminal violence since 1960 (with a slight drop between 1990 and 1995), but at least some of the increase might reflect changes in the recording of crime. As the nation has become more urban, informal social control processes have become less effective; consequently, formal social control agencies have expanded, thereby increasing reportability and detectability. Similarly, the integration of previously marginalized groups, such as African Americans, into the mainstream of American society has probably enhanced the willingness of members of these groups to go to the police to report victimizations. In sum, trends in official statistics of norm violations reflect some unknown combination of changes in actual levels of violations and changes in the recording of them.

Sociologists have increasingly turned to self-report surveys as a way to circumvent the limitations associated with official statistics on norm violations. The general logic of the survey approach is to bypass official agencies and contact persons who are more directly involved in the behavior under investigation. There are two basic types of self-report surveys used in research on norm violations. One type asks respondents to report on their own involvement in norm violations, while the other solicits information from persons who have been affected by norm violations. This latter technique has been applied most extensively in studies of crime and is referred to as a *victimization survey*.

Victimization surveys involve face-to-face and telephone interviews in which members of a household or representatives of a business are asked to reveal what crimes have been committed against them over some time period, generally within the last six months or year. In the United States these studies were initiated in 1966 by the Bureau of Social Science Research in a study of Washington, D.C., and by the National Opinion Research Center in a nation-wide study. Subsequently, the U.S. Bureau of the Census, in cooperation with the Department of Justice, has conducted extensive victimization studies. These studies include surveys of twenty-six cities during the 1972–75 period and an ongoing, national survey of the U.S. population that has continued up to the present. The national survey is based on a large probability sample of about fifty thousand households and is conducted annually. It was originally titled the "National Crime Survey" but it has been renamed the "National Crime Victimization Survey" (NCVS).

What have these victimization surveys discovered about crime, particularly regarding the issues of underestimation and biased estimation in the Uniform Crime Reports? Regarding the former, the victimization surveys suggest that the UCR underestimates the level of crime. The figures in Table 1.1 allow for a rough comparison of levels of violent personal crimes reported in the NCVS for 1994 with those recorded in the UCR for the same year (these comparisons are approximate because the populations covered by the two sources are not exactly the same). The victimization survey shows a considerably higher amount of crime than that shown in the UCR, although the exact difference depends on the type of crime. Rape is about five times higher in the survey than in the UCR, while robbery and aggravated assault are about two and a half times higher.

Do the victimization surveys describe the spatial and social distribution of crime differently than do the FBI reports? One approach to this question is to compare the ranking of cities by crime rates as yielded by the victimization surveys and the UCR. The results of such research indicate that the similarity in the rankings depends on the type of crime (Clarren and Schwartz 1976; Cohen and Land 1984). It is moderate to strong for property crimes (robbery, burglary, vehicle theft) but quite weak for personal crimes (rape and aggravated assault). Researchers have also compared the racial and gender characteristics of offenders across NCVS and UCR data sources for those incidents that involve contact between the offender and victim (Hindelang 1978; O'Brien 1995). The findings reveal very similar patterns for gender regardless of the data source—males constitute a much larger percentage of offenders than females. With respect to race, both data sources reveal an overrepresentation of African Americans among offenders. There is a noticeable tendency, however, for the UCR to underestimate (in comparison with the NCVS) the percentage of white offenders for rapes and assaults.

Victimization surveys, while avoiding some of the problems associated with official statistics, have their own validity problems. They are surveys and are thus hampered by the problems associated with all surveys. There are also problems with the use of households as the sampling units. Transients are ignored, which implies that crime is underestimated in cities with large transient populations. There are memory problems. People forget what has happened to them, and they may be unable to place victimizations within the time frames asked for by the interviewers. People also

TABLE 1.1 ESTIMATED CRIME RATES, 1994
(PER 100,000 POPULATION)[a]

OFFENSE	NCVS	UNIFORM CRIME REPORTS (UCR)	RATIO OF NCVS TO UCR
Criminal Homicide	—[b]	9.0	—
Forcible Rape	200	39.2	5.1
Robbery	610	237.7	2.6
Aggravated Assault	1,160	430.2	2.7

[a]National Crime Victimization Survey (NCVS) rates are based on the population age 12 and over.
[b]Not estimated in victimization surveys.

Source: Maguire and Pasture (1996, Table 3.1, 230; Table 3.109, 324).

lie. Many people do not wish to admit being victimized for certain types of crimes; others may wish to indulge the interviewer by fabricating incidents that never happened. Most importantly, victimization studies provide very little information about offenders.

This brings us to the use of offender self-reports. Sociologists have used both face-to-face interviews and anonymous questionnaires to ask people what norms they have violated over specific periods of time. For example, an interviewer may ask, "Over the last six months, how many times have you stolen things valued over five dollars (do not remember, never, once, twice, three or more times)." Hundreds of such studies have been conducted, commonly with student samples.

One of the most ambitious self-report studies is the National Youth Survey (NYS) carried out by Delbert Elliott and colleagues (Elliott et al. 1985). The NYS is based on a probability sample of U.S. households and is much more representative than the typical self-report study, which is often based on a single locale. Another valuable feature of the NYS is that it asks about a diverse range of delinquent activities. Table 1.2 reports the NYS estimates of the "prevalence" and "incidence" of various illegal activities by American youths, ages 15–21. Prevalence refers to the proportion of persons in the age group who admit to having engaged in the activity during the past year; incidence refers to the average number of acts reported per respondent during the past year. The figures in Table 1.2 indicate that some involvement in delinquent activity is fairly common. For example, approximately one in five respondents admit to acts of minor assault during the past year. At the same time, very serious delinquency is much less common. Only 2 percent of the respondents report involvement in robbery.

Self-report studies initially raised considerable debate about the use of official records to estimate the social correlates of crime. Official records

TABLE 1.2   PREVALENCE AND INCIDENCE RATES OF OFFENDING
FROM THE NATIONAL YOUTH SURVEY

OFFENSE	PREVALENCE[a]	INCIDENCE[b]
Felony Assault	9	.29
Minor Assault	21	1.20
Robbery	2	.10
Felony Theft	9	.44
Minor Theft	15	1.09
Damaged Property	15	.64
Hard Drug Use	17	5.79

[a]Prevalence refers to the percentage admitting to one or more offenses during the past year.
[b]Incidence refers to the average number of offenses per respondent during the past year.

Source: Robert M. O'Brien, "Crime and Victimization Data," in Criminology: A Contemporary Handbook, ed. Joseph F. Shelley, p. 70. © 1995 Wadsworth Publishing Company. Reprinted by permission of the publisher.

consistently reveal strong associations between delinquency and race and social class. The early self-report studies (Hirschi 1969; Gould 1969) did not confirm these findings, suggesting that official records overrepresent the delinquency of African Americans and members of the lower class. A widely accepted explanation for these discrepancies across data sources, however, is that the early self-report studies emphasized nonserious delinquencies, and race and class may not be related to the frequency of nonserious delinquency (Braithwaite 1981). Those self-report studies that inquire about serious as well as minor delinquency, such as the NYS, yield relationships between demographic characteristics and offending that are similar to those suggested by the official statistics (Elliott and Ageton 1980; Elliott et al. 1985).

In considering the validity of offender self-reports, the following should be noted. As surveys they are susceptible to some of the same types of problems as victimization studies: Transients are ignored, and respondents may have memory lapses, or they may lie. The latter may be more important in offender than in victim self-reports. While people may be willing to admit being the target of a serious offense, they may be much less likely to admit committing one. How many people would admit, even on a seemingly anonymous questionnaire, to having committed rape or homicide? Self-reports, therefore, may be inapplicable to the most serious offenses.

For nonserious offenses, there is considerable evidence to support the general validity of the self-report methodology. In an early study, Clark and Tifft (1966) reported that the ranking of juveniles on delinquency, using both self-reports and polygraphs (lie detectors), is highly similar. Hardt and Peterson-Hardt (1977) also found evidence of the validity of self-reports of delinquency. In their data, (1) there is only a minor discrepancy between juveniles' self-reports of being ticketed and arrested when compared with police records; (2) the tendency to give socially desirable, rather than correct, answers in interviews and questionnaires is unrelated to self-reports of delinquency; and (3) self-reports exhibit a high level of "questionnaire consistency." Hardt and Peterson-Hardt demonstrated such consistency by asking juveniles if they had ever been questioned by police in one part of the questionnaire, and then in another part, asking if they had ever been ticketed or arrested. Assuming that the latter implies the former, 98 percent of the juveniles responded consistently. Hindelang, Hirschi, and Weis (1981) reported similar conclusions concerning the validity of the self-report methodology, although they noted that self-report findings should be interpreted cautiously for hard-core delinquents. This is not because hard-core delinquents purposely refuse to disclose their delinquencies; rather, to those juveniles regularly disposed to delinquency, specific delinquent acts are not memorable events.

To circumvent the problems encountered with official records and self-reports, some researchers advocate direct or natural observation—the observation of norm violations in the day-to-day situations in which they normally occur. Such observation may be either "participant" or "nonparticipant." The nonparticipant observer locates himself or herself so as to be in a position to observe ongoing behavior. For example, in the study of prostitution, the researcher might spend time at certain street corners and bars; in the study of juvenile delinquency, the researcher might spend time with youth gangs. Such observational techniques, however, can sometimes alter the course of the interaction. An observer on a street corner may well be noticed and identified by prostitutes as a plainclothes detective or a journalist, thereby altering the interaction between prostitutes and clients; gang members may be more circumspect in their behavior when an outsider is present. One strategy is to participate in the action (participant observation) wherever possible. The observer can thus get very close to the action without being an outsider, learning things that might not be revealed to researchers.

While natural observation allows researchers to get very close to the action and perhaps to observe things that might not be revealed in self-reports or official records, this technique, like others, has its limitations. Natural observation is impractical for examining norm-violation rates across political and geographic units. Given the time involved in the observation of each case, natural observation is limited to very small samples in small geographical areas. It can also be quite unreliable, as the observations can easily reflect the values, concerns, and biases of the observer. Finally, only certain types of norm violations can be observed. Many norm violations occur infrequently and others are committed so as to go undetected, such as most crimes. There are also ethical (and commonsensical) limitations associated with participant observation; it is certainly not the recommended method for studying suicide.

To summarize, techniques of observing norm violations can be classified into three categories: official records, self-reports, and direct observations. Each has a unique set of advantages and disadvantages, making it suitable for the study of some research questions but not others. It is the responsibility of the researcher to know which techniques minimize error in the study of particular questions and norm violations.

Causal Inference   As noted earlier, many sociologists argue that causality is a critical component of a theoretical explanation. Their theories thus consist of assertions about the causes of social phenomena. To demonstrate causality, three general criteria must be satisfied.

1. Causal factors and the events or things to be explained should accompany one another (i.e., they should covary). In social research this rule is interpreted within a probabilistic framework. For example, if unemployment is asserted to be a cause of drug addiction, unemployed persons should have a higher probability of

drug addiction than employed persons. This relationship does not have to be a perfect one; not all unemployed persons need be drug addicts, and some employed persons may be drug addicts. What is important for causal inference is that the likelihood of drug addiction varies appreciably across employment status.

2. The causal factors must be temporally prior to the events or things that they explain. An effect cannot logically occur before its cause. Many of the associations reported in social research are compatible with alternative causal interpretations. For example, drug addiction may cause unemployment or unemployment may cause drug addiction. In addition to showing a relationship, then, observations should show that the causal factors precede the occurrence of the event or thing to be explained.

3. The association between a hypothetical causal factor and the events or things it causes must not be due to other factors. For example, unemployment and drug addiction may be related, not because one causes the other, but because another factor, low education, causes both. An observed relationship between two factors that merely reflects the influence of some other causal factor is referred to as a "spurious" relationship.

This description of the rules of causal inference is simplified, ignoring complications and complexities. Sophisticated methodological techniques have been developed to deal with these complexities. Regardless of the specific methodological approach, however, causal inference rests upon the demonstration of association, temporal order, and nonspuriousness.

SOCIAL POLICY

The term *social policy* refers to a directed course of action to change people or society. Concerning norm violations, actions are directed toward the prevention of norm violations and the treatment or rehabilitation of norm violators; and concerning societal definitions, actions are directed toward changing various social norms (e.g., drinking norms), changing the categories used to describe norm violators (e.g., medical versus criminal terms), and reducing the consequences of being publicly labeled a norm violator. While government policies are of central importance, the policies of other organizations should not be ignored. Business corporations have formulated programs to reduce norm violations (absenteeism and sexual harassment of employees); specific organizations have been formed by norm violators themselves to reduce norm violations (Alcoholics Anonymous).

While most, if not all, theories have implications for social policy, the implications of causal theories are most easily explicated. Quite simply, if a theory specifies social conditions as causing norm violations, the theory implies that changing these conditions is necessary to reduce norm violations. Although it is possible to alter problematic physical, biological, psychological, and social conditions without understanding how and why the course of action is effective, this book is concerned with how theory can assist in the construction of effective social policy. Policy implications provide the practical justification for theory and research.

Policy makers are not interested in more theories; if they are interested in theories at all, they are interested in those supported by social research. This raises the question: How much supporting research is enough before a theory can be used to guide social policy? No definitive answer can be given. On the one hand, it makes no sense to construct social policy, the implementation of which is expensive, unless the guiding theory is supported by some evidence. On the other hand, theories are never completely proven, especially social theories, and social conditions are frequently of such concern that policy makers must act. Clearly, the sensible position lies somewhere between waiting for all the evidence and acting without any evidence.

The link between policy implications and implementation is mediated by social technology, social values, and social power. Concerning technology, theory and research may identify causes of norm violations. For example, research may identify economic crises as the major cause of suicide. The policy implications are clear: Reduce economic crises. Yet social scientists may not know how. Theory and research may identify as the cause of norm violations social conditions that people are unwilling to change. For example, if research shows that certain religious beliefs cause delinquency, what should be done? The policy implications are clear—change the religious beliefs; yet Americans believe in religious freedom. This example illustrates a conflict of values, where the assumed causal conditions are valued more than the norm violations are disvalued. Finally, theory and research may identify as the cause of norm violations social conditions that contribute to the positions and careers of authorities. If research shows, for example, that the property crime rate is caused by the level of income inequality, what should be done? Will those with high incomes (usually in positions to influence social policy) sponsor social programs to equalize income? This seems unlikely.

The student should thus be aware that while theory suggests social policy, the implementation is constrained not only by research but by what is tractable to policy manipulation. In fact, policy makers are generally more interested in theory that, while not supported by research, suggests "practical" courses of action than with theory that is well-supported by research but suggests "impractical" courses of action—those that are difficult to implement, violate social values, or adversely affect authorities.

INTEGRATION

To summarize, a theoretical perspective is defined as an integrated conceptual scheme that includes subject matter, theory, research, and social-policy implications. The diagram in Figure 1.3 illustrates the various paths of influence between the components.

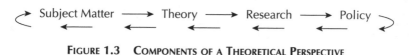

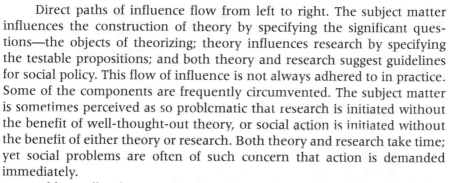

FIGURE 1.3   COMPONENTS OF A THEORETICAL PERSPECTIVE

Direct paths of influence flow from left to right. The subject matter influences the construction of theory by specifying the significant questions—the objects of theorizing; theory influences research by specifying the testable propositions; and both theory and research suggest guidelines for social policy. This flow of influence is not always adhered to in practice. Some of the components are frequently circumvented. The subject matter is sometimes perceived as so problematic that research is initiated without the benefit of well-thought-out theory, or social action is initiated without the benefit of either theory or research. Both theory and research take time; yet social problems are often of such concern that action is demanded immediately.

Additionally, direct paths of influence flow from right to left. The assumptions a theory makes about the nature of society and about the relationship between individuals and society shape the subject matter of study. The study of norm violations is premised on the assumption that society is essentially orderly, that social norms are clear, consistent, and stable, thus making it possible to define norm violations. Research also shapes both theory and subject matter. Nonsupportive research can be used to reject or reformulate theories, and available resources affect what aspects of the social world can be studied. For example, available government statistics have facilitated the study of some types of norm violations but not others, such as white-collar crime. Finally, social policy—the presumed end product of theory and research—frequently affects theory and research. As previously stated, various government programs exist because they are popular, beneficial to the interests of the powerful, or simple to implement. Government funds for research are in some cases made available to justify such programs.

OVERVIEW

Each of the next six chapters examines one perspective of the sociology of deviance. Each chapter is organized into three major sections—theory, research, and social policy—and a section critically evaluating the perspective. The book concludes with a final chapter that discusses historical patterns, current trends, and future directions in the study of crime and deviance.

THE STRUCTURAL/
FUNCTIONAL PERSPECTIVE

2

Structural/functionalism conceives of society as a system of interrelated parts. It assumes widespread consensus about core values and appropriate forms of behavior, and it examines how persistent patterns of behavior or social structures (statuses, roles, organizations, and institutions) function to implement society's values, thereby promoting the survival of the social system.

Some studies in the structural/functional tradition analyze the inter-dependencies between social institutions. For example, how does the Protestant religion contribute to the functioning of a capitalist economic system? How does the operation of a capitalist economy affect family relations? Other studies examine how particular institutions contribute to the realization of general social values. For example, to what extent do schools promote responsible citizenship? How do laws governing property rights contribute to economic productivity and social mobility as core American values?

Structural/functionalism distinguishes between manifest and latent functions. The former refers to those functions that are intended and readily recognized by most members of society. For example, to most Americans it seems rather obvious that strong religious institutions function to create and maintain social morality. Latent functions refer to those functions that are neither readily apparent nor widely recognized. For example, Piven and Cloward (1971) argue that the primary purpose of public welfare in the United States is not to provide relief to those in poverty but rather to regulate the political and economic behavior of the poor. In times of mass unemployment, welfare payments are instituted or made more generous to quell civil disorder. When political stability is restored, these payments are reduced to reinforce work norms. The largely unrecognized latent function of public welfare, according to Piven and Cloward, is to preserve a political and economic order characterized by extreme inequality.

How is social deviance studied from this general perspective? Given the assumption of a high level of consensus about basic norms and values, norm violations are considered to be clearly definable. Accordingly, the causes and consequences of norm violations constitute central foci of study, although deviance as a social definition is sometimes considered as well. Two major themes in structural/functional analyses of deviance can be identified. In the major thrust of the perspective, norm violations are explained with reference to disruptions of the social system, specifically, breakdowns in normative consensus and social integration. A second theme treats norm violations as any other persistent pattern of behavior; they are viewed as normal and are studied in terms of their functions in maintaining the existing social order. Recall that an underlying premise of structural/functionalism is that stable patterns of behavior persist precisely because they serve some function for the larger social system.

SOCIAL DEREGULATION

Structural/functional theories of deviance can be traced to Emile Durkheim, a French sociologist writing in the latter part of the nineteenth and early part of the twentieth centuries. Durkheim's work provides the historical foundations for the structural/functional approach to deviance and for structural/functionalism more generally. Durkheim wrote on a broad range of subjects, but one of his primary interests was the nature of the social changes accompanying the transformation of rural agricultural societies to urban industrial societies that was occurring in western Europe during the nineteenth century.

In his first major work, *The Division of Labor in Society*, Durkheim ([1893] 1964) considered the sources of social solidarity in different kinds of societies. He argued that in rural agricultural societies, people are generally involved in similar activities; the division of labor is minimal. Consequently, people tend to develop similar ideas, goals, and values. They share, in other words, a strong collective conscience. This shared conscience produces what Durkheim called "mechanical solidarity," which is the social force that holds rural agricultural societies together.

Industrialization and urbanization inevitably weaken the collective conscience by promoting a more specialized division of labor. People occupy different social positions and statuses, and as a result, they come to hold different thoughts, ideas, interests, and values. As the collective conscience weakens, mechanical solidarity disappears as a social force to bind the members of society together.

What then serves as the "social cement" in urban, industrial societies? Durkheim argued that the very division of labor that undermines mechanical solidarity gives rise to a new form of solidarity. As the division of labor becomes more and more specialized, people become highly dependent on one another for the satisfaction of their basic needs. This functional interdependence leads to a new kind of social bond, that of "organic solidarity." The different parts of a society with an advanced division of labor are interdependent just as are the different organs of the human body.

Durkheim believed that the normal developmental process of societies results in the substitution of this new form of solidarity—organic—for the old form—mechanical. He also suggested that an increasing division of labor would fail to yield organic solidarity under certain abnormal conditions. In one such condition there are few rules to regulate the interrelations between different roles in the division of labor (e.g., capital and labor). Durkheim referred to this situation as an "anomic" division of labor, because the division of labor does not yield organic solidarity. There is weak regulation in society because the collective conscience has largely disappeared while no replacement for it has emerged.

In a subsequent analysis, Durkheim examined how weak social regulation (deregulation) is related to a phenomenon that is typically explained in psychological terms—suicide. Durkheim ([1897] 1966) focused primarily on two sources of deregulation: egoism and anomie. Egoism refers to a situation where the individual is relatively free, independent, and nonintegrated into the larger society. For example, Durkheim reasoned that unmarried people are less integrated into society than married people. Married people are typically involved with spouses, children, and in-laws. These relationships are sources of both regulation and social support. The married man, for example, has numerous social responsibilities toward his wife, children, and so on, which constrain and limit his behavior, while the unmarried man is free of these obligations and, consequently, subject to less social control. Additionally, Durkheim argued that Catholics are more strongly integrated into the church than are Protestants and hence are more regulated. The Catholic religion provides extensive rules governing thoughts and behavior, and there are elaborate ceremonial occasions where such thoughts and behavior are reinforced. The Protestant religion, on the other hand, is more individualistic, emphasizing an individual's direct relationship to God. It provides comparatively few rules of thought and behavior and few ceremonial occasions in which rules are socially reinforced.

Throughout *Suicide* Durkheim discussed various psychological and social processes through which weak social integration and deregulation produce suicide. Generally, he suggested that group integration, by providing clear guidelines for behavior, makes life simpler and less stressful. It also provides a sense of social responsibility and social support during times of despair, thereby moderating stress and inhibiting its expression in suicide. For example, while both married and unmarried individuals may occasionally entertain suicidal thoughts, the married have more social responsibilities, which inhibits them from committing suicide, than do the unmarried, who have no one else to worry about and live for; and because Catholics are socially integrated, they receive social support (comfort, understanding, and sympathy), which lessens the pressure to commit suicide during times of despair.

Durkheim argued that rapid social change (economic, political, technological) causes another form of suicide—anomic suicide. He observed, for example, that the suicide rate varies with the business cycle. It is high not only during times of depression and contraction, which is not very surprising, but also during times of prosperity and expansion. Durkheim explained both observations with reference to an imbalance between people's goals and available means. During economic depressions people lose their economic means: Unemployment increases and wages decrease. As the discrepancy between goals and means widens, stress increases, leading to a high rate of suicide.

A similar discrepancy between goals and means occurs during economic expansion, but for different reasons. Durkheim believed that humans have no instinctual limits on what they desire. As a result, people can experience satisfaction only when they have accepted social restraints on their aspirations. Economic expansion is conducive to suicide because it erodes these social restraints. As the economy expands, people achieve and exceed their goals, and they begin to believe that anything is possible—the sky's the limit. Whatever means are available to people will be inadequate for their goals under such conditions, because limitless goals are by definition insatiable. Economic expansion, like contraction, thus creates a discrepancy between ends and means, which increases despair and leads to high rates of suicide.

Note the similarity between egoistic and anomic suicide. Both entail deregulation. The former reflects the influence of social statuses (e.g., marriage, religion) on deregulation, while the latter reflects the effect of social change (e.g., depression, prosperity) on deregulation. In developing this theme, Durkheim directed the sociology of deviance away from individual psychological causes of suicide (idiosyncratic psychopathologies and psychic states) toward the organization of social life.

Durkheim's work on the relationship between social deregulation and suicide has continued to stimulate sociological research and theorizing on suicide as well as on other patterns of deviance and socially problematic behavior. An influential example is provided by the work of Gibbs and Martin (1964) on status integration and suicide. Gibbs and Martin merged Durkheim's insights about deregulation with the concepts of status sets and role conflicts. A status is a position in the social structure characterized by patterned social expectations or social roles. People simultaneously occupy multiple statuses or status sets, which are integrated to varying degrees. A well-integrated status set is one in which the role demands of the constituent statuses are highly compatible; a poorly integrated status set is one in which the role demands are inconsistent.

Consider, for example, a woman with aging parents, young children, and a demanding occupation. Assume also that she is unmarried and trying to maintain an active social life. Can she possibly meet all the social demands of her parents, children, lover, and employer? Low conformity to some roles in this status set is inevitable.

Gibbs and Martin proposed that poor status integration is conducive to suicide because it undermines social relationships. Poor status integration entails inconsistent role demands, which implies that status occupants are unable to conform to expectations of all their role partners. When people involved in relationships fail to live up to expectations, the relationships break down. The likelihood of suicide, then, increases as the regulatory force of social relationships weakens. The basic thrust of the status integration theory is shown in Figure 2.1.

Another example of an effort to refine and recast Durkheim's theory of suicide is the work of Pescosolido and Georgianna (1989), which draws upon the tradition of network research in sociology. Their theory asserts that the suicide potential for a group varies in a curvilinear way with the density of religious networks. This potential is highest for groups with either extremely low or extremely high network density, and lowest for those with moderate density. When the density of religious networks is extremely low, people do not receive much collective support or regulation from their religious group. This increases the likelihood of suicide when individual crises occur. When the density of religious networks is extremely high, people are protected from individual crises, but they are highly susceptible to collective crises. They are prone to group suicide because they lack ties to others outside of the religious community (an example would be mass suicides of religious cults).

To summarize, Durkheim focused the attention of sociologists on the pattern of social relationships and social regulations. He emphasized the importance of the larger society in regulating the goals and means of individuals, and he identified social conditions that are conducive to either strong or weak regulation. Durkheim demonstrated the importance of social restraints in analyses of suicide. Gibbs and Martin extended Durkheim's work by relating suicide to status integration and unstable

Poor Status $\longrightarrow$ Inconsistent $\longrightarrow$ Low $\longrightarrow$ Unstable $\longrightarrow$ Suicide
Integration   Role Demands   Conformity   Relationships

FIGURE 2.1   THE STATUS INTEGRATION THEORY

social relationships. Pescosolido and Georgianna recast Durkheim's theory of suicide in terms of social networks. Although not tied together into a general theory of norm violations, these different theories are linked by the concept of social deregulation. They suggest that the level and pattern of norm violations are affected by the nature of the social regulatory system.

SOCIAL ORGANIZATION AND ANOMIE

One of the most influential efforts to formulate a general explanation of deviance based on Durkheim's insights is Robert K. Merton's ([1938] 1968) theory of "Social Structure and Anomie." Like Durkheim, Merton considered the relationship between goals and means to be critical to an understanding of the social sources of deviance. However, Merton discarded Durkheim's assumption that people are naturally prone to develop limitless aspirations. Merton viewed both ends and means as products of culture. In addition, Merton described the interconnections between culture, social structure, and deviance in much greater detail than did Durkheim.

The underlying premise of Merton's theory is that society is well-organized when its members are able to realize cultural goals using the culturally prescribed means. Under these conditions, culture and social structure are in harmony with one another; people receive satisfactions by conforming to cultural mandates (Merton 1968, 188). Societies are not always well-organized, however. Various elements of culture and social structure may be inconsistent or incompatible with one another, creating structural pressures for deviant behavior.

Merton cited the United States as an example of a society with fundamental inconsistencies in both its culture and its social structure. At the cultural level, there is an imbalance between the emphasis placed on goals and means. There is very strong cultural support for dominant goals, especially the goal of monetary success. People are strongly encouraged to accumulate wealth and acquire the good things in life that money can buy. American culture also provides guidelines about how the goal of monetary success should be pursued. The proper way to accumulate wealth is to get a good education, secure a well-paying job, save, and invest one's earnings. However, there is much less importance placed on using the proper means than on realizing the ultimate goal. What you have is more important than how you got it. American culture is, then, anomic in the sense that there is a disproportionate emphasis on goals in comparison with means.

At the structural level, there is also an imbalance or a "disjuncture" between cultural goals and structured opportunities. The cultural goals are universal. Children learn, informally and formally, from parents, the mass media, and schools that everyone can be president (figuratively speaking) and that everyone should aspire to be economically successful. However, because economic opportunities are limited, only a few can achieve and sat-isfy their culturally induced aspirations; others must settle for something less. Structural opportunities and cultural mandates are not well integrated. This type of dysfunctional social organization, or anomie, is conducive to high levels of deviance.

Perhaps one example of a structurally functional society is pre-World War II India. The culture did not extol economic achievement as a universal goal; rather, economic goals were culturally stratified, consistent with economic opportunities. Those who did not achieve by the standards of the upper castes were not necessarily judged by those standards; their accomplishments and achievements were evaluated by their own subcultural standards. In terms of Merton's logic, since the level of cultural/structural integration was high, frustration should have been low, even though the level of poverty may have been high by Western standards.

Having described the social organizational conditions leading to anomie, Merton proceeded to discuss the different ways that people adapt to such an anomic environment. He introduced a typology, or classification system, that describes different adaptations based on the acceptance or rejection of goals and means. (See Table 2.1.) According to Merton, the most common adaptation is conformity. The conformist continues to accept the cultural goals and abide by the proper means despite the organizational pressures for deviance. If conformity were not the most prevalent adaptation, there would be no social order and thus no society (Merton 1968, 195).

Merton devoted primary attention to the four deviant adaptations, especially that of *innovation*. The plus sign under goals in Table 2.1 for innovation signifies that the innovator adheres to the culturally prescribed goals. He or she tries to achieve monetary success. The minus sign under means indicates that he or she rejects the normative means for achieving this goal. The innovator uses the most technically expedient means to success, which are often illegal. An illustration is the drug dealer who perceives no realistic opportunity for wealth and status through legitimate means and who innovates by selling an illegal product that is in high demand. In many ways, the successful criminal innovator manifests the characteristics of the

TABLE 2.1   MERTON'S FIVE ADAPTATIONS

ENDS	MEANS	RESOLUTIONS
+	+	Conformity
+	−	Innovation
−	+	Ritualism
−	−	Retreatism
±	±	Rebellion

Note: Each resolution is an adaptation to high ends-means discrepancy.

successful business person: ambition, drive, hard work, and shrewdness (see, for example, Adler and Laufer 1995).

Ritualism refers to a psychological process of goal de-escalation. Goals and means are brought into alignment by striving for what is possible. An example of this pattern is the low-level bureaucrat who has become aware that he or she is not going to make it to the top of the organization and who has come to accept this. He or she no longer tries to get ahead but simply comes to work each day and does his or her job. Many people do this; perhaps we all do to some extent. While no behavioral rules are violated, Merton maintained that the ritualist is deviant nevertheless because in the United States people are expected to strive continuously to advance. To do otherwise is deviant. Ritualism is represented in Table 2.1 by a minus sign under cultural goals (designating that goals are abandoned) and a plus sign under means (designating that conventional means are adhered to). Because this pattern of deviance causes few problems for other people and organizations, it has generated little discussion and research.

Retreatism refers to an adaptation whereby both the culturally approved goals and socially acceptable means are rejected. In Table 2.1, minus signs appear under both cultural goals and means. In a sense, retreatists drop out of society and are in a different social world. Mental illness, drug addiction, and alcoholism can be viewed as forms of social retreatism.

Rebellion refers to an adaptation whereby cultural goals and acceptable means are rejected, like retreatism; but unlike retreatism, new goals and means are advocated. The rebel does not drop out of society but tries to change it. He or she has an image—however vague—of the "good" society. The minus signs in Table 2.1 refer to the rejection of both cultural goals and conventional means, and the plus signs refer to the advocacy of alternative goals and means.

Although Merton formulated an explicit system for classifying norm violations, he was somewhat vague in explaining why one adaptation occurs rather than another. One of the more important efforts to describe in more detail why certain patterns of deviance emerge rather than others is the work of Richard A. Cloward and Lloyd E. Ohlin (1964), which focuses specifically on juvenile delinquency. Their primary contribution is to extend Merton's notion of a legitimate opportunity structure to encompass the concept of an illegitimate opportunity structure. Merton implicitly assumed that people who lack access to legitimate means have access to illegitimate means. Cloward and Ohlin argued, on the contrary, that to innovate successfully requires more than motivation; it also requires the opportunity to learn and use illegitimate means. A juvenile who wants to be a successful burglar must learn how to identify lucrative sites, how to gain entry through locked doors or windows, how to avoid getting caught, and how to dispose of stolen merchandise. Not all juveniles have the opportunity to learn these things. In short, access to illegitimate opportunities is differentially distributed just as is access to legitimate opportunities.

Cloward and Ohlin were primarily concerned with collective or subcultural adaptations, that is, adaptations that characterize neighborhoods rather than individuals. They argued that innovation becomes a subcultural adaptation in neighborhoods that lack legitimate opportunities but have a well-developed illegitimate opportunity structure. In these neighborhoods, "criminal subcultures" emerge. Juveniles interact with successful adult criminals who provide illegitimate role models and who offer instruction in the techniques for committing crimes. The presence of a well-developed illegitimate opportunity structure presupposes a level of integration between criminal and conventional business activity. For example, there must be ties between criminals and retail outlets for stolen goods, between criminals and lawyers, between criminals and the police, and between criminals and politicians.

Neighborhoods that lack such integration between the conventional and unconventional worlds fail to provide a well developed illegitimate opportunity structure. Youths in these neighborhoods are not tied very closely to any adults, and as a result, they are virtually free from adult supervision. These neighborhoods often give rise to "conflict subcultures" that encourage violence, vandalism, and other forms of unrestrained behavior.

There is a third type of subculture, *retreatist*, that emerges among youths who lack access to legitimate and illegitimate opportunity structures, and who are unwilling or unable to participate in violence. Juveniles in these subcultures turn to escapist behaviors such as drug and alcohol use. The *retreatist subculture* is essentially the collective counterpart to Merton's retreatist mode of individual adaptation.

Merton's original anomie theory and subcultural elaborations such as those of Cloward and Ohlin and others (e.g., Cohen 1955) dominated the sociological study of deviance in the 1950s and 60s. The popularity of this general perspective decreased substantially through the 1970s, due in part to influential critiques of its logical and empirical foundations (Hirschi 1969; Kornhauser 1978). Since the early 1980s, however, there has been a resurgence of interest in the anomie perspective. This is reflected in critical reappraisals of the earlier critiques, empirical studies informed by the perspective, and efforts to elaborate the general theory (Adler and Laufer 1995; Bernard 1984; Burton and Cullen 1992; Agnew 1992).

One of the more influential of these efforts at resurgence is Robert Agnew's (1992) general theory of strain. According to Agnew, the distinctive contribution of the strain approach is to call attention to the importance of negative social relationships. These negative relationships produce negative emotions, especially anger. Crime and delinquency are common ways of expressing them.

Agnew proposed that there are three general sources of strain. One is the failure to achieve positively valued goals. This is the type of strain recognized by those who study the discrepancy between aspirations and expectations. A second source of strain is the removal of positively valued life events. This type of situation involves a variety of unpleasant events, such as the loss of a friend, divorce of one's parents, getting fired from one's job, or suspension from school. The third general source of strain is the experience of negative or aversive events. This encompasses experiences such as child abuse, criminal victimization, and physical and verbal punishment. Agnew hypothesized that these factors create a psychological predisposition for crime and delinquency. Whether or not crime and delinquency actually occur depends on the nature of the "coping strategies" adopted by individuals and on the different constraints they experience in their social environments.

While the early work applied anomie theory to deviance among the lower class, more recent studies also apply it to deviance among the well-to-do. For example, Nikos Passas (1990) argued that, because economic success is assessed in relative rather than absolute terms, the strong cultural pressures for economic success in the United States tend to produce pressures for deviance throughout the social structure. Members of the upper classes have much greater means to succeed than those of the lower classes, but their standards for success also tend to be higher. They are thus still susceptible to relative deprivation even if they receive considerable financial rewards in an absolute sense. Accordingly, pressures to innovate and employ illegitimate means to realize the goal of monetary success diffuse throughout the social structure, although the forms of innovation vary depending on opportunities for illegitimate activity. High-status people experiencing a means/end discrepancy are more likely to embezzle, for example, while low-status persons are more likely to resort to muggings.

Further elaborating anomie theory, Diane Vaughn (1983) and Deborah Vidaver Cohen (1995) argued that this theory is particularly well suited for explaining corporate deviance. Corporations must be able to generate profits to survive in the marketplace. Some corporations, however, inevitably confront structural obstacles—they lack the legitimate resources (capital, technical expertise, etc.) to compete effectively. Under such structural conditions, an organizational culture often emerges that condones the use of technically expedient but illegal means to ensure market share, such as price-fixing, theft of trade secrets, false advertising, and bribery (Vaughn 1983, 62).

Messner and Rosenfeld (1997) extended Merton's theory by describing the broad institutional foundations for anomie. They agreed with Merton that American culture encourages people to strive for monetary success with relatively little regard for the means that are used. They went on to argue that this exaggerated emphasis on monetary success and the accompanying de-emphasis on means occur because the market economy has become the dominant social institution. Other institutions—such as families, the schools, and political organizations—that could offer alternative success goals and temper the pecuniary mentality of the marketplace have been rendered subservient to the economy.

The dominance of the economy is reflected in three principal ways. First, noneconomic roles are devalued in comparison with economic roles. For example, while education may be viewed as a helpful tool for getting a good job, there is little status attached with being a "good student" per se. Second, noneconomic roles are accommodated to economic roles when role conflicts emerge. Consider how families tend to adjust their schedules and routines to the demands of the workplace rather than vice versa. Finally, the logic of the marketplace penetrates into noneconomic realms. This is manifested in the widespread use of market language and metaphors to characterize all social relationships. For example, spouses are "partners" who "manage" the family household; education is an "investment" in "human capital" (see also Schwartz 1994). Messner and Rosenfeld concluded that economic dominance at the institutional level reflects and reinforces anomie at the cultural level, resulting in high levels of crime in society at large.

In summary, Merton presented a theory of social organization and anomie, a typology for classifying deviant adaptations, and an incipient theory of deviant adaptations. He argued that the combination of universal success goals and inequality of opportunity generates pressure toward anomie and high levels of deviance. Cloward and Ohlin introduced the concept of illegitimate means and identified distinct subcultural adaptations to blocked opportunities. Recent work applies the anomie perspective to deviance by the upper class and relates anomie to an institutional order where the economy dominates other noneconomic institutions.

FUNCTIONS OF DEVIANCE

As previously noted, a second major theme of the structural/functional perspective is that norm violations can be viewed as any other persistent pattern of behavior in terms of their contributions for maintaining the existing social order. An underlying premise of the perspective is that stable behavior persists precisely because it serves a function for the larger society. Durkheim reasoned that if patterns of norm violations persist, like all persistent patterns of normative behavior they too must perform certain functions for society. For example, the violation of commonly held values and sentiments (the rape of an elderly woman, the kidnapping and molestation of a young child, the murder of a respected citizen) may unite people in an expression of common outrage and contempt. As the mass media publicize the incident and as people talk to each other about it, their common values about what is good and bad are reconfirmed. The deviant, in a sense, is the common enemy who unites the community. In Durkheim's words:

> Crime brings together upright consciences and concentrates them. We have only to notice what happens, particularly in a small town, when some moral scandal has just been committed. They stop each other on the street, they visit each other, they seek to come together to talk about the event and to wax indignant in common. ([1893] 1964, 102)

Kai Erikson extended and elaborated this thesis (Erikson 1966; Dentler and Erikson 1959). Erikson argued that the identification of deviants serves the important purpose of affirming and reinforcing the cultural identity of social groups. The deviant provides an opportunity for other group members to come together in pursuit of a common goal—bringing the deviant back into the fold. This reminds group members of what they share in common and strengthens social cohesion.

Additionally, Erikson argued that deviance clarifies norms. Frequently, the general norms of correct and proper behavior are vague. The social reaction to rule violators functions to clarify the meaning of these norms. Others learn "how far they can go." Consider the rule, "do not cheat on examinations." What does it mean for specific examinations? In the case of take-home examinations, it clearly means that students should not copy another student's answer. Does it also mean that students should not work together or talk over the assignment at all? How does the rule apply to term papers? Does it mean that students should not seek assistance from other students or other professors? Does it mean that one term paper should not be submitted in two classes? When some students "go too far" and exceed the educational community's boundaries or tolerance limits, the community reacts. It is these reactions that define the specific situational application of the rule.

Durkheim and Erikson also suggested that deviance highlights and accentuates the rewards for conformity. Punishing some people for norm violations reminds or makes salient to others the rewards for conformity. What social respect is given to saintly behavior in a community of saints? A little deviance by some makes saintly behavior stand out and become the object of respect. People can feel virtuous about their own conformity by contrasting themselves to the violations of others.

In sum, Durkheim and Erikson directed our attention to three functions of deviance: (1) Deviance increases group cohesion; (2) deviance clarifies the situational applications of general norms; and (3) deviance highlights the rewards of conformity.

For the most part, Durkheim and Erikson studied small rural communities where the moral consensus was very high and crime rates were very low by today's standards. In these societies deviance may do what Durkheim and Erikson say that it does. But what about contemporary urban communities (cities and neighborhoods) where moral consensus is weak, and deviance rates are very high? In these situations, further increases in the rate of deviance may produce fear. People may avoid shopping, working, and living in high crime neighborhoods; and those who cannot avoid them may constrain their behavior within them to a few safe places at a few safe times. Indeed, rather than increasing the intensity of social interaction and social cohesion, the fear of crime may decrease social interaction and weaken community cohesion in these settings.

Hence, a few acts of deviance in otherwise low-deviance communities, as experienced in rural communities, may well function to maintain the social order by clarifying social norms and increasing solidarity; but consistently high rates of deviance and crime, as experienced in many contemporary neighborhoods, may function to erode the social order by reducing social interaction and weakening solidarity. Starting from a level of zero deviance, increases in deviance may positively affect social life, as described by Durkheim and Erikson; but as deviance continues to increase, at some point the negative consequences outweigh the positive ones.

RESEARCH

Structural/functionalism has stimulated a large body of research on a variety of norm violations. Much of the contemporary work focuses on the social causes of suicide, crime, and delinquency, and on the consequences of crime for social organization.

SUICIDE

Durkheim's work on structural integration and regulation has inspired a distinctive tradition of research on suicide. Some of these studies follow the original Durkheimian tradition rather closely, whereas others elaborate and extend Durkheim's core ideas in new directions.

A key social factor in Durkheim's explanation of suicide is economic change. Durkheim was one of the first to study the relationship between the economic cycle and suicide. Using data on Western Europe at the end of the nineteenth century, he reported that suicide rates rise both in periods of depression (as measured by bank failures and bankruptcies) and in times of prosperity (as measured by productivity). For example, between 1874 and 1886 the average yearly increase in the French suicide rate was 2 percent; in 1882, a year of an economic crash, the rate climbed by 7 percent. In Italy, industrial expansion started in approximately 1870 with sharp increases in horsepower, salaries, the number of steam boilers, and the general standard of living. Immediately prior to that period (1866 to 1870), the suicide rate had been stable, but from 1871 to 1877 it increased by 36 percent, and from 1877 to 1899 it increased another 28 percent.

Durkheim provided numerous such examples to support his thesis that disruptions in the normative order (anomie) associated with the peaks and troughs of the business cycle lead to suicide. For the most part, however, the research findings are more illustrative than conclusive. Cases that are contrary to his theory are frequently explained away or even ignored. In an influential reanalysis of Durkheim's data, Pope (1976) found that the evidence in support of the theory is much more marginal and less conclusive than Durkheim suggested. Nevertheless, Durkheim's general point that economic change is a potentially disruptive force conducive to suicide has proven to be an insightful one.

Durkheim also directed attention to marital status in the explanation of suicide. Durkheim assumed that marriage is socially integrating and, thus, that it lowers the risk of suicide. In support of this hypothesis, he cited statistics from various countries during the latter part of the nineteenth century showing that married people have much lower suicide rates than unmarried people (single and widowed). More recent research generally confirms Durkheim's proposition that married people are at relatively low risk of suicide (Danigelis and Pope 1979; but see Kposowa, Breault, and Singh 1995). Contemporary studies also indicate that suicide rates increase along with divorce rates, an indicator of marital breakdown (Breault 1986; Stack 1980).

Durkheim noted a striking exception in his data to the general relationship between marital status and suicide. Married people under twenty do not exhibit low levels of suicide. The fact that age alters the association between marriage and suicide is central to Gibbs and Martin's status integration theory of suicide discussed earlier. To reiterate, Gibbs and Martin argued that a poorly integrated status set leads to inconsistent role demands and high levels of stress. For example, being married at age seventeen creates a malintegrated status set. The role demands of adolescent statuses, such as student, are inconsistent with the role demands of adult statuses, such as spouse and parent. At the same time, most people marry, and by middle age, social activity is centered around the family. Those who remain single beyond the normal ages of marriage experience difficulties meeting the social demands of their age group. Early widowhood is also a problematic status set. Young widows experience difficulties not experienced by those widowed at the "normal" time (during the elderly years). They frequently have children to rear and demanding economic responsibilities to bear; further, there are few other widows in their age group to console them. Those widowed in their later years are beyond those responsibilities and usually know other widows in their age group who can offer emotional support.

The notion of status integration is easily described with illustrations, but measuring it systematically poses a formidable challenge for research. Gibbs and Martin developed an ingenuous technique for quantifying the degree of malintegration associated with a status set. They argued that people avoid status sets that generate stress: People tend not to move into them, and if in them, they try to move out. Thus, the occupancy rate of a status set can be used as a measure of its integration.

Gibbs and Martin (1964; Gibbs 1969), in their early work, examined the occupancy rate of status sets composed of only two statuses, typically marital status and age. In a study using a sample of white males, Gibbs (1969) calculated the occupancy rates across marital status categories for specified age groups, and related these rates to the corresponding suicide rates. He found that for the fifteen to nineteen age group, single persons had the highest occupancy rate (96.1 percent of the persons in this age group were single) and the lowest suicide rate. For the twenty-five to twenty-nine age group, married persons showed the highest occupancy rate (78.1 percent of the persons in this age group were married) and the lowest suicide rates. These results support the theory: High occupancy implies strong integration of the status set, which is associated with a low risk of suicide. Of all the possible age and marital comparisons, 72 percent conformed to the theoretically expected pattern.

Gibbs and Martin argued that their predictions of suicide rates were not 100 percent accurate because people occupy more than two statuses. In addition to marital and age statuses, people occupy gender, racial, occupational, and educational statuses, as well as many others. Subsequent research (Stafford and Gibbs 1985) on status integration and suicide has considered multidimensional status sets. The results of this research offer some support for the theory but also indicate the need for its modification. Evidently, all statuses do not contribute equally to the prediction of suicide rates. Research also reveals that the relevance of different statuses is not the same in different historical periods (Stafford and Gibbs 1988). A major challenge for status integration theorists is to explain why the influence of status varies from status to status (e.g., age, occupation, marital status) and over time.

Research on suicide following in the Durkheimian tradition has also considered the role of religion. Durkheim cited statistics indicating lower suicide rates among Catholics than among Protestants, and he explained this differential with reference to the greater integration of Catholics into a collective entity—the organized Church—and the greater regulation associated with this integration. More recent research has built upon Durkheim's insights by extending the analysis to other religious groups. For example, Simpson and Conklin argued that Islam is a religion that "binds its adherents to a daily ritual of prayer and intrudes into all facets of life" (Simpson and Conklin 1989, 961). Given the logic of Durkheim's theory, then, populations with large numbers of followers of Islam should exhibit low suicide rates, all other things being equal. Conklin and Simpson found support for this hypothesis in an analysis of suicide rates for a sample of seventy-one contemporary nations. After statistically controlling for demographic and socioeconomic characteristics of nations, the relative size of the Islamic population was inversely related to the national suicide rate.

One of the more innovative attempts to extend Durkheim's work on suicide and religion is the research by Pescosolido and Georgianna (1989). Their research is based on the premise that the role of religion in society has changed considerably since Durkheim's time. Secularization has occurred in some denominations, blurring previous distinctions between religious groups. In addition, there has been an evangelical revival in many areas of the United States. These changes imply that the simple contrasts between the religious life of Protestants and Catholics upon which Durkheim's theory rests are no longer applicable. An adequate analysis of the effect of religious affiliation on suicide in contemporary American society requires the use of a more detailed classification of religious denominations.

Recall that, according to Pescosolido and Georgianna's social network theory, the protective influence of religion against suicide derives from participation and integration in a religious network. To test this hypothesis, they collected information on the strength of these social networks (e.g., the percentage of the members of the denomination who attend weekly services, and the percentage of members who are married to a spouse of the same denomination) for twenty-seven different religious groups (Catholics, Jews, and twenty-five Protestant denominations). They then examined the relationship between a denomination's suicide rate and the strength of its social network. Consistent with their theory, they found that denominations characterized by relatively strong social networks exhibited more powerful protective effects against suicide than did denominations characterized by weak networks. (They did not test for the hypothesized relationship between extremely high network density and high suicide rates.)

To summarize, sociologists following in the Durkheimian tradition have published a large volume of work on the relationship between social structure and suicide. While the work has been criticized (Pope 1976; Poppel and Day 1996), it strongly suggests that the nature of the social order (degree of social integration) is important in understanding suicide rates in both the nineteenth and twentieth centuries. This is not to say that suicide is unaffected by interpersonal relationships and psychological factors; however, in emphasizing these factors, psychologists and psychiatrists have frequently neglected the social order. The work of Durkheim and his followers reminds us that the nature of the social order and people's integration in it are important factors as well.

JUVENILE DELINQUENCY AND CRIME

Merton's work on social structure and anomie has had a major influence on studies of juvenile delinquency. These studies have commonly employed a "stress" or "strain" model of the underlying causal dynamics linking social structural conditions with individual acts of delinquent behavior. According to this model, youths who perceive means/end discrepancies experience psychological stress and turn to delinquency as a way to cope with this stress. Figure 2.2 illustrates the basic logic of the strain model.

The critical issue in testing hypotheses derived from the strain model has been measuring its core concepts. For the most part, the intervening variable of individual stress has not been measured directly. Researchers have instead constructed measures of the means/ends discrepancy and related these measures to indicators of delinquent involvement.

The most widely used measure of the means/ends discrepancy in research on juvenile delinquency is the perceived gap between aspirations and expectations. With respect to a desired outcome, such as the amount of schooling attained, youths are asked about what they aspire to—how much they want to get—and what they expect to end up with. Strain theory implies several predictions about levels of delinquent involvement for youths with different combinations of aspirations and expectations. Delinquency should be high when youths have lofty aspirations and low expectations. Such a discrepancy between what people want and expect presumably creates the psychological stress that leads to delinquency. In contrast, youths who have high aspirations but also high expectations should experience little strain and should exhibit low levels of delinquency. Finally, youths with both low aspirations and low expectations should also feel little stress and should have low levels of delinquency. (The combination of low aspirations and high expectations is a logical possibility, but does not occur very often.) Early research, however, provided little support for the strain hypothesis (Liska 1971; Burton and Cullen 1992).

In a critique of this research, Farnworth and Lieber (1989) argued that most efforts to test strain theory have been seriously flawed because they fail to measure the means/ends discrepancy in a way consistent with the original theory (see also Menard 1995). The common approach to measuring this concept has been to calculate the aspirations/expectations gap with

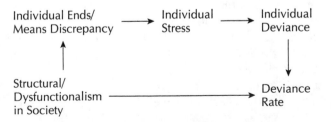

FIGURE 2.2　MERTON'S THEORY OF DEVIANCE
The diagram illustrates that the structural dysfunctionalism in society causes ends/means discrepancy in people, which in turn causes stress, which is expressed in deviance. Hence, a society with a high level of structural dysfunctionalism will have a high rate of deviance.

reference to levels of schooling. However, in Merton's formulation of anomie theory, the central cultural goal is monetary success—getting rich. Education is essentially a means to that goal. "If strain is recast entirely in the educational realm, the educational means in Merton's original theory become both goals and means, and the central importance of economic goals is lost" (Farnworth and Lieber 1989, 265).

Farnworth and Lieber introduced a measure of strain based on the perceived discrepancy between economic aspirations (wanting "to make lots of money") and educational expectations. They used this measure to predict levels of delinquent involvement for a sample of adolescents in Seattle, Washington. Consistent with their hypothesis, the proposed measure of strain was significantly related to delinquent involvement. Youths who expressed a strong desire for financial success but who expected limited educational achievement exhibited comparatively high levels of delinquency. The effect of their measure of strain was particularly strong for utilitarian forms of delinquency (i.e., acts with an economic component). Farnworth and Lieber concluded that the failure to find support for strain theory in previous research is due to improper measurement of the principal theoretical concept (for a critique of this study, see Jensen 1995).

The research on strain and delinquency has been conducted for the most part at the individual level of analysis. There have also been "macrolevel" studies of variation in crime rates that draw upon the general logic of the structural/functional perspective. Recall that structural/functionalism directs attention to the *malintegration* of the different parts of the social system in the explanation of deviance. In Merton's theory, it is disjuncture between cultural and social structure that ultimately creates pressures for high levels of deviance. This general insight has been applied in research on the relationship between racial inequality and crime rates across U.S. metropolitan areas.

The most influential study of racial inequality and crime is that of Blau and Blau (1982). The Blaus argued that inequalities based on "inborn" characteristics are illegitimate in societies with a formal commitment to democratic principles. In a democracy, political rights and economic opportunities should be available to all; access to them should not depend on membership in social groups. The dependence of economic opportunities on race in a democratic society such as the United States is thus contrary to basic society values. It represents a social structural arrangement that is poorly integrated with the culture. The Blaus hypothesized that this kind of structural/cultural malintegration is likely to lead to diffuse hostility, weak integration, and high levels of violent crime.

To test this hypothesis, the Blaus collected data for a sample of the 125 largest metropolitan areas in the United States. They calculated a measure of racial economic discrimination based on the difference in socioeconomic status for nonwhites and whites and examined the effects of this measure on the violent crime rates included in the FBI's crime index. The results supported their main hypothesis: Metropolitan areas with high levels of racial inequality exhibited comparatively high rates of violent crime, controlling for a wide range of other characteristics of these areas. Subsequent studies have offered only mixed support for the Blaus' thesis. Evidently, the observed effect of racial inequality on metropolitan crime rates is sensitive to measurement procedures (Messner and Golden 1992).

Some cross-cultural evidence also supports the structural/functional hypothesis that economic structures can have different effects on levels of deviance depending on the larger cultural setting. For example, a fairly large body of research has documented a relationship between economic inequality and homicide rates for samples of contemporary nations: Nations with high levels of inequality tend to exhibit high homicide rates (Krahn, Hartnagel, and Gartrell 1986). This empirical pattern does not generalize to all types of societies. Social inequality bears little systematic relationship to homicide rates in "simple," preindustrial societies typically studied by anthropologists.

Rosenfeld and Messner (1991) proposed a structural/functional explanation for these disparate observations. They argued that simple and modern societies differ in basic value orientations, and as a result inegalitarian structures have different implications for social integration. Similar to the case of pre-World War II India referred to earlier, simple societies are organized around traditional status hierarchies where assignment to social roles is based on ascribed characteristics—basically "who you are." Under these arrangements, inequalities are largely inherited and taken for granted. Modern societies, in contrast, are more oriented toward achievement. Inequalities are accordingly not "natural" in the same sense that they are in simple societies; they must be explicitly justified and legitimated (Parsons 1970, 18). Given these value differences across types of societies, it is reasonable to expect that extreme levels of inequality will pose a much greater threat to social integration in modern than in preindustrial societies, and that inequality will emerge as a more powerful predictor of crime rates in the former than in the latter.

To summarize, Merton's anomie theory and the structural/functional perspective more generally have inspired a large volume of research on delinquency and crime. In delinquency studies, researchers have formulated and tested a "strain" model that predicts high levels of delinquent behavior as a result of a gap between aspirations and expectations. Early work in the strain tradition offered only limited support for the strain model, but the results of recent studies using new measurement procedures have been more promising. The structural/functional perspective has also informed research on crime rates across cities, states, and nations. The distinctive contribution of this perspective has been to sensitize researchers to the importance of considering structural conditions in conjunction with prevailing cultural orientations.

FUNCTIONS OF DEVIANCE

Research within the structural/functional perspective has considered not only the causes of deviance but also its consequences or functions for the social order. As previously argued, we suspect that deviance has positive consequences in rural and agricultural societies where deviance rates are generally quite low, but has negative consequences in urban and industrial societies where deviance rates are quite high.

Research on the positive consequences of deviance falls into two categories: observational studies of small informal groups and historical studies of communities.

Dentler and Erikson (1959) studied small friendship groups of army recruits and various Quaker work groups. These groups functioned as if they were organized to encourage or sustain deviance. In most of the groups, one or two people violated the norms by not doing their share of the work. Yet the other group members did not isolate or ostracize them. Rather, they sustained them by doing their assigned work and covering up their mistakes, and frequently they united to bring them back into the fold. Why? Dentler and Erikson offered a functional explanation: The deviants were sustained by the group because of what they contributed to it. Their deviance provided an opportunity for the other group members to come together in pursuit of a common goal, thereby increasing group cohesion and reminding group members of what they shared in common.

Erikson (1966) extended this analysis to deviance in the Puritan community of the Massachusetts Bay colony. He examined three crises confronting the colony. Each crisis initially reduced the solidarity and cohesion of the community and increased its internal conflict, and each was followed by an increase in deviance as recorded in official statistics. One crisis involved the rise and fall of recorded instances of witchcraft, arrests for witchcraft, and punishment of witches. Does a crisis cause people to misbehave more than in times of stability? Erikson argued "no." Rather, during a crisis people's tolerance for deviance constricts; they tolerate less deviance when the group itself seems to be threatened. Recorded instances of witchcraft are particularly useful to illustrate this point. Its rise and fall cannot reflect the underlying variation in actual acts of witchcraft; it must reflect something else, such as a community's values and tolerance of deviance. Whatever it reflects, Erikson maintained that it is functional. By identifying specific norm violations as witchcraft and specific people as witches, the Puritans came together to "wax indignant," to condemn the action, and to control it. Initially torn by internal conflict, this "coming together" reminded them of what they shared in common and reaffirmed their collective identity; it also increased their cohesion and solidarity. Here Erikson's work reminds us that it is not the act of deviance itself that is directly functional but rather the reaction to it. Deviance is functional insofar as it illicits a common public outrage and collective response.

Now what happens if the deviance grows out of control, as it seems to have in many contemporary cities and neighborhoods? Considerable research shows that, while deviance may continue to lead to outrage, it also leads to fear. While common outrage may bring people together, which increases cohesion, fear of walking the streets keeps them apart, which decreases cohesion. Many researchers have examined this issue, using surveys that ask people about their social behavior (walking streets, shopping, socializing around their home) and about their fear of being victimized in their neighborhood. In one such survey of city residents, Liska et al. (1988) found that the fear of crime severely constrains social activity, which in turn further increases the fear of crime, leading to a vicious cycle. In a further study, Liska and Warner (1991) reported that robbery, more than any other crime, imparts fear. This is understandable, because robbery is the only crime of violence committed primarily by strangers. This is what people fear about crime. If the negative consequences of crime on community life operate through fear, then the above findings have important public policy implications.

While one response to the fear of crime is to constrain activity to a few safe places during a few safe times, another is to move. In a recent study, Liska and Bellair (1995) examined the impact of crime on the social composition of cities from 1950 to 1990. They found that many people respond to their fear of crime by simply moving to safer places—the suburbs. Not only does this effect contribute to the decline of city populations and to the growth of suburban populations, but it changes the social composition of both. Those who move in response to the fear of crime are those with the resources to do so—the well-off who also tend to be white. Liska and Bellair (1995) reported that from 1950 to 1990 city crime rates, especially robbery rates, played a major role in reducing the white urban population, thereby increasing the percentage of the urban population that is nonwhite.

In sum, then, research clearly suggests that crime has consequences, not only for the individuals victimized, but for the community at large. The consequences can be positive, or functional, such as when crime rates are low as they frequently are in rural communities; but the consequences can also be negative, such as when rates are high as they frequently are in contemporary urban communities.

SOCIAL POLICY

The theoretical arguments and the research findings in the structural/functionalist tradition carry implications for the social changes that would be required to reduce levels of crime and deviance in society.

Some of these changes could conceivably be achieved through modest social reforms, whereas others would require a radical restructuring of the social order.

Durkheim argued that social disintegration or deregulation causes norm violations. The policy implications are reasonably clear in principle: Increase social integration and regulation. For example, Durkheim identified being married as a status that provides strong regulation. Presumably, then, social policies that encourage marriage (e.g., tax credits) and discourage divorce (e.g., strict alimony laws) would foster lower levels of crime and deviance. Durkheim also argued that economic instability causes stress that leads to suicide. This argument implies that policies that help smooth the business cycle should also decrease general levels of social stress and self-destructive behavior. An example of such policies would be the regulation of interest rates by the Federal Reserve Board. Although it is possible to identify social policies such as these that would be consistent with Durkheim's theoretical arguments concerning societal disintegration and deregulation, Durkheim's work has not, in fact, been a direct source of much social policy in the United States.

Merton's anomie theory, in contrast, has had a major influence on social policy. Merton suggested that the rate of deviance is directly linked to the degree of cultural/structural integration of the social system. He attributed the high level of deviance in American society to the unequal distribution of opportunities to realize the culturally prescribed goal of monetary success. A policy implication that logically follows from this perspective is to expand access to economic opportunities, thereby making the social structure more compatible with cultural values.

A number of social policies have been implemented that attempt to provide greater opportunities for the disadvantaged. One of the most ambitious of these was the Mobilization for Youth Program, which was largely inspired by Merton's anomie theory. In fact, the program was partially organized by Richard Cloward, a prominent theorist within the anomie tradition. The program began in the early 1960s and was financed by the National Institute for Mental Health, the Department of Health, Education and Welfare, the New York School of Social Work, and the Ford Foundation. Based on the theoretical proposition that economic and social obstacles to goal achievement are the causes of crime and delinquency, the program sought to expand work and educational opportunities in a sixty-block area on the lower East Side of Manhattan—an area composed largely of poor nonwhites. It proposed vocational training for hard-to-place juveniles and employment for those without jobs. To overcome educational barriers confronting the slum student, it proposed educational laboratories and the use of high school students to tutor low-income elementary school children. In addition, it proposed assisting slum dwellers to organize themselves to solve their own problems.

How did the program work in practice? By most accounts, the program was a failure (Arnold 1964; Quinney 1975). The political aspects of the program led to considerable controversy and turmoil, preventing its full implementation. For example, the community organization program helped to generate rent strikes, demonstrations, and marches, and it encouraged welfare clients to retain lawyers. Much of this activity disturbed local and state authorities. Moneys for the program were sometimes impounded; the FBI began an investigation into the program; and program files were confiscated. The fate of the Mobilization for Youth program highlights a dilemma confronting those advocating policies informed by anomie theory: Changing social conditions to help the disadvantaged means changing the lives of those in power, and they resist.

The basic logic of Merton's anomie theory nevertheless continues to underlie a variety of social policies for dealing with crime and deviance. Interestingly, the influence of anomie theory can be detected in policies associated with both liberal and conservative political agendas. Liberals and conservatives agree that economic opportunity is essential for social stability, but they disagree on how to maximize such opportunity. Liberals generally prefer a proactive role for government; they thus favor programs such as preschool education (Head Start) to compensate for disadvantages in the home, publicly supported child-care to enable poor people to work, and government-sponsored recreational programs to "keep kids off the streets." Conservatives, in contrast, prefer policies such as enterprise zones to encourage private investment in targeted areas and across-the-board tax cuts to spur economic growth ("a rising tide lifts all boats"). In either case, however, the shared assumption is that at least part of the solution to the problems of crime and deviance is to be found in expanded economic opportunity. The principal difference between liberal and conservative approaches to securing greater opportunities revolves around the extent and nature of the role of government.

Although Merton's anomie theory is usually associated with policies designed to expand opportunities within the framework of the existing social order, recent formulations of the perspective are also consistent with more radical proposals. Theories that emphasize the role of *relative* deprivation in the origins of anomie lead logically to proposals for a more egalitarian distribution of economic outcomes. This implies, in turn, movement away from a free market economy, an economy that relies on appreciable differentials in rewards to serve as incentives for work and investment. Similarly, to the extent that anomie derives from an institutional structure that is imbalanced, with excessive priority given to the economy, the solution to the problem of crime and deviance will entail a restructuring of social institutions. Of course, whether or not there is any political support for such fundamental social changes remains to be seen.

CRITIQUE

THEORY

After dominating the sociological study of deviance in the 1950s and early 1960s, structural/functionalism has come under considerable criticism. Various sociologists have argued that structural/functionalists exaggerate the degree of value consensus and harmony in American society (Lemert 1967). Instead, the United States is characterized by value pluralism, dissensus, and conflict among social classes, ethnic groups, racial groups, geographical regions, and age groups.

This criticism carries significant implications for theories of deviance built on the assumption of societal consensus and integration. First and foremost, if the critics' charges are valid, the definition of deviance as a norm violation becomes problematic, for conformity from the viewpoint of one group then constitutes a norm violation from the viewpoint of another group. Structural/functionalists sidestep this issue by implicitly assuming the normative perspective of dominant groups.

As Merton's theory has been the most prominent of the structural/functional theories of deviance, it has elicited the most rigorous criticisms (Kornhauser 1978; Pfohl 1985). Merton assumed that most people value economic success, and he thus focused on class differentials in economic opportunity. Critics have charged that Merton's theory ends up exhibiting a class bias: It exaggerates lower-class deviance and ignores upper-class deviance. As noted earlier, recent researchers have tried to respond to this criticism by bringing in the notion of relative deprivation. This offers an explanation for deviance among members of the upper classes. They may be *relatively* deprived even if they are well-off in an absolute sense. However, this extension of the theory threatens to stretch it to the point that it fails to yield any distinctive predictions. If all conceivable distributions of deviance across the class structure can be rendered consistent with the theory, the theory offers no particular insight about the class patterning of deviance.

Merton has also been criticized for not providing a theory of deviant adaptations (Cullen 1983). While classifying patterns of deviance (innovation, retreatism, ritualism, and rebellion), Merton never clearly indicated the conditions under which each of these adaptations occurs. Why does one person become a retreatist and another a ritualist? To some extent, Cloward and Ohlin addressed this problem, specifying the conditions under which innovation and retreatism occur. Yet they did not identify the conditions under which ritualism and rebellion, rather than innovation and retreatism, occur.

The theory can also be criticized for its vague and incomplete account of social psychological processes. Some formulations imply that an ends/means discrepancy exerts pressures on individuals and creates deviant motivations that would not otherwise arise; others imply that the ends/means discrepancy erodes inner psychological controls and frees individuals to express preexisting deviant motivations (see Bernard 1995; Cullen 1983; Messner 1988). In general, the theory does not provide a clear description of the linkage between macrolevel conditions and the psychological reactions to them.

Durkheim's theory of suicide has also been criticized. Pope (1976), for example, charged that the theoretical link between deregulation and suicide is vague. Exactly how is deregulation experienced by people so as to produce suicide, or how is regulation experienced so as to deter suicide? Pope argued that throughout the monograph, *Suicide*, a variety of unconnected and sometimes inconsistent processes, such as ends/means discrepancy, stress, meaninglessness, and social irresponsibility, are said to be induced by social deregulation and to culminate in suicide.

In addition, feminists have criticized Durkheim's application of the theory to explain gender differences in suicide (Lehmann 1995). Durkheim observed that marriage has a less protective effect on suicide for women than for men, and he interpreted this finding by claiming that women's sexuality is essentially "physical," whereas men's is more "mental." As a result, women do not have as great a need for marriage to regulate their sexual activity—it is regulated naturally. Durkheim's interpretation of the gender differential in suicide thus rests on highly problematic assumptions about "natural" differences between men and women.

The functions of deviance thesis has also been criticized. Perhaps the main criticism is the tendency to ignore the dysfunctions of deviance. A hypothesis is needed that specifies the conditions under which deviance is functional and under which it is dysfunctional.

RESEARCH

Many of the central concepts of structural/functional theories have not been measured, and many others have not been validly measured. At the individual level, an obvious example is *stress*, a central concept in Durkheim's and Merton's theories. Very few researchers have measured it directly. Rather, they have measured the hypothesized causes of stress (economic crises, marital status, status disintegration, and blocked opportunities) and the alleged outcomes of stress (suicide, crime, delinquency). Similarly, at the aggregate level, anomie typically remains an unmeasured concept that is supposed to intervene between structural conditions, such as economic or racial inequality, and rates of deviance.

Criticisms have also been leveled at structural/functional research for the tendency to rely on official records of deviance (police files, court records, coroners' reports, and the like). For example, Durkheim, in support of his theory, reported that Catholics show a lower suicide level than Protestants. Douglas (1967) challenged this finding, arguing that it may simply reflect a bias in official records. Suicide is regarded as more sinful in the Catholic than in the Protestant religion. Thus, Catholic families and friends may cover up suicides, disguising them as natural deaths. These actions may produce the official statistics that show Protestants to have a higher suicide rate than Catholics. Research by van Poppel and Day (1996) in the Netherlands is consistent with this interpretation. They reported that the Catholic-Protestant differential in suicide rates can be explained entirely by the common practice of classifying large numbers of deaths among Catholics as "sudden deaths" or "deaths from ill-defined or unspecified causes" that would have been recorded as suicides if they had occurred among Protestants. Although some other research paints a more positive picture of the utility of official suicide rates for the evaluation of social theories (Pescosolido and Mendelsohn 1986), clearly care must be taken when using official reports of deviance to indicate actual levels of deviant behavior. (See Chapter 6 for a further discussion of the limitations of official records of deviance.)

Time order is another important problem. Some research suggests a relationship between ends/means discrepancy and norm violations. Researchers frequently assume that the ends/means discrepancy occurs first and causes norm violations yet the reverse may be true in many cases. Norm violations may lower economic and educational opportunities. Alcoholics or drug addicts, for example, may have little time for educational or economic pursuits and may be discriminated against in educational and economic organizations.

Measurement and time order have to do with the quality of research. The quantity of research is also important. For several decades, relatively little work on deviance was done within the structural/functional perspective. Despite the recent resurgence of interest in structural/functional approaches, more research is clearly needed before we can have confidence in these theories of norm violations.

POLICY

Concerning social policy, a theoretical perspective can be criticized on two counts: (1) The policy implications are vague, and (2) the policy implications are not subject to implementation. Structural/functional theories are subject to both criticisms. Those who have extended Durkheim's social deregulation theory tend not even to discuss social policy, perhaps because their theories often imply policies that are in conflict with basic American values. For example, Durkheim identified Protestantism as a status that provides a low level of social regulation. The logical policy implication is to encourage people to shift their religious affiliations from Protestantism to some other, more regulative religion. Such a proposal would clearly be unacceptable to most people because Americans place a high value on freedom of religion. Similarly, with respect to the functions of deviance thesis, it is unlikely that policy makers or members of the general public will be responsive to the recommendation of increasing norm violations, specifically those that violate the common social consciousness, to strengthen social cohesion and moral boundaries.

Merton's theory, on the other hand, has had a considerable influence on policy. As noted earlier, programs inspired by Merton's theory are usually designed to provide greater opportunities to the disadvantaged by increasing their educational and vocational skills. Assume for a moment that these programs are successful at increasing skills among the disadvantaged. What would be the effect on the norm-violation rate? A policy of improving educational and economic skills assumes that the economy can absorb these people. That may be true in an ever expanding economy; but what about an economy that is contracting, or stagnant, or exhibiting very slow growth? Consider the issue in these terms. If an economy generates jobs for 95 percent of those who wish to work, 5 percent must be unemployed. These people will probably be the least educated and the least skilled. Improving their education and skills may not reduce the level of unemployment; rather, it may simply rearrange the ranking of people in the job queue. Thus, if successful, these programs may not lower the rate of norm violations; they may only shift the propensity for norm violations from some people to others.

Generally, social policies like Mobilization for Youth, Head Start, and other skill-enhancing programs assume that economic opportunities exist but that some people are ill-equipped to take advantage of them. These types of social policy are geared toward accommodating people to the existing system. More radical recommendations have also been put forth by proponents of anomie theory, recommendations that call for changing the basic social order, especially the economic order. Those who are doing well in the present system are unlikely to be very responsive to these recommendations, and these are the very people who control social policy. Hence, if the more radical extensions of Merton's theory are valid, high norm-violation rates will remain with us for some time to come.

3 ECOLOGICAL PERSPECTIVES: SOCIAL DISORGANIZATION, CONTROL, AND LEARNING PROCESSES

THEORY

American sociology emerged at the University of Chicago in the late nineteenth century. The university opened its doors in 1892 and, with substantial grants and endowments by the Rockefellers and others, appointed many of the most prestigious scholars of the day. The situation at the time was perfect for the development of sociology as an academic discipline, and the university became an instant success and academic leader. Unlike the situation in the East, Chicago, as a new university, had no established departments with control over money and curricula that could hamper the formation of a new department.

Sociology at Chicago encompassed a diverse set of concerns about society and human behavior, but the dominant concern that pulled together much of the research, giving it shape and form, was social ecology.

At the most general level, the study of *social ecology* deals with the distribution of social activities across space and time. Applying the ecological perspective, Chicago school theorists focused on two basic issues: how the spatial-temporal distribution of activities facilitates or impedes the realization of collective goals, and how this distribution influences the social experiences to which people are exposed. In addressing these issues, the Chicago school theorists inspired research and theorizing on both the macrolevel processes that lead to variation in rates of deviance across communities and the microlevel (or social psychological) processes that underlie the macrolevel processes.

MACROLEVEL THEORY: SOCIAL DISORGANIZATION
AND DIFFERENTIAL SOCIAL ORGANIZATION

With the publication of Charles Darwin's epic works, *On the Origin of Species* (1859) and *Descent of Man* (1871), natural and physical scientists became increasingly interested in the relationship between the organization of living matter and the external environment. The structure or order of living matter was thought to depend on the nature of the environment, defined as all factors external to an organism. The study of this relationship between organism and environment constitutes the science of ecology.

In studying this relationship, ecologists emphasize the survival and adaptation of organisms—organisms survive through adaptation. In addition, since some organisms constitute part of the environment, organisms must adapt to each other. Ecologists refer to these interrelationships between organisms as the "web of life." Some forms of life are compatible; some are not. Over time only compatible organisms survive. Food chains are instances of compatible interrelationships between organisms. For example, in North America deciduous trees support or initiate a number of food chains. Mice and squirrels feed on fruit and leaves; mice are eaten by skunks, who are eaten by red foxes, and so on. A change in one part of the chain results in necessary adaptations in other parts (Hawley 1950). These interdependencies produce *biotic communities,* that is, discernible patterns of interrelationships between organisms. Biotic communities are located in distinct geographical spaces called *natural areas.* Ecologists study how biotic communities and natural areas develop and change. What happens, for example, when the physical features of an area are altered, or when new forms of life appear? According to the ecological framework, changes vibrate through biotic communities because of their interdependent character. Ecologists describe these processes in terms of invasion, competition (for resources), and succession.

In a rather loose manner, the Chicago sociologists used the ecological model to conceptualize their research on the city of Chicago. They argued that the social order of the city can be understood from an ecological viewpoint as a product of various social processes, such as symbiosis (mutually beneficial relationships), cooperation, competition, and cyclical change. They also argued, however, that humans, unlike other animals, develop a culture (customs, values, norms) that restricts or limits ecological processes. Within this general framework, research focused on a variety of specific topics, attempting to describe and explain the spatial distribution of persistent patterns of urban activity, such as commerce, industry, residence, and unconventional behavior (crime, delinquency, mental illness, and prostitution).

One of the more prominent examples of an ecological theory of urban activity is the zonal theory proposed by Ernest Burgess (1925). Burgess argued that the development of a city approximates a pattern of concentric circles, whereby certain activities cluster in distinctive spatial zones (see Figure 3.1). The central zone is occupied by commerce and industry. The second zone is transitional. It is in the process of being taken over by commercial interests but includes areas where the poor, migrants, and immigrants reside. The third zone is a working-class residential district dominated by multifamily houses. The fourth zone is a residential zone consisting

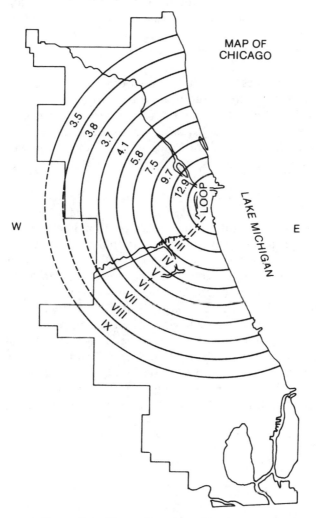

FIGURE 3.1 ZONAL PATTERN OF DELINQUENCY

This map of Chicago includes nine zones, and Burgess' hypothesis includes only five zones. On this map, Burgess' zone I is equal to zone I; his zone II is equal to zones II and III; his zone III is equal to zones IV and V; his zone IV is equal to zones VI and VII; and his zone V is equal to zones VIII and IX. The numbers refer to rates of delinquency.

Source: C. R. Shaw, F. M. Zorbaugh, H. D. McKay, and L. S. Cottrell. *Delinquency Areas.* © 1929 by University of Chicago Press. Reprinted by permission of the publisher.

primarily of single-family houses. Finally, the fifth zone is a commuters' residential area. Burgess did not conceive of this zonal pattern as literally describing all cities (Faris 1967). In fact, it only roughly described Chicago, as Lake Michigan cuts the pattern into a half circle. Burgess depicted an ideal or classical pattern of city development from which actual patterns could be analyzed as departures.

The zonal pattern was thought to emerge through ecological processes, particularly competition for real estate. The highest land values tend to be those in the center of the city, where transportation networks are concentrated. This land is purchased and used by commerce and industry, which have the resources to afford it. Over time, business activity tends to grow and expand. It "invades" surrounding territory. Areas adjacent to the industrial/commercial zone are in the process of "turning over" from residential to commercial land use. These areas are not particularly desirable places to live, and they are thus occupied primarily by the poor and by immigrants. Generally, the value of land increases with distance from the transitional zone, and the pattern of use, including residential, changes accordingly.

Social Disorganization Theory   The Chicago theorists also studied the patterning of deviance in physical space. Their studies of delinquency, mental illness, and suicide showed that unconventional behavior tends to concentrate in cities, particularly in the transitional zone where residential and business activity intermesh. They proposed a theory of *social disorganization* to account for both the relatively high rates of deviance in urban areas compared to rural communities and for the high rates of deviance in the transitional zones of cities. The core argument of their theory maintains that ecological conditions associated with urban life disrupt traditional social controls, thereby promoting unconventional and deviant behavior.

Various Chicagoans (Wirth 1938; Shaw and McKay 1931) attempted to specify exactly how an urban environment leads to deviance. Their explanation for the comparatively high rates of deviance in urban settings is depicted schematically in Figure 3.2. Industrialization creates a need for

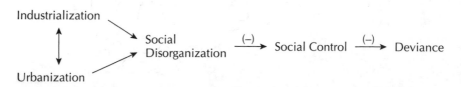

FIGURE 3.2   CAUSAL STRUCTURE UNDERLYING THE THEORY OF SOCIAL DISORGANIZATION
Arrows show the direction of causal effects, double-headed arrows indicate that the effect flows in both directions, and a minus sign means that the effect is negative (an increase in one variable results in a decrease in another variable). Generally, the figure shows that industrialization and urbanization increase social disorganization, which decreases conventional social controls, which in turn increases deviant behavior.

concentrations of labor, thereby increasing population size and density (urbanization) by migration and immigration. Both of these social processes, industrialization and urbanization, in turn produce social and cultural conditions that can be described as socially disorganizing. (1) Industrialization produces a division of labor. As people specialize in their productive activities, they develop different and sometimes conflicting values and norms. In addition, the specialization accompanying the division of labor segments social relationships in urban areas—people interact with others only briefly in isolated contexts. In rural communities, in contrast, friends and neighbors may also be economic associates and fellow church members. The resulting interaction with the same people in a variety of social contexts strengthens primary relationships. (2) Compared to rural areas, urban areas are characterized by a high degree of social and geographical mobility. Such mobility contributes to cultural heterogeneity and value conflicts and makes it difficult to maintain close, primary relationships. (3) Because many urbanites have migrated from rural areas, their cultural values and norms are not well-adapted to urban life. For example, in dealing with formal municipal bureaucracies, new migrants from the countryside have little cultural background relevant to these institutions.

These conditions are more prevalent in urban than in rural areas, and within urban areas they are most pronounced in the zone of transition. Mobility and population heterogeneity, for example, are highest in this area because this is where new immigrants and migrants congregate (housing is least expensive). In addition, people are eager to move out of the transitional zone to more desirable locales as soon as possible, so social relationships with neighbors within the zone of transition tend to be tenuous. Finally, given the widespread poverty in the transitional zone, residents have difficulty mobilizing resources that might be used to combat and deter norm violations.

The concept of social disorganization thus refers to social and cultural conditions—value and norm conflicts, mobility, cultural change and vacuums, and weak primary relationships—that undermine internal and external social control and, in turn, promote deviant behavior. Internal social control refers to a process whereby people accept cultural norms and values as right and proper and thus do not violate them; and external social control refers to a process whereby people do not violate social norms because of rewards for conformity and punishments for violations.

The internal process is weakened by normative conflicts, cultural change, and social mobility. People are more likely to accept cultural standards as right and proper when they are not exposed to alternatives. In a small town characterized by a stable standard, people learn it as *the* standard; they accept it as the only way. On the other hand, in urban areas, because of cultural conflicts and social mobility, people come into contact with others who accept and practice different standards.

External social control is also weakened by cultural conflicts and a lack of primary relationships. For example, a girl growing up in a small town for one reason or another may not accept the standard. She may conform to it, nonetheless, because there are no unconventional groups to join and the goodwill of relatives and friends is important. What about the same child or teenager growing up in a large city? Since the strength of primary relationships is weak, she may be less interested in the good will of others and be able to locate groups who approve and practice what she believes.

While offering significant insights into the social distribution of deviance, the disorganization theory often failed to distinguish between the condition of social disorganization and its alleged consequences (Pfohl 1985, 167). For example, the Chicagoans argued that social disorganization causes a community to develop a high rate of delinquency, but they also regarded a high rate of delinquency as evidence for the presence of social disorganization. This argument is tautological: It is true by definition and cannot possibly be falsified. More generally, the Chicago school theorists failed to articulate the concept of social disorganization very clearly. This conceptual ambiguity made it difficult to construct adequate measures of social disorganization and to subject the theory to empirical tests.

In an effort to overcome this deficiency of the classical social disorganization theory, Robert Bursik Jr. (1988) attempted to further clarify the meaning of social disorganization. Bursik defined social disorganization as "the capacity of a neighborhood to regulate itself through formal and informal processes of social control" (p. 527). Community "self-regulation" depends on two factors: supervision and socialization. A community with strong supervisory capacity is one in which residents are willing and able to monitor the daily activities that take place within community boundaries and intervene in cases of suspicious behavior. A community with strong socialization capacity is one in which community standards are consistently expressed in local institutions, such as families, schools, and churches. Bursik argued that it should be possible to develop measures of these two dimensions of social disorganization that are independent of the hypothesized consequences of social disorganization. These measures can then be used to test the predictions of the theory.

Sampson and Groves (1989) also elaborated the concept of social disorganization. They argued that community organization depends on a network of friendship and kinship and on the involvement of community residents in community organizations. A community with strong social organization (and little disorganization) is one in which residents are interconnected by extensive friendship and kinship ties and in which neighbors participate actively in local organizations. These network ties and organizational activities enhance the supervisory capacity of the community, especially its capacity to monitor the behavior of youths.

Differential Organization Theory When theorizing about deviance, the primary focus of the ecological/Chicago theorists was on the breakdown of the social order. The very term *disorganization* implies the absence of patterned behavior. At the same time, however, some theorists in the ecological/Chicago tradition generated vivid ethnographic accounts of the "seamy side" of life in the city. These ethnographies suggested that there were, in fact, patterned, orderly forms of deviance. Some Chicagoans accordingly began to conceptualize deviant areas as *differentially organized* rather than socially *disorganized*. A principal proponent of this point of view was Thorsten Sellin (1938). Sellin examined the causes and types of cultural conflict and specified its relationship to crime and deviance. He argued that different groups in a pluralistic society have different cultural values or conduct norms, some of which are incompatible. Only one set of values becomes incorporated in the law. Crime can thus be understood in terms of cultural conflict; it is behavior that conforms to cultural values that are inconsistent with the formal criminal law.

Research within the cultural conflict tradition did not focus on the dynamics or structure of cultural conflicts and the associated power struggles between groups (this is the focus of the conflict perspective, discussed in Chapter 7). Instead, the primary concern was with explaining the social process by which unconventional forms of organization (norms and values) are transmitted from generation to generation. Shaw and McKay (1931) were among the first Chicagoans to discuss this process. They argued that when social disorganization disrupts the conventional forces of social control, with time, deviance can become a patterned or an organized way of life. Once established, these patterns or traditions are passed on from one generation to the next through personal and group contacts. Shaw and McKay referred to this process as one of *cultural transmission*.

This ethnographic tradition continues today. It can be seen, for example, in the work of Elijah Anderson (1978, 1990). Anderson described how themes in the ghetto culture of the urban black underclass, such as "going for bad," "having fun," and "getting big money," coexist with conventional values and encourage various forms of defiance (teenage pregnancy and street violence).

A related recent development in the ecological tradition is the *routine activities* theory of criminal victimization by Cohen and Felson (1979). Cohen and Felson argued that ecological researchers have concentrated on the spatial dimension of crime but have neglected the temporal dimension, and that they have concentrated on criminals, but have neglected victims. To understand crime, it is necessary to consider the distributions of both criminals and victims and their routine activities across both space and time.

Cohen and Felson identified three indispensable elements of a criminal victimization: (1) a motivated offender (someone who wants to commit the crime); (2) a suitable target (a person or an article of property of suffi-cient desirability or value to victimize); and (3) the absence of a capable guardian (someone who could effectively intervene to thwart the victim-ization). For a crime to occur, all three of these elements must converge in space and time: A motivated offender must come into contact with a suit-able target in a setting where there are no capable guardians. The probabil-ity that these three elements will converge depends, in turn, on the nature of routine, everyday activities—the ways in which people earn a living, sat-isfy basic needs (e.g., shop for groceries), and spend their leisure time. Thus, the level of crime may change over time because routine activities have changed, resulting in greater or lesser opportunities for criminal victimiza-tion. To illustrate, improved transportation facilities have allowed people to spend more time away from the household. This may be responsible for higher rates of burglary and theft because more and more households are left unprotected.

In sum, the Chicago theorists applied an ecological perspective to explain variation in levels of deviance across different types of communities (urban versus rural) and across neighborhoods within urban areas. They borrowed concepts like competition, struggle for survival, invasion, and natural area to describe social processes and order. Also, because they real-ized that people are culture-bearing animals, they examined the link between ecological processes and culture, and the extent to which cultural and ecological processes operate to produce social order. They identified ecological processes that spatially distribute activities, including deviant activities.

Two distinct theories of deviance were developed within the perspec-tive. The social disorganization theory attributes high rates of deviance to weak conventional institutions that are unable to exert much control over people. The differential organization theory explains high levels of deviance as the product of reasonably strong deviant traditions that compete with the conventional order. Both of these theories focus on macrolevel variation in behavior, that is, variation in rates of behavior across different social group-ings (small towns versus cities; poor, inner-city neighborhoods versus more affluent neighborhoods). However, each theory also implies certain social psychological or microlevel processes that underlie the development of deviant behavior. The key process for social disorganization theory is social control, whereas for differential social organization theory, the key process is socialization or social learning.

MICROLEVEL THEORY:
SOCIALIZATION (LEARNING) AND SOCIAL CONTROL

Socialization In an effort to describe more fully the socialization processes associated with the cultural transmission of deviant behavior, Edwin Sutherland (1939) proposed a *theory of differential association.*

Sutherland was one of the leading criminologists of his time, and his textbook on criminology (published in multiple, revised editions) dominated the discipline for decades. Sutherland's theory attempts to articulate in nine propositions the social psychological processes involved in deviant socialization (Sutherland and Cressey 1970), but the thrust of differential association theory can be stated more succinctly than these nine propositions. Indeed, some of the propositions are completely or partially redundant, and others criticize competing theories, specifying what differential association theory is not. Reduced to its core, differential association theory asserts that deviant behavior is an expression of definitions favorable to deviant behavior learned in association with others in intimate social relationships. Note that the theory does not say that deviance is the result of simple exposure to deviant definitions. Everyone is exposed to some deviant definitions; the critical factor is the *ratio* of deviant to nondeviant definitions.

Several revisions and extensions of Sutherland's theory have been proposed over the years to compensate for alleged limitations of the original formulation. The most important revisions are those originally advanced by Burgess and Akers (1966) and subsequently extended by Akers (1985). Burgess and Akers advanced two general criticisms of Sutherland's theory: (1) Its core concepts (favorable and unfavorable definitions) refer to mental phenomena, which are intrinsically difficult, if not impossible, to measure; and (2) the processes of learning deviant behavior are only vaguely described. In Burgess and Akers' view, differential association theory would be on firmer theoretical and methodological ground if it were reconceptualized in terms of behaviorist psychology—a body of theory de-emphasizing the study of mental phenomena.

Behaviorists have traditionally argued that mental phenomena cannot be part of scientific inquiry because they cannot be readily observed. Researchers should focus their attention on what can be observed—behavior. Various behaviorist theories have been developed that direct attention to different kinds of learning processes. The most important of these learning processes in Burgess and Akers' theory is operant conditioning. In operant conditioning, an organism learns behavior through reinforcements, or the application of rewards and punishments. As rewards that follow a behavior increase and punishments decrease, the frequency of that behavior increases; and as rewards that follow a behavior decrease and punishments increase, the frequency of the behavior decreases. Deviant behavior is thus likely to occur when it has been differentially reinforced in comparison with conventional behavior. Akers (1994) elaborated on the learning process, introducing additional elements of modeling and symbolic cues or signals, and applied his theoretical framework to diverse forms of deviance. His theory is commonly referred to as *social learning theory*.

Akers considers his theory to be a general theory of deviance that effectively subsumes differential association theory. However, his reformulation transforms Sutherland's theory in important ways. Reflecting the concerns of sociologists at the University of Chicago, Sutherland gives priority to cultural meanings or definitions. These are assigned much less importance in behaviorist reformulations where mental phenomena are de-emphasized. Furthermore, the thrust of Sutherland's theory, that socialization takes place through social interaction in intimate groups, is also less central to Akers' social learning theory. In social learning theory, behavior is learned when it is followed by rewards, whatever the source of those rewards might be. These rewards might take the form of an impersonal medium, such as money, or they might involve nonsocial, physiological reactions that are reinforcing (e.g., the euphoric sensations produced by drugs).

Both differential association theory and social learning theory are based on the implicit assumption that there are conflicting social orders. Some groups must embrace deviant values and norms to serve as a source of prodeviant definitions and prodeviant reinforcements. This conceptualization makes the concept of deviance as a norm violation problematic. What constitutes a norm violation depends on which group's norms are adopted as the frame of reference. Sociologists in the differential association and social learning tradition have resolved this issue by essentially ignoring it. Rather than dealing with the question of social conflict, they implicitly or explicitly assume the normative order of dominant groups in society. Research thus focuses on violations of the dominant norms, while the status of these norms as "dominant" is regarded as unproblematic.

Social Control   Whereas socialization theories are the microlevel complement of differential organization theories, social control theories are the microlevel complement of social disorganization theories (Kornhauser 1978). Social disorganization theories specify the macro conditions (e.g., social heterogeneity) that weaken conventional social bonds and thus lead to high rates of deviance; and social control theories specify the micro processes by which weakened conventional bonds lead to deviance. While logically tied to social disorganization theory, control theories can stand alone; that is, control theories are not necessarily concerned with the macro causes and consequences of social disorganization; rather, they are interested in how a weakening of conventional social ties, whatever the cause, leads to a weakening of conventional controls which in turn leads to deviance. Neighborhood social disorganization, for example, may be sufficient to weaken social controls, but it is not necessary. Even in a well-organized neighborhood some people may not be strongly tied to the institutions and organizations that control the behavior of most people.

Social control theories differ from socialization theories in many ways, most important of which is the role of motivation. Socialization theories assume that deviants differ from conformists by possessing deviant motivation. These theories examine how some people, but not others, come to acquire deviant motives. The general explanation is that some people learn attitudes and values that motivate or "push" them into norm violations. Thus, deviants are still moral actors whose behavior is guided by norms and values; they simply march to the beat of a different drummer. Social control theory, in contrast, assumes that norm violations are generally so attractive, exciting, and profitable that virtually everyone is motivated to violate the norms. It is not necessary to explain deviant motivation; rather, it is necessary to explain why everybody does not act on his or her deviant motives and violate the norms. Social control theorists examine the social forces that control or inhibit people from acting upon widely shared deviant motives.

Control theorists distinguish between two types of social control referred to earlier: inner (or internal) and outer (or external). To recapitulate, the former refers to those societal rules or norms that people internalize as their own. Internalized rules control behavior because people experience self-righteousness and satisfaction when they conform to them; they experience guilt, self-reproach, and self-condemnation when they violate them.

Equally important are outer controls—the rewards foregone and punishments experienced upon being identified as a norm violator. While various punishments associated with being identified as a norm violator are well known, social control theorists remind us that rewards in different sectors of life are tied to maintaining an acceptable public identity. People identified as deviants may lose their jobs and the respect of their family and friends (social rewards foregone) and may be fined and imprisoned (punishments). It is the prospect of these rewards foregone and punishments incurred that inhibits the expression of deviant motivations. For example, which of the following would be more likely to patronize a prostitute: an unemployed and unmarried man or an employed and married man? From the viewpoint of social control theory, while both men may find such an encounter equally appealing, the former is more likely to patronize a prostitute. The unmarried, unemployed man has little to lose upon being publicly identified as a "john." The married, employed man is more committed to conformity by virtue of his link to society—he has a greater "stake in conformity" (Toby 1957). Being publicly identified as a "john" may adversely affect his career and his marriage. According to social control theory, then, people conform not because they lack deviant motivation but because they are restrained by inner and outer social controls.

Various specific control theories were developed in the 1950s and early 1960s (Reiss 1951; Toby 1957; Nye 1958; Reckless 1961). One of the more influential of these was the work of Sykes and Matza (1957) on juvenile delinquency. They challenged the claim that delinquent youths are socialized into a distinctive value system at odds with the dominant culture.

Most youths, they argued, actually believe in the moral validity of the dominant norms. How, then, can these youths engage in delinquent acts? Sykes and Matza pointed to the use of techniques of neutralization. Techniques of neutralization are excuses or justifications that temporarily suspend the applicability of general norms to specific situations. Sykes and Matza identified five common techniques of neutralization: denial of responsibility ("I couldn't help myself"), denial of injury ("nobody got hurt"), denial of victim ("the victim had it coming"), condemnation of the condemners ("what right do they have to criticize me?"), and appeal to higher loyalties ("I did it for someone else"). By such techniques youths are able to maintain a commitment to the dominant norms while neutralizing their controlling effect on deviant behavior.

In the late 1960s, Travis Hirschi (1969) introduced a formulation of control theory that incorporated many of the insights of earlier theories and that has become the most influential version of the perspective. Hirschi's theory maintains that social control operates through the "bond" developed between the individual and the larger society. This bond comprises four elements: belief, attachment, commitment, and involvement. *Belief* refers to the extent to which the conventional norms are internalized. Hirschi's theory proposes that the more people believe in the moral legitimacy of the conventional norms, the lower the probability that they will violate these norms. *Commitment* refers to the extent to which people's social rewards are tied to conformity. Here, the theory incorporates the notion of stakes in conformity. People who have more to lose upon being publicly identified as a deviant are less likely to violate social norms. *Attachment* refers to people's sensitivity to the opinions of others. People unconcerned with the respect and status afforded them by others are not very susceptible to outer controls. The respect and status associated with conformity are sources of control only for people sensitive to the feelings and opinions of others. *Involvement* refers to the amount of time people devote to conventional activities. People involved in conventional pursuits simply have little time available for deviant activities. For example, an adolescent whose day is occupied with school activities, sports, adult-sponsored recreation, and homework has little time to get into trouble. Generally, belief increases inner control (personal satisfaction following from conformity and personal dissatisfaction following from norm violations), and attachment, commitment, and involvement increase outer control (social rewards following from conformity and punishments following from norm violations).

Despite the immense popularity of social bonding theory, Hirschi, in collaboration with Michael Gottfredson (Gottfredson and Hirschi 1990), subsequently reformulated Hirschi's earlier work on social control. They proposed a "general theory of crime" that emphasizes the concept of self-control. The key postulate of self-control theory is that individuals exhibit differential propensities to engage in deviant and criminal acts regardless of the circumstances in which they find themselves. Those who are prone to commit crimes are low in *self-control*. Gottfredson and Hirschi (1990, 89) enumerated the following "elements" of low self-control. People with low self-control are unable to defer gratification; they lack diligence and tenacity; they tend to be adventuresome, risk-seeking, and physical; they are impulsive and uninterested in long-term pursuits; and they tend to be self-centered and insensitive to the needs of others. Low-self-control people are attracted to deviance and crime because it provides them with what they want, when they want it.

The primary cause of low self-control is ineffective child rearing. If parents fail to monitor behavior, to recognize improper behavior when it occurs and to punish it, the child will not develop self-control. According to Gottfredson and Hirschi, self-control is a stable property. Once established in childhood, it continues to determine behavior into adulthood. The principal focus of Gottfredson and Hirschi's theory is criminal behavior, but the theory presumably applies to other forms of behavior that involve the pursuit of immediate pleasure with little regard for future consequences. The theory predicts, for example, that people with low self-control "will tend to smoke, drink, use drugs, gamble, have children out of wedlock, and engage in illicit sex" (p. 90).

Another important elaboration of control theory is the "life-course" theory of social control proposed by Sampson and Laub (1993) to explain both stability and change in deviant and criminal behavior. Whereas Gottfredson and Hirschi focused on the stability of crime and deviance over the life-course, Sampson and Laub emphasized both stability and change, which they explained in terms of life-course trajectories and transitions. *Trajectories* refer to stable patterns of behavior over the life span; *transitions* refer to key life-events, such as getting married or entering the labor force. When people undergo major transitions, they adapt to their new situations, which can lead to significant changes in behavioral trajectories.

Sampson and Laub combined insights from the life-course perspective with conventional control theory. They theorized that structural background factors (e.g., social class, family structure) affect social control processes in childhood and adolescence. Youths who are exposed to weak social controls are predisposed toward juvenile delinquency. Involvement in delinquency, in turn, sets people on the path of future criminal behavior in adulthood. However, in contrast with Gottfredson and Hirschi's self-control theory, Sampson and Laub argued that these trajectories are subject to change. Transitions in adulthood, such as getting married and settling down, can lead to the formation of new social bonds that impose informal controls, thereby reducing the likelihood of criminal behavior.

In sum, the core insights of the Ecological/Chicago perspective are as follows: Deviance and crime are distributed spatially and temporally, and to understand these distributions it is necessary to understand the social organization (or disorganization) of social life. Social disorganization theory emphasizes the role of macro structures in weakening social control, and recent theories call attention to the role of neighborhood networks and ties in this process. At the microlevel, theories of social control (external and internal, and enduring from childhood or mutable over the life-course) have elaborated the details of these control processes. Self-control theory emphasizes inner controls that are formed early in life and that continue to serve as restraints against norm violations throughout adulthood. Both external and inner controls have been incorporated in a life-course theory of control that explains persistence and change in deviance with reference to social bonds that are formed (or not formed) at different stages of the life-course.

Once high rates of deviance are established in an area, differential organization theory focuses on how they take on the properties of a normative social order, become an integral part of organized social life, and are passed on from one generation to the next. At the microlevel, socialization (learning) theories elaborate the interpersonal processes by which deviance is learned and thus passed on. Recently some scholars have also focused on the spatial and temporal distribution of the routine activities of potential victims as well as criminals, and how their intersection leads to crime.

While not all of these theories are always thought of as part of one general perspective—the ecological perspective—and while many of them can certainly stand alone, they share an emphasis on the ecological distribution of deviance and crime or on the microprocesses that underlie these distributions.

RESEARCH

SOCIAL DISORGANIZATION

Social disorganization research has consisted of ecological and case history studies. Ecological studies examine the relationship between deviance and social disorganization across communities within a city and across different cities, while case history studies describe the experience of living in socially disorganized neighborhoods.

The work of Clifford R. Shaw and Henry D. McKay et al. set the pattern for future work. Their classic study, *Delinquency Areas* (1929), analyzed the court records of 55,998 juveniles in the city of Chicago and reported the following:

> 1. *Spatial Concentration*: Ecological areas with the highest rates of school truancy have the highest rates of delinquency and adult crime.

2. *Zonal Pattern*: Crime and delinquency rates are highest in the center of the city and decrease progressively from the center to more remote areas.

3. *Persistence*: High rates of delinquency have persisted in the same ecological areas, even though the ethnic composition of the residents has changed. This suggests that high rates are produced by the prevailing social conditions of areas and not personal characteristics, such as the ethnic backgrounds of the residents.

4. *Structural Correlates of Deviance*: High-rate areas are characterized by population instability, high percentage of families on public assistance, low median income, low home ownership, high percentage of foreign born, and high percentage of nonwhites—structural determinants of social disorganization.

Shaw and McKay (1931) extended this work to other cities and continued the analysis of Chicago (1942). With some exceptions, these latter works confirmed the original findings. Additionally, in *The Jack-Roller* (Shaw 1930), *The Natural History of a Delinquent Career* (Shaw 1931), and *Brothers in Crime* (Shaw et al. 1938), Shaw, McKay, and their associates showed how the social conditions described in their ecological studies were experienced by juveniles and thus led to delinquency.

The ecological studies by Shaw and McKay inspired other researchers to apply the social disorganization framework in a variety of contexts. Faris and Dunham (1939) reported that mental illness was not distributed randomly throughout the city of Chicago; instead, it exhibited a distribution similar to that observed for crime and delinquency. Rates were highest in the most disorganized areas of the city. In the 1950s and 1960s, several studies attempted to further replicate patterns previously observed for Chicago in Baltimore (Lander 1954), Detroit (Bordua 1959), and Indianapolis (Chilton 1964). The results of these studies were somewhat inconsistent, but they offered partial support for the disorganization perspective. During the 1960 through 1980 period, social disorganization theory was often applied to the explanation of deviance in developing countries—countries where urban conditions resembled those of U.S. cities during the late nineteenth and early twentieth centuries. These studies revealed that some of the findings of the Chicago school were not generalizable to cities in other countries, such as the zonal model of the distribution of crime and delinquency (e.g., Weinberg 1976). However, researchers reported that the general process of social disorganization could explain the increases in property crime rates accompanying societal modernization (Clinard and Abbott 1973, 1976; Shelley 1981).

In the 1980s, a number of studies once again reported findings consistent with the logic of social disorganization theory. Structural variables such as population size, population mobility, racial heterogeneity, and family disruption were consistently associated with community and city crime rates in multivariate statistical analyses (e.g., Blau and Blau 1982;

Crutchfield, Geerken, and Gove 1982; Messner and Tardiff 1986; Sampson 1986a). These empirical associations were commonly interpreted rather loosely with reference to social disorganization, but the precise causal processes were not specified very clearly, and social disorganization itself was not measured directly.

In a highly influential study, Sampson and Groves (1989) attempted to overcome these limitations. They proposed that social disorganization be conceptualized in terms of three dimensions. One is the ability of a community to supervise and control teenage groups. Youths are particularly susceptible to the temptations of crime, and if they are allowed free rein, rates of crime and delinquency are likely to be high. The second dimension of social disorganization involves the extensiveness of local friendship networks. Strong ties between neighbors should increase their capacity to supervise and monitor the neighborhood, thereby reducing the frequency of crime. The third dimension of social disorganization is local participation in formal and voluntary organizations. Such organizations enable a community to mobilize and defend itself against the "criminal element." Accordingly, low levels of organizational participation should be associated with high rates of crime and delinquency.

Sampson and Groves tested their hypotheses with data from the British Crime Survey. This survey collected information on friendship patterns, organizational involvement, and the presence of unsupervised teens from respondents in 238 local communities in Great Britain. Sampson and Groves summed the survey responses for each community to construct community-level indicators of each of the three key dimensions of social disorganization. In a similar manner, they used information from the survey to measure the following hypothesized determinants of social disorganization: low economic status, ethnic heterogeneity, residential mobility, and family disruption. Finally, they used the survey responses to construct rates of criminal victimization and self-reported offending.

The results of their analyses are largely consistent with social disorganization theory. The hypothesized determinants of social disorganization are generally related to the disorganization indicators (sparse friendship networks, unsupervised teens, low organizational participation) in the theoretically predicted manner, and these disorganization indicators are related to victimization and offending rates. In addition, the associations between structural characteristics and crime rates are reduced when the disorganization measures are taken into account, suggesting that the effects of the structural characteristics are "mediated by" (i.e., they "work through") the disorganization processes. Sampson and Groves concluded that social disorganization theory has "renewed relevance for explaining macro-level variations in crime rates" (p. 799). (For a review of subsequent research, see Bursik and Grasmick 1993.)

Recently, some studies of urban neighborhoods have raised questions about the relevancy of traditional social disorganization theory to contemporary neighborhoods. For example, in a study of Boston neighborhoods, Warner and Pierce (1993) reported that among poor neighborhoods the highest crime rates are found in the most homogeneous (non-white) and stable neighborhoods. Remember that, according to disorganization theory, stable and homogeneous neighborhoods should have the highest levels of social control. Warner and Pierce argued, instead, that stability and homogeneity in these neighborhoods (which are mainly nonwhite) means that the residents are isolated from the mainstream of society, and it is this isolation that leads to high crime rates.

Shihadeh and Flynn (1996) further elaborated the processes by which the social isolation of poor minorities associated with residential segregation leads to high crime rates. They argued that the geographical concentration of poor minorities separates them from people with the strongest investments in the conventional order and with the strongest commitments to controlling crime. It separates them, in other words, from conventional role models and from conventional cultural norms. Consistent with expectations, their research showed that cities where such geographical isolation is most prevalent exhibit the highest rate of black violent crime.

→ ROUTINE ACTIVITIES

Research by Cohen and Felson (1979) illustrates the utility of the routine activities perspective for explaining changes in national crime rates in the United States. They developed a "household activity ratio" based on female labor force participation and the prevalence of nontraditional households (i.e., households without a husband and wife) to indicate the extent to which activities are dispersed away from the family household. Routine activities theory implies that increases in the household activity ratio should be accompanied by increases in crime rates because persons are at a comparatively high risk of victimization when they venture beyond the security of the home (they are more likely to come into contact with motivated offenders), and because household property is at greater risk of victimization when occupants are not present to serve as guardians. Cohen and Felson found support for their hypothesis in an analysis of changes in serious crime for the United States over the 1947–74 period. Their household activity ratio was positively related to each of five crime rates: homicide, rape, aggravated assault, robbery, and burglary.

Cohen and Felson's household activity ratio largely reflects routine involvement in work-related activity. Messner and Blau (1987) extended the routine activities perspective by examining the implications for crime of variation in the nature of leisure activities. They hypothesized that leisure activities have opposite effects on levels of crime depending on where those activities typically occur. A high volume of leisure activities that occur outside the household should be positively related to crime rates because nonhousehold settings carry relatively high risks of victimization, whereas a high volume of leisure activities that occur within the household should be negatively related to crime rates.

They tested these hypotheses with data on official crime rates for the 124 largest metropolitan areas of the United States. To measure household leisure activity, they constructed an index of aggregate levels of television viewing, based on the assumption that television viewing typically takes place at home. They measured nonhousehold leisure activity with a composite index of the availability of sports and entertainment establishments in the metropolitan area. The results of their analyses were consistent with expectations. For six of the seven crime rates studied, communities with high scores on the television viewing measure exhibited relatively low crime rates, while communities with high scores on the nonhousehold leisure activities index exhibited relatively high crime rates.

Routine activities theory has also been used to interpret the "hot spots" of crime—locations within the city that generate unusually high levels of criminal activity. In one such study, Roncek and Maier (1991) argued that bars and taverns are commercial facilities that promote hot spots by sustaining routine activities conducive to crime. Patrons of these establishments are likely to be carrying cash and are thus attractive targets for victimization, especially if they are intoxicated. Intoxication also promotes a wide range of troublesome behavior, such as arguing and brawling. In addition, bars and taverns tend to bring unacquainted persons together, which heightens the sense of anonymity and weakens social control. Finally, bars and taverns tend to attract persons who are generally predisposed to crime, thereby increasing the supply of "motivated offenders" in an area.

Roncek and Maier examined the relationship between the presence of bars and taverns and the frequency of crimes across different blocks in Cleveland. Consistent with their hypothesis, they found that crimes were significantly more frequent on blocks with bars or taverns than on blocks without them. In addition, they reported that the number of bars and taverns on blocks was positively associated with the number of crimes, even after statistically controlling for other characteristics of blocks that are related to crime.

SOCIALIZATION AND SOCIAL CONTROL

Research on deviant socialization during the 1930s and 40s relied largely on case histories and field observations. In the mid-1950s, survey methods became popular, leading to the emergence of a systematic research paradigm for testing deviant socialization theories.

The work of James F. Short (1957, 1958) on testing differential association theory is particularly noteworthy. Short argued that exposure to deviant definitions can be indirectly measured by exposure to deviants. Although exposure to deviant definitions and exposure to deviants are not equivalent (someone can learn deviant definitions from conventional people and conventional definitions from deviants), the relationship is strong enough so that exposure to deviants may be used to measure exposure to deviant definitions.

Short focused specifically on juvenile delinquency. He measured delinquency with a variety of self-report items (e.g., driving without a license, buying or drinking alcoholic beverages, cutting school, taking property that belongs to others, sexual relations, defying parents' authority). To operationalize the various "modalities" of deviant associations, he used the following questionnaire items:

> *Frequency*: Think of friends you have been associated with most often. Were (or are) any of them juvenile delinquents?
> *Duration*: Think of the friends you have known for the longest time. Were (or are) any of them juvenile delinquents?
> *Priority*: Think back to the first friends you can remember. Were any of them juvenile delinquents?
> *Intensity*: Have any of your best friends been juvenile delinquents while they were your best friends?

Short's first study (1957) used a sample of boys from a training school. The results supported the theory, showing a moderately strong relationship between exposure to delinquents and delinquent behavior. For both sexes, intensity and frequency were the most significant dimensions of association. While a sample of juveniles in training school is certainly not representative of the juvenile population at large, other studies using different samples throughout the United States reported similar results, generally supporting differential association theory (Short 1958; Voss 1964; Reiss and Rhodes 1964; Stanfield 1966; Matthews 1968).

By the mid-1960s, these studies had generated considerable data consistent with the thrust of deviant socialization theories. They established a clear link between delinquency and association with delinquent peers. These studies did not, however, establish the causal process underlying the link. Differential association theory stipulates a learning process whereby juveniles learn prodelinquent definitions and attitudes from delinquent associates (see Figure 3.3, Model A). Other theories stipulate still different causal processes that would also create a relationship between delinquent associations and delinquent involvement.

Social learning theory (Akers 1985) implies that adolescents emulate the behavior of peers not primarily because they come to accept delinquent attitudes as right and proper but because of differential reinforcement of

A. Differential Association Model
    Deviant Associations ———► Deviant Attitudes ———► Deviant Behavior

B. Social-Learning Model
    Deviant Associations ———► Deviant Behavior

C. Differential Association/Social-Learning Model
              ———► Delinquent Attitudes ———➤
    Deviant Associations ———► Deviant Behavior

D. Social Control/Social-Selection Model
    Conventional Bonds ———► Deviant Behavior ———► Deviant Associations

FIGURE 3.3 CAUSAL STRUCTURES UNDERLYING THE LINK
BETWEEN DEVIANT ASSOCIATIONS AND DEVIANT BEHAVIOR

delinquency, which often takes the form of peer pressure (Figure 3.3, Model B). On the other hand, social control theory (Hirschi 1969) argues that delinquency comes about because of weak ties to conventional institutions, like the family and school, and that delinquents then select other delinquents as friends. "Birds of a feather flock together." Hence, from this theory, delinquent associations and delinquency are related, not because delinquent associations cause delinquency but because delinquency causes delinquent associations (Figure 3.3, Model D).

Various research studies have attempted to assess the relative merits of the causal structures in Figure 3.3 in explaining the established link between deviant associations and deviant involvement (Jensen 1972b; Liska 1973; Matsueda 1982; Matsueda and Heimer 1987; Warr and Stafford 1991). Research has focused on three major issues: (1) To what extent are deviant-peer associations a cause (Models A, B, and C) or effect (Model D) of deviant behavior? (2) To what extent is the effect of deviant associations on deviant behavior mediated by deviant attitudes learned in association with deviant peers (Model A) or mediated by other processes, such as peer pressure (Model B)? (3) What is the relative influence of deviant-peer associations (Models A, B, and C) versus social bonds (Model D) on deviant behavior?

Gary F. Jensen's work (1972b) provides one of the first rigorous efforts to assess these causal structures. He examined a sample of high school males from Richmond, California. Delinquency involvement was measured with a self-report inventory; delinquent associations were measured in terms of the number of close friends picked up by the police; and delinquent attitude was measured in terms of approval of the police and the law. Consistent with past findings, the data showed moderately strong positive relationships between delinquent attitudes, associations with delinquent peers, and delinquency. The critical test, however, is the extent to which the relationship between delinquent associations and delinquent involvement persists when delinquent attitude is statistically controlled. If delinquent attitude mediates the relationship between delinquent associations and delinquent involvement, this relationship should disappear when delinquent attitude is controlled. Upon including such controls, Jensen found that the relationship between delinquent associations and delinquency did not change. His data were thus most consistent with the social learning model (Figure 3.3, Model B), wherein delinquent association affects delinquent behavior directly (e.g., via social pressure). Jensen's data also offered some support for control theory (the first causal link in Model D): Parental attachment (supervision and emotional support) reduces delinquency independently of its effect on delinquent attitudes.

A decade later, Matsueda (1982) reanalyzed the Richmond data, using a much more sophisticated statistical technique. Contrary to Jensen, he concluded that differential association theory is supported (Model A). He found that peer associations and parental attachment only affected delinquent behavior because they affected delinquent attitudes. Controlling for the effect of delinquent attitudes essentially eliminated the effects of differential associations and parental attachment. A later study by Matsueda and Heimer (1987) used similar procedures to assess whether the causal mechanisms underlying delinquency are similar for different racial groups. Consistent with Matsueda's earlier research, they found that delinquent definitions mediated the effects of parental attachment and peer associations on delinquency for both black and white youths. They also reported that the effects of definitions were the same for both racial groups. Both of these findings are consistent with differential association theory.

Recently, Warr and Stafford (1991) introduced another technique for testing the causal processes underlying the link between delinquent peer associations and delinquency. They noted that the distinguishing feature of Sutherland's theory is the notion that delinquency is learned through "attitude transference." The prodelinquent attitudes of one's peers foster prodelinquent attitudes for oneself, which then leads to delinquency. Social learning theory, in contrast, provides a rationale for expecting that peers' behaviors might be equally or more important than peers' attitudes in affecting behavior. Friends who engage in delinquency serve as models who can provide vicarious reinforcement for delinquent behavior, regardless of the friends' attitudes. While past research has repeatedly documented an association between delinquent peers and delinquency, it has not determined whether it is primarily peers' attitudes (as suggested by Sutherland's theory) or peers' behavior (as suggested by social learning theory) that predicts delinquency.

Warr and Stafford addressed this issue with data from the National Youth Survey, a panel study of a national probability sample of youths. The survey collected information on the delinquent attitudes and behaviors of both the respondents and their friends. Warr and Stafford were thus able to examine the relative effects of friends' attitudes versus friends' behavior on respondents' behavior. They reported that, contrary to differential association theory, friends' behavior had the stronger effect on delinquency. The important factor appeared to be what friends do, not what they say. In addition, Warr and Stafford found that friends' behavior had a significant effect on respondents' delinquency even with respondents' attitudes controlled, contrary to the claim that the learning of deviance consists entirely of "attitude transference." Overall, the authors concluded that Sutherland's theory is incomplete and that other social learning mechanisms need to be considered to explain the widely observed relationship between deviant associations and deviant behavior.

Now, let's review. Socialization theory suggests that people learn deviance from their peers, frequently organized into groups and subcultures. A series of studies, initiated in the late 1950s, has clearly shown a strong relationship between delinquent behavior and peers' delinquency. Recent research has focused on the causal process that underlies this relationship. Some research shows that delinquent peers are a source of delinquent attitudes; other research shows that they serve as role models; and still other research shows that they are a source of social rewards for delinquent behavior. All of these processes may operate.

As Model D of Figure 3.3 suggests, differential association theory has also been criticized for mistaking cause and effect. Involvement in deviance may cause individuals to associate with deviants, rather than vice versa. A similar challenge concerning causal order has been leveled at social control theory. A large body of research indicates that people with tenuous ties to the conventional order engage in comparatively high levels of deviance. But, do weak bonds lead people to deviance, or does involvement in deviance weaken bonds to conventional society?

Researchers have addressed this issue by using longitudinal data. A longitudinal design involves repeated observations on the subjects under investigation. It is thus possible to examine how variables measured at one point in time affect variables measured at a later point in time. Agnew (1985) used such a design to assess the effects of different dimensions of the social bond (parental attachment, involvement, commitment, and belief) on later delinquency, controlling for earlier delinquent involvement. Contrary to social control theory, the effects of social bonds were rather trivial. Agnew concluded that support for control theory has been exaggerated in past research because the effect of delinquency on bonds has been confounded with the effect of bonds on delinquency. Matsueda (1989) arrived at a similar conclusion in his longitudinal analysis of the effect of moral beliefs or conventional attitudes on delinquency. He concluded that the previously observed association between beliefs in the conventional order and minor forms of delinquency is largely the result of a causal process opposite to that of control theory. Rather than conventional beliefs or attitudes restraining delinquency, delinquent involvement induces youths to abandon their conventional beliefs.

Certainly these issues regarding the causal processes that underlie the relationships between deviant associations, attitudes, social controls, and behavior are far from settled. Future research may even reveal additional causal processes, or it might indicate that the causal processes specified by these theories operate to a greater or lesser degree at different stages of the individual's development. For example, social controls may play an important role early in life in the development of predispositions toward deviance, whereas learning processes may influence the kinds of deviant behavior that such persons become engaged in at later ages. Although the exact causal processes are yet to be unraveled, it is clear that deviant associations and weak social bonds are consistently correlated with high delinquent involvement.

GENDER AND POWER-CONTROL THEORY

The ecological tradition draws attention to two basic features of social life in the explanation of deviance: social structure and socialization. The work on social disorganization and differential organization emphasizes social structure, whereas research on control and learning highlights the role of socialization. An important effort to join these two features of social life into a single theory is the "power-control" explanation of gender differences in delinquency, developed by John Hagan and colleagues (Hagan et al. 1985; Hagan et al. 1987).

Hagan et al. set out to explain the widely observed pattern of high rates of delinquency for males in comparison with those for females. They proposed that this gender differential reflects the varying socialization experiences of the two sexes, which in turn is determined by the organization of the family. In patriarchal families (i.e., families where the father is "king of the castle"), girls are subjected to high levels of control, especially from mothers. This control is intended to promote a "cult of domesticity"; it prepares daughters for their future social roles as mothers and homemakers. Girls in patriarchal families tend to become "risk averse." They shy away from risky behaviors, many of which are delinquent, because they fear detection and punishment.

The socialization experiences of boys in patriarchal households are quite different. They are awarded a high degree of power and are relatively "free to deviate." Under these circumstances, boys develop a preference for risk and are attracted to risky behaviors, including delinquent behaviors. The gender differential in delinquency is accordingly very pronounced in patriarchal families.

In contrast, when the wife/mother shares power more equally with the husband/father, daughters are less likely to be socialized into the "cult of domesticity." Girls are not subjected to particularly intense control.

Rather, they are given a degree of power similar to that of boys, and they develop orientations toward risk similar to boys. The gender differential in delinquency is therefore much narrower in egalitarian families than in patriarchal families.

Hagan et al. related these differences in family organization to the larger social structure and to the class system in particular. The class position of the household depends on the occupational roles of husbands and wives and on the extent to which these roles provide for similar or different levels of authority. When husbands and wives experience similar levels of authority (i.e., they both either exercise authority over others or lack authority over others in the class system), the class position of the household is "balanced." When the husband exercises greater authority over others in the class system than does the wife, the class position of the household is "unbalanced." Power-control theory stipulates that unbalanced class relations promote patriarchal relations within the family and thus create large gender differences in delinquency. In contrast, balanced class positions are conducive to egalitarian family arrangements, which lead in turn to a relatively narrow gender differential in delinquency.

Hagan et al. (1987) tested power-control theory with survey data from the Toronto metropolitan area. They classified families into different categories reflecting greater or lesser class balance and examined the effect of gender on delinquency for the respective class categories. Their results were generally supportive of the theory. Gender differences in delinquency were significantly larger for families with an unbalanced rather than a balanced class situation. In addition, the effect of gender on delinquency was mediated by measures of parental control and preferences for risk, consistent with theoretical expectations.

Research on power-control theory is quite limited at present, and its empirical adequacy remains a matter of considerable controversy (see Jensen and Thompson 1990; Hagan et al. 1990). Some supportive evidence is also provided by a study by Grasmick et al. (1996). Using an Oklahoma sample, Grasmick et al. (1996) studied the relationship between patriarchal households and the effect of gender on risk preference (as measured by such questionnaire items, as "I like to test myself every now and then by doing something a little risky" and "Sometimes I take a risk just for the fun of it"). Sure enough, they, too, found that males had a stronger risk preference than did females, but only if they were raised in patriarchal families. As their sample included people of all ages, they could also compare those born in different eras. Their results showed precisely what many suspect, that the percentage of patriarchal families decreased from 45 percent of all families in the 1940s to 27 percent in the 1970s (the era during which the youngest cohort was growing up) and that risk preferences increased. This research supports the claim that the gender discrepancy in risk preference is decreasing as families become less patriarchal. While it thus suggests that female delinquency and crime will continue to increase, approaching that of males, it also suggests that more recent cohorts of females will be personally suited for those high status occupations and professions that require a tolerance of, if not a preference for, risk.

SOCIAL POLICY

This section examines the policy implications and implementations of the two main schools of the ecological perspective: social disorganization and differential organization.

SOCIAL DISORGANIZATION, DISORDER, AND COMMUNITY CONTROL

Classical social disorganization theory states that social processes, such as industrialization and urbanization, create disorganization in communities, which reduces social control, resulting in deviant behavior. The policy implications are clear: The chain of events leading up to deviance must be broken. Policy makers can concentrate on the more immediate causes—the weakened regulatory capacity of communities—or the more remote causes—industrialization and urbanization. Given the rather unlikely prospects for reversing processes of industrialization and urbanization, the Chicagoans focused on the more immediate causes. They tried to strengthen social control by building urban community organizations.

Community organization projects were initiated by Clifford R. Shaw in Chicago and came to be known as the Chicago Area Projects. Three types of projects were established. Some dealt with general community improvement, including schools, sanitation, traffic safety, physical conservation, and law enforcement. Some were designed to improve community recreational facilities for juveniles. They used community volunteers to establish recreational space through the conversion of storefronts and unused space in churches, police stations, and homes. Other projects, specifically designed to reduce crime and delinquency, emphasized helping police and juvenile courts to develop supervision plans for delinquent youths, visitations to youth training schools and reformatories, working with gangs in the neighborhood, and assisting parolees in their return to the community (Kobrin 1959).

The exact nature and content of these projects is less theoretically important than their underlying logic. The Chicagoans were concerned with organizing conventional residents so as to strengthen social control. They believed that such projects, whatever their specific goals, function to bring together the responsible and respectable adults of an area and to provide them with a vehicle for organization and social control. What were the accomplishments of these projects? They showed that urban community organizations can be formed and can function autonomously. Their effectiveness in reducing norm violating behavior, however, is less certain. The Chicagoans did not conduct rigorous evaluation studies of their programs, although later research suggests that they may have been at least partially successful in reducing delinquency (Schlossman et al. 1984).

Recently there has been a growing interest in the relationship between "disorder" and neighborhood decline, and in community-based strategies for combating disorder (Skogan 1990). *Disorder* refers to both social and physical characteristics of neighborhoods. It encompasses a variety of "uncivil" behaviors such as panhandling, prostitution, vandalism and the writing of graffiti, as well as unattractive surroundings such as boarded-up buildings, abandoned cars, broken windows, and inoperative street lights. These social and physical conditions allegedly weaken the capacity of residents to exert control because they undermine any mutual sense of territoriality in a neighborhood—no one feels obligated to take responsibility for such areas (Skogan 1990). In addition, neighborhoods that exhibit disorderly conditions attract trouble-makers, who regard the persons and property within them as fair game.

One popular strategy for dealing with the problems of disorder and decline is citizen self-help. These self-help projects attempt to mobilize communities to deal with the problems of disorder and decline on their own. Examples include "inspirational meetings, block-watch groups, neighborhood patrols, property marking, home security surveys, escort services for the elderly, educational programs, leafletting, and marches to 'take back the night'" (Skogan 1990). The logic underlying these programs is essentially the same as that of the earlier Chicago Area Projects. As the conventional residents of a community participate in collective action, they develop a stronger sense of territoriality, and they are more likely to look out for their neighborhood. Social control is thereby strengthened.

How successful are these contemporary programs informed by social disorganization theory? Evaluation studies of community self-help projects in Chicago and Minneapolis reported that these projects were likely to be successful when implemented in communities with strong, pre-existing forms of organization. In other words, communities that confronted the most serious problems of disorder and decline—the poor, disadvantaged neighborhoods—were the ones least amenable to the successful implementation of self-help policies.

The conclusion to be drawn from research on policies inspired by social disorganization theory is that there are no "silver bullets" (Skogan 1990, 18). Social disorganization theorists may have correctly identified weak ties among community residents and impotent local institutions as important factors leading to high levels of crime and deviance (Bursik and Grasmick 1993). However, the formulation of effective strategies for promoting strong neighborhood ties and establishing vital community institutions remains a daunting task.

DIFFERENTIAL ORGANIZATION: OPPORTUNITY STRATEGIES

In addition to the focus on socialization processes, the differential association variant of the ecological perspective calls attention to the kinds of situations that enhance the *opportunities* for deviance. The policy implication that follows from this research is to alter situations so that these opportunities are minimized, if not eliminated.

An example of such an approach to dealing with crime is a set of policies commonly referred to as *environmental criminology* (Winfree and Abadinsky 1996, 148–151). Environmental criminology identifies features of the architectural design and the physical layout of communities that affect social interaction. The core idea is that a proper use of commercial and residential space can foster a greater sense of territoriality among residents and promote high levels of surveillance, thereby reducing the opportunities for crime. For example, using gates to divide areas of a city into "minineighborhoods" counteracts the anonymity typically associated with modern urban life. In addition, encouraging residents to mark off their territory with iron gates rather than solid walls enables neighbors to keep watch over other's property. These type of arrangements help to "design out crime" (Clarke and Mayhew 1980) by making criminal behavior much more risky.

A similar logic underlies efforts to reduce crime by encouraging citizens to take "routine precautions" (Felson and Clarke 1995). These refer to the everyday activities of self-protection such as locking doors, not leaving property unattended, avoiding dark alleys, and so on. While much of this seems very commonsensical, some routine precautions may, in fact, be ineffective, and others may be temporarily forgotten. The responsibility of the experts is to determine which routine precautions are worth the time and inconvenience, and to alert citizens to the importance of following them. Note that underlying all of these "opportunity" strategies is the assumption that it is extremely difficult, if not impossible, to prevent the formation of motivations for crime (or deviance). Rather, a realistic policy objective is to alter situations so that crime (or deviance) is simply not a very attractive option for the potential offender.

DIFFERENTIAL ORGANIZATION: SOCIALIZATION

By the 1930s, many Chicagoans conceptualized the city as differentially organized, rather than disorganized, and studied the socialization process by which unconventional forms of behavior are learned. The policy implications of socialization theory and research are less concerned with reorganizing communities than with resocializing those at risk of deviance. Specifically, differential association theory suggests that deviant behavior comes about because of deviant definitions, and research suggests that such definitions are learned in association with deviants. Thus, to reduce deviance, policy makers must increase the ratio of nondeviant to deviant associations and definitions.

How can this be done? Two general types of programs will be discussed here: (1) programs in which conventional people, like parents, teachers, and exemplary peers, try to cultivate personal qualities that enable individuals to resist deviant opportunities and influences; and (2) programs in which deviants organize themselves into groups to control their own behavior—self-help groups.

An early example of the first type of program is a project that grew out of the self-concept theory developed by Walter Reckless and his associates. They argued that adolescents with positive self-concepts can resist the influence of delinquent peers. To test this hypothesis, Reckless and Dinitz (1967) organized a self-concept building program in an inner city area of Columbus, Ohio. A sample of junior high boys who had been identified by their teachers as "bad" was randomly divided into an experimental group that participated in the program, and a control group that did not participate. Teachers of those youths in the experimental group were trained to provide positive feedback and positive role models to enhance self-concept. What were the results? The teachers were very pleased with the results, noting marked improvement in the "bad" boys; however, objective data on arrests, school dropouts, school attendance, grades, school achievement scores, and even self-concept measures showed no differences between the experimental and control groups (Lundman et al. 1976).

Recent drug use prevention strategies have also emphasized the importance of providing adolescents with the personal qualities to resist deviant social influences. These programs often involve "resistance skills training" or "personal and social skills training" (Gorman and White 1995). Both types of programs are based on the premise that youths in U.S. society are bombarded with many prodrug messages and that they must be given the skills to be able to resist the pressures to use drugs. In other words, they must learn how to "just say no."

An example of such a program is Project ALERT. This project was administered to seventh-grade students in Oregon and California. Participating schools were randomly assigned to one of three treatment groups: a social influence program led by teachers; a social influence program led by teachers and assisted by peers; and a control group with no intervention. In the schools with the social influence programs, students attended sessions with discussions about the reasons for using drugs, the dangers of use, and techniques for countering pressures to use drugs. Students in the program were monitored for subsequent use of alcohol, marijuana, and cigarettes. The effectiveness of the project has been the subject of considerable controversy. Whereas some researchers reported that the programs basically worked, other evaluators concluded that the effects are highly variable across different types of students, and that the few significant differences between experimental subjects and controls appear for those youths who are at the lowest risk for drug use—those who were nonusers or infrequent users at the start of the study (Gorman and White 1995, 141).

Self-help programs are somewhat different. They bring together deviants who themselves wish to change their lives and who wish to help each other to change. There are usually no professional helpers involved to stimulate or guide group discussion and activities, although in recent years there has been a trend toward greater involvement by professionals. The best-known such group is Alcoholics Anonymous; similar groups have been formed for drug addicts, gamblers, debtors, and others with problem behaviors (see Reissman and Carroll 1995).

Theoretical justifications for these groups are varied and abundant. From the vantage point of socialization theories, they organize deviants to provide nondeviant definitions to each other. The active involvement of the deviants themselves is held to be critical for the success of these programs, because such involvement fosters a sense of "empowerment" among the participants, enabling them to take control of their own destinies (Katz and Bender 1990, 250–251). Self-help programs should be effective resocialization agents to the extent that they become a significant part of people's lives, affecting the frequency, duration, and intensity of social relationships. It is important to note, however, that self-help groups are limited to deviants who wish to change their lives and to deviants who are willing and able to confront the traumas that frequently accompany membership in self-help groups.

CRITIQUE

SOCIAL DISORGANIZATION

Theory The original social disorganization theory formulated by the Chicagoans reflects an ecological model of urban dynamics. This model is based on the assumption that the distribution of urban activities results from the operation of "natural" ecological dynamics. The impersonal operation of the market presumably determines the outcome of the competition for commercial and residential space, yielding a distinctive pattern of social relationships such as Burgess' zonal model of the city.

This natural model of urban dynamics has been called into question because it neglects critical factors of the political economy (Bursik 1989; Bursik and Grasmick 1993). Residential and commercial patterns in a city are created not only by market processes but also by conscious decisions by influential actors. Public officials decide where to locate public housing projects; they also choose which neighborhoods to demolish to allow for the construction of new highways. Similarly, financial institutions determine who is loaned money for mortgages, while real-estate agents are able to steer different kinds of people into different kinds of neighborhoods. In short, classical social disorganization theory is largely insensitive to the role of politics in the construction of human environments.

In addition, while classical social disorganization theory situates neighborhoods within a larger urban system, the internal characteristics and dynamics of neighborhoods are emphasized in the explanation of deviance (Heitgard and Bursik 1987). Neighborhoods with heterogeneous, mobile, and poor populations supposedly have difficulty exerting social control over their residents. However, the level of control in a neighborhood is also likely to depend on "extracommunity" dynamics. Some neighborhoods are more integrated into the larger urban system and are thus better able to garner the kinds of resources that help control deviant behavior (e.g., funds to support community organizations). In addition, features of the national economy, such as the movement of jobs to the suburbs and the "deindustrialization" of cities (see Wilson 1987), undoubtedly influence the control capabilities of urban neighborhoods.

Research   A persistent problem for research informed by social disorganization theory is the operationalization of the core theoretical concept: social disorganization. Recent proponents of the perspective (e.g., Bursik and Gramick 1993) have proposed that social disorganization is best conceptualized in terms of the social relationships and networks linking the residents of a neighborhood to one another. Unfortunately, readily available data sources (e.g., census data) do not contain information on such social phenomena. Researchers can, in principle, use survey techniques to collect data on personal ties, but such efforts must be rather massive in scope to ensure that sufficient numbers of respondents are surveyed across an appreciable number of·neighborhoods. As a result of these rather demanding research requirements, very few studies have been able to measure social disorganization directly. The evidence in support of the theory is thus necessarily indirect. Most studies are able to demonstrate merely that the hypothesized determinants of social disorganization are associated with the hypothesized consequences of disorganization.

In addition, some of the available evidence runs counter to the claims of the theory. As noted earlier, recent research suggests that crime rates may be highest in neighborhoods with little population turnover but very high levels of nonwhites (Warner and Pierce 1993), which contradicts the prediction of social disorganization theory that population heterogeneity and residential instability promote crime. It may be that in some cities, especially those in the East and Midwest, we are witnessing a decline in the urban dynamics, expressed in social disorganization theory, wherein poor immigrants and migrants move into low-rent housing in low-income neighborhoods; in time are replaced by newer immigrants and migrants in an ongoing cycle, leading to social instability and heterogeneity, which in turn produces low social control and high rates of deviance. (These processes may still be prevalent in southern and western cities.) Neighborhoods where only poor minorities permanently reside because they have no other place to go may be conducive to high crime rates via a different process. The homogeneity and stability of these neighborhoods might not produce cohesiveness and, consequently, social control; rather, the social isolation of their residents may build resentment, frustration, hopelessness, and apathy that reduces their motivation to enforce conventional standards. Cultural standards of the mainstream society may seem irrelevant to the survival demands of everyday life.

Social Policy Social disorganization theory implies that deviance can be reduced if disorganized communities are reorganized. While the logical basis of this proposition is readily apparent, obstacles to the successful reorganization of communities are formidable. In the first place, we have very little knowledge about how to organize communities through deliberate planning, and very little experience in doing so. Indeed, the very idea of "planned communities" is not easily reconciled with basic commitments to individualism, personal autonomy, and privacy, commitments which are at the core of the American value system.

It is also important to recognize that while social disorganization might be detrimental to some, it might be highly beneficial to others. Disorganized neighborhoods are unlikely to get their fair share of the services and amenities of urban life, which implies that there is more to be distributed to the better-off neighborhoods. In other words, reorganizing disorganized communities might very well threaten the interests of powerful groups. Gathering the social support necessary to pursue meaningful social reorganization is thus likely to be highly problematic.

Accomplishments Most critics of the disorganization school also acknowledge its major accomplishments, and there were many. For example, the research findings did much to counter the eugenics movement based on the growing prestige of the biological sciences. Eugenics proponents argued that the high crime and deviance rate associated with urban slums is a result of generations of selective breeding of defectives. Many suggested fertility-reduction remedies, including sterilization. The Chicago researchers showed that high levels of deviance are associated with the slum, not the inhabitants who reside there. They are linked to sites and situations, to the ecological and social situations confronted by the residents, whether they be Poles, Italians, Germans, or as is common today, African Americans (see Stark 1987).

DIFFERENTIAL ORGANIZATION

Theory   While many Chicagoans rejected the concept of social disorganization by the mid-1930s, in favor of differential organization, they
never fully developed this alternative concept and placed it within a general theoretical framework. Does differential organization reflect processes of
social conflict? If so, what are the relevant dimensions of conflict (cultural,
economic, and/or political)? Why are the norms of some groups but not
others translated into law? For the most part, these questions were ignored.
With the exception of Sellin (1938) and a few others, it was not until 1958
that Vold's monograph on crime and social conflict appeared; even this
work included only a few chapters on social conflict and crime. (More
about this will be said in Chapter 7.) Instead the Chicagoans developed and
inspired a social psychology of deviance that focused on the process by
which people are socialized and operate in social worlds that conflict with
the conventional order. Similarly, while recent work within the routine
activities approach calls attention to the importance of different types of
association for criminal opportunities, there is no general theory of social
structure associated with this approach that explains why routine activities
tend to be patterned in one way rather than another.

Range of Application   Socialization theories are most applicable to
deviance that is subcultural, describing the processes through which
deviant definitions are learned. Yet not all deviance is subculturally supported. Certain acts lack subcultural support in the United States in the
sense that no groups actively encourage involvement (e.g., necrophilia).
Many acts are not actively supported by groups, although subcultural
norms may indirectly contribute to their occurrence (rape and homicide).
Acknowledging the scope conditions of socialization theories of deviance
(i.e., the conditions to which they apply) may enhance their usefulness in
directing research and social policy.

SOCIAL POLICY

The policy recommendations from the routine activities tradition seem
highly plausible, if not downright commonsensical. If people take greater
precautions, they should be less likely to be victimized. However, the efficacy of concrete precautions is less obvious than it appears (Felson and
Clarke 1995, 182–183). Some precautions may be based on folk wisdom
that is simply invalid—do lights really deceive burglars into thinking that
someone is home? Other precautions may simply displace victimization
onto other "targets" that are not as well-hardened, resulting in no net gain
for the community at large. Some precautionary measures may actually
enhance risks of victimization (e.g., walling off yards, thereby providing
potential burglars with privacy). In sum, knowledge about precisely how to

reduce the "opportunities" for crime is more limited than is often recognized.

Socialization theories have been criticized for focusing on so-called root causes of deviance that are not tractable to policy implementation (Wilson 1975). Manipulating social definitions is difficult compared, for example, to manipulating the penalties for law violations. Moreover, programs designed to resocialize persons who have reached the stage of adulthood, or even advanced adolescence, are likely to be of limited effectiveness given the extensive learning that has occurred prior to that time. Nevertheless, there is evidence to suggest that family-based programs that attempt to influence early childhood socialization can have lasting benefits for the children involved (Gorman and White 1995). Also, studies of various self-help groups such as Alcoholics Anonymous suggest that it is possible, if not easy, to change the behavior of adults as well. Policy makers might build upon these types of programs to develop both preventive and rehabilitative programs to deal with deviance.

THE RATIONAL CHOICE/DETERRENCE PERSPECTIVE

THEORY

The rational choice/deterrence perspective has its roots in utilitarian social philosophy and a body of ideas often referred to as the "classical" school (Beccaria 1963; Bentham 1843). Proponents of the classical school adopted a distinctive view of human nature that emphasized hedonism, rationalism, and free will. They believed that human beings choose to behave in certain ways after rationally calculating the potential pleasures (benefits) of behavior as well as the potential pain that might result from being punished for that behavior (costs).

CONTEMPORARY RATIONAL CHOICE THEORY

Rational choice theory follows in the tradition of the classical school by assuming that behavior is the product of a rational assessment of costs and benefits. It focuses generally on how people weigh costs relative to benefits of both law-violating and law-abiding alternatives. In addition to legal costs, contemporary rational choice theorists consider other costs, including informal sanctions and the painful emotions (e.g., shame and embarrassment) that may accompany law violations (Grasmick and Bursik 1990; Grasmick et al. 1993; Nagin and Paternoster 1994), as well as the benefits associated with them. They also consider the cost/benefits of law abiding alternatives. In sum, according to rational choice theory, the probability of committing a given act (a crime) depends on the potential pains of the punishments and on the potential pleasures of the rewards associated with law violations (Piliavin et al. 1986), relative to those of law-abiding alternatives.

The most sophisticated formulations of rational choice theory have drawn heavily on contemporary economics (Becker 1968; Cornish and Clarke 1986; Rubin 1978). According to the economic approach, criminals are fundamentally no different from everyone else. They seek to maximize personal utility given the constraints ("prices") in their environment. Some persons become criminals for the same reason others become doctors, lawyers, or social scientists. The net "payoff" of crime for these persons simply exceeds that of other available alternatives. Similarly, the level of crime is higher in one place than in another because crime is a more profitable enterprise in the former than in the latter.

Rational choice theory has been used to describe how crime depends on the interaction between offenders and victims (Cook 1986). The theory assumes that offenders are attracted to crime targets that provide a high payoff with little effort and low risks of legal punishments. Victims, on the other hand, desire to be safe from victimization, and they take a variety of precautions to reduce the attractiveness of crime. They try to make it more difficult for offenders to successfully complete their crimes; they try to increase the likelihood that offenders will be detected and apprehended; and they try to reduce their loss if they are victimized.

Offenders and victims thus have competing interests, just as buyers and sellers do in the marketplace. The interaction between buyers and sellers ultimately yields a market price for goods and services, which determines how much of these goods and services will be produced. In an analogous manner, offenders and victims interact in the "crime market" to determine the volume of crime. Offenders "supply" more or less crime depending on the net return ("price") that they are able to receive. Victims "demand" more or less safety depending on how much time and effort is required to secure it (the "price" that they must pay for a given level of security). As offenders and potential victims interact and respond to one another, they arrive at a "going rate" for crime (its net payoff), which determines how much crime will be produced.

DETERRENCE THEORY

Conventional deterrence theory can be viewed as a special case of rational choice theory. Whereas the rational choice perspective calls attention to both costs and benefits, deterrence theory specifically emphasizes the role of "costs" in explaining law violations. An increase in the costs of crime should logically reduce the volume of crime. The type of punishment that receives principal attention is state-administered punishment. Given that legal punishment is a significant cost of crime, it follows that a higher level of such punishment should be associated with a lower level of crime.

Two basic types of deterrence processes have been studied: general and specific. General deterrence refers to a process by which the punishment of some law violators provides information about the costs of crime to those who have not been punished (the general public), thereby reducing the latter's law violations. Specific deterrence refers to a process by which punishment reduces the law violations of those who have been punished.

Three different dimensions of punishment are relevant to deterrence: severity, certainty, and celerity. *Severity* refers to the harshness or degree of punishment, such as the length of incarceration or the amount of a fine. *Certainty of punishment* refers to the probability of experiencing punishment, such as the chances of being apprehended, prosecuted, convicted, and sentenced. *Celerity of punishment* refers to the swiftness of punishment (i.e., the time interval between committing a law violation and experiencing punishment). The central claim of deterrence theory is that law violations are low when the severity, certainty, and celerity of legal punishments are high (see Figure 4.1). Although the basic thrust of deterrence theory seems straightforward, there are ambiguities concerning the relative effects of these three dimensions, the nature of each effect, and the combined effects of the three dimensions.

First, the theory does not specify the relative importance of the three dimensions. Which has the strongest effect and which the weakest? With respect to social policy, would it be more effective to increase severity (length of prison sentence) or certainty (probability of a prison sentence) by a given amount?

Second, the nature of the effect of each dimension is unclear. We frequently assume a linear relationship—each increment in punishment yields a steady reduction in law violations. However, the effect may be nonlinear. For each dimension, increases in punishment may have no effect until a certain level is reached. For example, an increase in the arrest rate clearance rate (i.e., the proportion of known crimes that results in an arrest) from 10 percent to 25 percent may produce no meaningful decrease in the level of law violations; but a further increase to 40 percent may produce a substantial decrease in law violations (Tittle and Rowe 1974). People may not think of punishment probabilities in precise, quantitative terms (10, 11, 12 percent); rather, they may think more qualitatively. Low probabilities of 1 to 20 percent, for example, may be perceived as "little probability of being

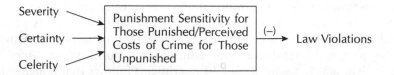

FIGURE 4.1   CAUSAL STRUCTURE OF DETERRENCE THEORY
The figure shows that severity, certainty, and celerity of punishment positively affect the punishment sensitivity of those punished and the perceived costs of crime for those unpunished (the general public), which in turn negatively affects the level of law violations. Therefore, a high level of punishment should result in a low level of law violating.

caught." Perhaps a 25 or 30 percent objective level of certainty is needed before people think that being punished is a viable possibility. The effects of severity and celerity may also be nonlinear.

Third, although each dimension of punishment is analytically distinct from the others, they may operate in conjunction. For example, the effect of severity of punishment may depend on the certainty of punishment (Gibbs 1975). In other words, the level of severity may not enter into people's decision-making when the certainty of punishment is trivial. Reasonably high levels of certainty may be necessary before people seriously consider the severity of punishment. Similarly, the effect of certainty may also depend on severity.

Table 4.1 illustrates how the effect of punishment might depend on both severity and certainty. The table shows a hypothetical crime rate for two levels of severity and certainty. The figures outside the parentheses show that at a low level of both severity and certainty (lower-right corner), the crime rate is high (10); a high level of either severity or certainty reduces the crime rate by 50 percent (5); and a high level of both severity and certainty reduces it by 100 percent (0). These figures illustrate an additive model, where the effects of severity (50 percent crime reduction) and certainty (50 percent crime reduction) can be added together to estimate the combined effects of severity and certainty (100 percent crime reduction). The figures inside the parentheses illustrate an interactive model, where the effects of punishment certainty and severity operate in combination (they interact). When both are low, the crime rate is high (10), as in the additive model. However, contrary to the additive model, the figures inside the parentheses show that an increase in either the level of severity or certainty has no effect on the crime rate when the other dimension is low; the crime rate remains high (10). Both severity and certainty must be high before the crime rate decreases (upper-left corner).

In sum, both deterrence theory and rational choice theory assume that behavior is the result of a rational decision-making process. People make judgments about likely benefits and costs and then act in ways that maximize benefits and minimize costs. Deterrence theory focuses on one particularly important component of this rational calculus: the costs associated with legal sanctions. The theory stipulates that the more severe,

TABLE 4.1   ADDITIVE AND INTERACTIVE MODELS FOR ESTIMATING
THE COMBINED EFFECTS OF SEVERITY AND CERTAINTY

	HIGH SEVERITY	LOW SEVERITY
HIGH CERTAINTY	(0) 0	(10) 5
LOW CERTAINTY	(10) 5	(10) 10

certain, and swift the punishment by the state, the lower the crime rate will be. Rational choice theory incorporates additional costs of crime beyond those of legal punishments and also examines the likely benefits of crime.

RESEARCH

This section reviews research on general deterrence and the rational choice model of offending. The general deterrence section is divided into two major subsections: objective properties of punishment and individual perceptions of punishment. Specific deterrence research will be discussed in Chapter 5, in conjunction with the labeling perspective. Research that examines the consequences of legal punishment for those punished also, in effect, examines the consequences of public labeling for those labeled. Thus, research on specific deterrence and labeling bear directly on one another.

GENERAL DETERRENCE: OBJECTIVE PUNISHMENT

Recall that general deterrence refers to a process by which the punishment of some people reduces the law violations of those not punished, the general public. Relevant research is extensive, varied in methodological rigor, and difficult to synthesize. In studies focusing on objective properties of punishment, two methodological designs are commonly used: comparative and time series. The former compares the crime rate of jurisdictions with different levels of punishment at a particular time; the latter compares the crime rates and levels of punishment in a single jurisdiction over time.

Comparative Most studies include three basic concepts: the crime rate, severity of punishment, and certainty of punishment. (Celerity of punishment has been largely ignored.) Although procedures vary somewhat from study to study, these concepts are usually measured as follows: The crime rate is measured as the ratio of reported crimes to the population in a jurisdiction. Severity of punishment is measured as the average (mean or median) length of sentence (time served in prison) in a jurisdiction. Certainty of punishment is measured as the ratio of the number of arrests or prison admissions to the number of crimes reported in a jurisdiction (this ratio expresses the probability of being arrested or incarcerated upon committing a crime). According to deterrence theory, the crime rate should decrease as the average length of sentences increases and as the ratio of arrests or prison admissions to reported crimes increases.

Researchers have confronted four general issues. The first involves the relative importance of severity and certainty of punishment. The evidence indicates that certainty is the more important of the two (Cook 1980), but it also suggests that the two dimensions of punishment are interrelated. For example, Charles H. Logan (1972) found that states with high severity tend to have low certainty. He speculated that judges and juries are reluctant to find people guilty and incarcerate them when punishment is very severe. He also suggested that severity alters the effect of certainty: Certainty has the greatest impact when severity is high.

A second issue involves the nature of the widely observed certainty effect on crime. Is it linear or nonlinear? The issue was first stimulated by Tittle and Rowe (1974). Studying Florida cities and counties, they reported a "tipping" effect: An appreciable level of certainty must be reached before any reduction in the crime rate occurs. Their data showed that certainty of arrest made a substantial difference in crime rates only after a 30 percent certainty rate had been reached (30 percent of reported crimes were cleared by arrest). Below that level, changes in certainty had little effect on crime rates. Brown (1978) extended Tittle and Rowe's research by comparing large cities and counties in California to small ones in Florida and by comparing different tipping points (25 percent, 30 percent, and 35 percent). He found a tipping effect at 25 percent that was restricted to small cities and counties. More recently, Chamlin (1991) further extended these findings in two analyses: a monthly time series of seven Pennsylvania cities varying in population size from 5,000 to 2 million, and cross-sectional analysis of all U.S. cities. For both analyses he found a negative effect of certainty rates on crime rates with a tipping point at about 40 percent, but only for small cities. Clearly, the studies suggest that a tipping effect exists, but it may be limited to small cities. Why small cities? A plausible interpretation is that, because people in these places are intensely involved in primary relationships, the news of punishments is spread more efficiently and rapidly through personal communication than it is in large cities.

If this interpretation is correct, then we should also expect to find that people are affected more by the certainty rates of their neighborhood than of their state, and more by the certainty rates of members of their age cohort, class, and race than of all people within the state. Yu and Liska (1993) addressed this issue by disaggregating a city's certainty and crime rates into the certainty and crimes rates for whites and for blacks, separately. They found that the crime rate of whites is always more affected by certainty rate of whites than blacks, and conversely that the crime rate of blacks is always more affected by the certainty rate of blacks than whites.

A third issue pertains to the causal process that accounts for the consistently observed negative relationship between certainty and the crime rate. Deterrence theory implies that high certainty of punishment causes a low crime rate. Another possibility is that the level of crime affects the certainty of punishment. When the crime rate is low, police can devote considerable time to each case, increasing the probability of arrest and conviction. On the other hand, when the crime rate is high, police are unable to spend much time on each case, decreasing the probability of arrest and conviction. This latter interpretation is often referred to as the "overload" hypothesis. It implies a negative association between certainty and the crime rate, but the association is attributed to a causal process that is the reverse of that implied by deterrence theory.

Greenberg, Kessler, and Logan (1979) addressed the issue of causal order in a longitudinal study of 98 U.S. cities. They estimated the effects of past and present certainty levels on present crime rates and the effects of past and present crime rates on present certainty levels over a six-year period for index crimes. The results were startling: Neither deterrence theory nor the overload hypothesis was supported. They concluded that while crime and certainty of punishment are negatively related, the relationship is brought about not by the causal effects of one on the other but by unknown conditions which affect both crime rates and certainty.

A final concern in the general deterrence literature is the scope of its applicability: Is it limited to only certain types of crime? Geerken and Gove (1977) argued that deterrence effects should be expected only for crimes that occur in situations where people have the time and motivation to calculate the rewards and costs of alternative behavior. They differentiated between economic crimes (robbery, burglary, larceny, and auto theft), which tend to be committed in circumstances where rewards and costs are calculable, and crimes of violence (assault and homicide), which tend to be committed in emotional states that inhibit thoughtful assessment of consequences. Rape falls somewhere between economic and emotional crimes, as it is a crime of violence which is frequently planned. They examined the correlation between certainty of punishment (measured as the arrest clearance rate) and crime rates for all U.S. metropolitan areas over five hundred thousand population. The data support their hypothesis: The correlations for the four economic crimes are substantial and negative; the correlation for rape is moderately negative; and the correlations for the two "emotional" crimes are small and nonsignificant.

Sampson (1986a) also discovered differential effects of indicators of punishment risk for different types of crimes in a study of 171 U.S. cities. He examined three indicators of the probability of legal punishment: police aggressiveness (arrests per police officer for "social control" offenses such as disorderly conduct); jail incarceration risk (jail population per offenses); and state prison risk (state prison admissions per offenses). His analyses support the deterrence perspective for robbery but not for homicide. While none of the indicators of legal sanctions exhibits the expected association with homicide rates, jail incarceration risk is consistently associated with robbery rates in an inverse direction. Cities with high risks of incarceration exhibit low robbery rates, controlling for socioeconomic and demographic characteristics of cities.

Time Series To reiterate, time-series analysis examines the relationship between crime rates and punishment levels for a single jurisdiction over time. A special type of time-series study in the deterrence literature compares crime rates of a jurisdiction before and after some change in either the severity of punishment (e.g., an increase in prison sentences) or certainty of punishment (e.g., an increase in the number of police per capita). This approach has been used extensively to study the effects of legal interventions to reduce drunk driving (DD), which have occurred in numerous jurisdictions not only in the United States but in other nations as well. H. Laurence Ross (1984, 1992) has reviewed much of this literature, and the following discussion relies heavily on his review.

Changes in the severity of punishment (length of imprisonment) for those convicted of drunk driving generally show little effect on the rate of drunk driving. In one of the first efforts to control this behavior, Finland significantly increased prison sentences for violations in 1950; subsequent incidents of fatal and serious injuries in vehicle crashes, however, showed no clear deterrence effect. Similar conclusions have been reached on the basis of analyses of increased legal penalties in a number of cities, although there are exceptions (Voas and Lacey 1990). Ross cited an unanticipated consequence of some of these efforts, however: Increases in severity of punishment tend to decrease the certainty of punishment. As the severity of punishment increases, conviction rates, charges by police, and reports of crashes to police and insurance companies decrease. It seems that when penalties are very severe, judges and juries are reluctant to convict, police are reluctant to charge, and those accused use all possible legal opportunities to avoid conviction, thereby overloading the criminal justice system. The reluctance to impose harsh penalties on drunk drivers may be diminishing, however, as a result of efforts to increase public awareness of the social harm associated with drinking and driving by citizen activist groups, such as Mothers Against Drunk Driving (MADD) and Remove Intoxicated Drivers (RID).

Findings for the certainty of punishment are much more supportive of deterrence theory. Norway in 1936 and Sweden in 1941 passed laws that defined drunk driving in terms of blood-alcohol concentrations, which can be measured exactly. These types of laws have been adopted in many countries. They significantly increase the certainty of punishment since specific blood-alcohol levels are taken as prima facie evidence of drunk driving. Evidence documenting the effectiveness of these laws was first reported in Britain (Ross 1984). The British Road Safety Act of 1967 allowed police to demand a test of blood alcohol (breath analyzer) of anyone stopped for a traffic violation or involved in an automobile accident. The effect was dramatic. The number of fatal and serious auto injuries occurring on weekend nights, when alcohol-impaired driving is most frequent, dropped from twelve hundred per month to four hundred per month. The fact that no such drop was observed during weekday commuting hours, when alcohol-impaired driving seldom occurs, further suggests that the drop in nighttime weekend injuries was a result of the law. The passage of similar laws in other countries (France, the Netherlands, Canada, Australia, New Zealand, Germany, Austria, and the Czech Republic) appears to have had similar consequences, although the size of the effect varies from country to country. It is likely that the impact of these laws depends on the publicity surrounding their passage (Ross 1984). When the legal change is highly publicized, people are aware of the increased probability of punishment for DD, which affects their decision whether to drink and drive.

An increasingly popular law enforcement strategy for raising the certainty of punishment for drunk driving is the use of checkpoints. In this approach, all drivers passing through a designated spot are stopped and screened for the presence of alcohol. The State of New Jersey implemented a "strikeforce" program during the 1983–85 period in which checkpoints served as a major component. An evaluation of the program found that there was a drop of 10–15 percent in the single vehicle nighttime crash rate (Voas and Lacey 1990). Moreover, the impact of checkpoints was greater than that of the other elements of the strikeforce program, such as public information and traditional police patrols.

The main problem revealed in many of the studies on drunk driving crackdowns is that the deterrent effect tends to be short-lived. In the British case, it lasted for only a few months. Generally, after a relatively short period of time, the rate of serious and fatal auto accidents climbs back to about the level that existed before the enactment of the law. Apparently, drivers initially scared by the law learn from day-to-day experience that they are unlikely to be stopped and tested for blood-alcohol levels.

An exception to this general pattern is provided by an intervention in the Australian states of New South Wales and Tasmania (Ross 1992). The Australian program involved the establishment of unannounced checkpoints where all motorists were stopped and given a breath test. This approach differs from the common practice in the United States, where the police initially "screen" motorists at checkpoints and administer a breath test only to those who display evidence of alcohol impairment. An evaluation of the study revealed that traffic deaths declined by about 20 percent and that death rates remained relatively low for a follow-up period of five years. The ultimate duration of the reduction in fatalities is uncertain, however. As Ross (1992, 70–71) cautioned, long-term deterrence is likely to require rigorous enforcement over a sustained period of time, which is difficult to achieve.

Three basic conclusions are suggested by the DD studies: An increase in the certainty of punishment can have a deterrent effect; it is often short-lived; and it depends on the publicity given to the increase in certainty.

A related line of research has examined the deterrent effect of capital punishment. The early death penalty studies employed a comparative approach, contrasting jurisdictions with and without the death penalty. The results of these studies generally failed to support the deterrence perspective (Sellin 1955, 1961). More recent studies have adopted time-series designs. For example, Phillips (1980) examined the effect of executions on weekly homicide rates in London from 1858 to 1921. He compared the homicide rate during the two weeks before an execution (the statistical control period), the week of the execution, and the week following the execution. He found that the average number of homicides (thirty per week) for the prior two weeks dropped 35 percent during the week of the execution and the following week. Furthermore, the size of the decrease in the homicide rate was positively correlated with the degree of newspaper coverage of the execution, as measured by the number of column inches devoted to the story in the London *Times*. The effect, however, was short-lived. In the third, fourth, and fifth weeks following the execution, the homicide rate increased by an average of nineteen homicides above the normal rate and then returned to the normal level of thirty per week. (These findings are controversial: See Zeisel 1982; Kobbervig, Inverarity, and Lauderdale 1982; Phillips 1982a, 1982b.)

Several studies have considered the generalizability of Phillips' research on London during the 1858–1921 period to the contemporary United States. Stack (1987) examined the effect of newspaper publicity of executions on the monthly homicide rate for the United States between 1950–80. He classified an execution as "highly publicized" if it was covered in both *Facts on File* (an index of the daily press throughout the nation) and the *New York Times*. Consistent with deterrence theory, Stack's results revealed that months with highly publicized executions had lower homicide rates than months without highly publicized executions. Subsequent research by Bailey and Peterson (1989), however, challenged Stack's conclusion. After controlling for determinants of homicide neglected by Stack and correcting some technical coding errors, Bailey and Peterson found no evidence to support the claim that national publicity of executions in newspapers has any appreciable deterrent effect on homicides. Research by Bailey (1990) on television publicity yielded similar results. Measures of the amount and type of television publicity surrounding executions had no effect on monthly homicide rates over the 1976–87 period.

Note that the absence of a *deterrent effect* in these studies of execution publicity and homicide does not necessarily discredit *deterrence theory*. Executions are uncommon, and they might have to occur with a greater frequency to deter potential killers (as with other offenses, there may be a "tipping effect"). Indeed, as Bailey has observed, "what television news coverage may be *communicating* to the public is that the certainty of capital punishment for murder is quite low" (1990, 633). The safest conclusion to draw from this research, then, is that executions as currently employed and publicized appear to have little effect on the national homicide rate.

To summarize, the comparative and time-series studies of general deterrence suggest two basic conclusions: (1) There is little consistent evidence for a severity effect, although some data suggest that an effect may be present when the certainty level is high. Severity of punishment may not be important to people unless they feel that the chances of getting caught are reasonably high. (2) There is evidence of a certainty effect, although the nature, size, and duration of it remain unclear.

GENERAL DETERRENCE: INDIVIDUAL PERCEPTIONS

General deterrence studies are frequently criticized for assuming that people are able to perceive accurately the objective level of severity and certainty of punishment, which seems unlikely. It may thus be useful to test deterrence theory by examining the relationship between the perception of punishment and law violations. Deterrence theory implies that as perceived severity and certainty decrease, law violations increase.

The early studies of perceptual deterrence were based on cross-sectional surveys. These studies generally supported the deterrence hypothesis for the certainty of punishment but not for severity. Consistent with deterrence theory, respondents perceiving high risks of legal sanctioning typically report lower involvement in various types of criminal behavior (see Paternoster 1987 for a review). An important limitation of these cross-sectional studies is that it is difficult to infer cause and effect. Deterrence theorists assume that the level of perceived certainty affects the level of violations; however, it seems equally plausible to argue that the level of law violations affects perceptions of certainty. Those who violate the law may come to realize that the chances of formal sanctioning are actually rather low.

Two influential studies attempted to disentangle these causal effects by examining changes in perceptions of certainty and levels of self-reported crime over time with panel data (Saltzman et al. 1982; Minor and Harry 1982). The research of Saltzman et al. was based on self-reports of petty theft, shoplifting, marijuana use, and writing bad checks by 300 college students over a one year period; the study by Minor and Harry was based on self-reports of marijuana use, shoplifting, cocaine use, fighting, cheating, and drunk and disorderly conduct by 488 college students over three months. Both studies examined the effect of perceptions of certainty of punishment at time one, on changes in law violations between times one and two, and the effect of law violations between times one and two on perceived certainty at time two. This makes the direction of causal influences clearer than in most studies. The results revealed that law violations affected perceptions of certainty more than perceptions of certainty affected law violations. Indeed, the findings indicated little deterrence effect, suggesting that past findings of a negative relationship between perceptions of certainty and law violations have been misinterpreted as evidence of deterrence when in fact they are probably evidence of an "experiential effect."

Research by Horney and Marshall (1992) provides further support for the experiential interpretation. They noted that previous studies often focused on samples of college students and on minor forms of offending. As a result, the generalizability of the findings to high-risk populations (serious offenders) is open to question. In addition, Horney and Marshall argued that an adequate test of the experiential effect requires that involvement in crime be related to experiences with sanctions. High involvement in crime should lead to low perceptions of certainty only if the person actually goes unpunished for these acts. For a sample of 1,046 convicted male offenders in Nebraska, Horney and Marshall computed a "relative sanctions" measure based on the ratio of arrests for a type of crime to the number of times that crime was committed. They examined the effect of this measure on perceived certainty of punishment (the respondent's estimate of the likelihood that he would be arrested if he committed the crime). They found that among active offenders (those who report any involvement in a given crime), the relative sanctions measure was significantly related to certainty perceptions, with low estimates of risk for those who were rarely arrested for offending. These findings suggest that serious offenders formulate perceptions of punishment probabilities on the basis of their past experiences with legal sanctions.

In sum, research on individual perceptions offers mixed support for deterrence theory. Most studies have not detected an association between severity of punishment and law violations, but most have found a relationship between certainty of punishment and law violations: Persons who perceive that the chances of being punished are high tend to report low levels of criminal involvement. The causal processes underlying this relationship, however, are ambiguous. The evidence suggests that persons who commit law violations and go unpunished adjust their perceptions of risks accordingly. In other words, the inverse relationship between perceived certainty and law violations appears to reflect, at least to some extent, past experiences with legal sanctions—an "experiential effect." Future research should attempt to estimate more precisely the relative magnitudes of deterrent and experiential effects in the creation of a relationship between perceived certainty of punishment and law violations.

RESEARCH ON RATIONAL CHOICE

Rational choice theory incorporates traditional deterrence processes but considers additional factors that influence the choice of crime beyond those of legal punishments. For example, Williams and Hawkins (1986, 1989) argued for an expanded conception of deterrence that allows for "indirect" as well as "direct" costs of legal sanctions. Direct costs refer to the pains and deprivations associated with legal penalties, such as fines, imprisonment, and loss of life through execution. Indirect costs reflect the more general ramifications of legal punishment for an individual's life. The most important of these, according to Williams and Hawkins, are "stigmatic costs" (i.e., humiliation for the individual and his or her family), "attachment costs" (i.e., damage to interpersonal relationships), and "commitment costs" (i.e., reduced returns on investments and foreclosed opportunities).

Williams and Hawkins (1989) applied this expanded conception of deterrence to explain the social meaning of arrest for wife assault. Using survey data for 494 cohabitating males, they addressed three questions: (1) What costs do men perceive as resulting from an arrest for wife assault? (2) How do the various costs affect their overall fear of arrest? (3) What is the effect of these perceived costs on involvement in wife assault? The legal or direct cost of arrest was measured by perceptions of the chances of going to jail. Indirect costs were measured by potential damage to attachments with others (the partner leaving, friends and relatives disapproving, or losing respect of others), by potential loss of job, and by anticipated stigma for oneself and one's family. Overall fear of arrest was measured by the respondents' rating of "how bad it would be for them if they were arrested for hitting their partner," and involvement in wife assault was measured by a scale indicating whether people use violent tactics to deal with conflicts with their partners.

With respect to the first question—the perceived costs of an arrest for wife assault, Williams and Hawkins found that the stigmatic and attachment costs were most important. The majority of respondents reported that self-stigma, family stigma, and social disapproval would follow from an arrest. In contrast, the direct legal cost (doing time in jail) was not perceived as very likely to happen (nor was loss of a job). To answer the second question, Williams and Hawkins examined the association between the various costs and overall fear of arrest (ratings about how bad it would be to be arrested). The results indicated that self-stigma was the strongest determinant of fear of arrest, followed by social disapproval, loss of job, and loss of partner. Jail time had no significant effect. Thus, the major reason that men feared arrest appeared to be "the likelihood of personal humiliation and potentially damaged relationships with friends, relatives, and partners" (1989, 173). The final question deals with the relationship between perceived costs and actual involvement in wife assault. In a multivariate analysis, Williams and Hawkins discovered that self-stigma was the only significant determinant of wife assault. They concluded that the prospect of this personal humiliation serves as the key intervening variable through which other perceived costs of arrest deter criminal behavior.

Whereas Williams and Hawkins expanded the conception of deterrence by including informal sanctions that are activated by a legal punishment (an arrest), Grasmick et al. (1993) extended the approach further by conceptualizing as deterrents the painful emotions (shame and embarrassment) associated with the violation of social norms. Shame refers to painful emotions that people experience when they violate internalized norms; and embarrassment refers to painful emotions that people experience when they violate norms embraced by others whose opinions are valued. Grasmick et al. proposed that shame and embarrassment reduce the utility of behavior that evokes them. Shame and embarrassment, therefore, can be thought of as potential costs analogous to legal punishments that vary along the dimensions of severity and certainty, just as do legal threats. The overall perceived threat of shame and embarrassment is a function of their perceived certainty (the likelihood that these emotions will be evoked) and their perceived severity (the degree of discomfort that will be experienced if they are evoked).

Grasmick et al. applied their expanded deterrence/rational choice framework in research on drinking and driving. Their analyses were based on two random surveys conducted in Oklahoma City in 1982 and 1990. Respondents were asked about their intentions to drink and drive. In addition, the surveys elicited information permitting the construction of the following measures: legal certainty (perceived likelihood of getting caught for driving under the influence), legal severity (perceived problems for the respondent if he or she were to get caught and be punished), shame certainty (likelihood of feeling guilty if the respondent were to drink and drive), shame severity (perceived problems for the respondent that would be created by feelings of shame), embarrassment certainty (likelihood that valued persons would lose respect for the respondent), and embarrassment severity (perceived problems for the respondent if people were to lose respect for him or her). Grasmick et al. combined the certainty and severity scores to create measures of the perceived threat of legal sanctions, the perceived threat of shame, and the perceived threat of embarrassment. In their analysis, they estimated the effect of each of these perceived threats on intentions to drink and drive. Their results indicated that the threat of shame exhibited a relatively strong deterrent effect on intentions to drink and drive, and that the increase in the perceived threat of shame over the 1982–90 period was the primary cause of a general reduction in these intentions. The threat of legal sanctions also exerted a modest deterrent effect on intentions to drink and drive, although it did not account for the change over time. (The effect of threat of embarrassment was not significant.) Grasmick et al. concluded that rational choice models of criminal behavior can be made more powerful by joining considerations of moral "costs" with the traditional focus of deterrence theorists on legal punishments.

In addition to calls for expanding the types of "costs" considered in the analysis of the criminal decision-making process, researchers have argued for explicit consideration of the "benefit" component as well. For example, Piliavin et al. (1986) proposed a theoretical model that identifies both benefit (reward) factors as well as legal risk factors as determinants of criminal behavior. They assessed the importance of these factors using survey data from three samples of respondents: adult offenders who had been incarcerated, adults who were known drug users, and adolescents age 17–20 who had dropped out of school. Two types of legal costs were measured: formal risk (perceived chances of legal punishment) and personal risk (perceived chances of losing a spouse or one's friends if sent to prison). Measures of benefits (legal and illegal) included estimated earnings that could be made from illegal sources relative to those for a "straight" job, belief that there are frequent opportunities for crime, and respect for conventional jobs over illegal jobs. Their results revealed that, contrary to conventional deterrence theory, the legal costs variables had no effect on criminal behavior (measured as self-reported crime and arrests). In contrast, the measure of perceived opportunities for crime had a substantial effect on criminal behavior across all three samples, and respect for illegitimate jobs relative to legitimate ones had a significant effect in the offender and addict samples. Piliavin et al. concluded that the benefit or reward component of the rational choice model was supported, whereas the cost or punishment component was not.

In subsequent research, Decker, Wright, and Logie (1993) arrived at different conclusions. Using a street-based field worker in St. Louis, they recruited forty-eight "active" burglars (i.e., nonincarcerated individuals who considered themselves to be actively involved in burglary at the time of the interview) to participate in a study of perceptual deterrence. The respondents were presented with hypothetical scenarios that described situations in which a burglary might be committed. These situations were manipulated to vary according to penalty, risk, and anticipated reward. The categories for penalties were two years on probation, six months in a work camp, one year in the city jail, and five years in state prison plus five years on parole. The categories for risk of apprehension were 1 percent, almost no chance of being caught; 10 percent, only a slim chance; 50 percent, an even chance, and 90 percent, almost certain to be caught. The categories for anticipated reward were $200, $500, $1,000, and $5,000. Respondents were presented with different combinations of penalties, risk, and anticipated reward and were asked whether or not they would commit a burglary under those situations.

The results of the analysis indicated that penalty had no effect on its own, but it did influence offending in combination with other factors. Consistent with other research on the severity of punishment, penalties deterred offending when risk (certainty) was high. Penalties also affected offending when anticipated rewards were relatively high. Contrary to the research by Piliavin et al., Decker and colleagues found that risk of arrest had a strong effect on intention to commit a burglary, even controlling for anticipated reward. They suggested that the reason for the discrepancy in results across studies is the way in which certainty of punishment was measured. Piliavin et al. asked respondents for their subjective evaluations of risk of punishment. These risk levels were likely to be relatively low, given the low clearance rates for property crimes in large cities. In contrast, Decker et al. "imposed" risk levels in their hypothetical scenarios and included very high levels of risk. This could account for the different findings because "it is at high levels of risk that the greatest deterrent effects are to be found" (1993, 146).

SUMMARY

What does the research imply about the deterrence/rational choice perspective in general? On the one hand, it is clear that legal punishments matter. Most studies indicate that certainty of legal punishment deters law violations. The comparative studies suggest that this deterrent effect is non-linear (the tipping effect) and dependent on the level of severity and the type of crime. The time-series studies of drunk driving indicate that interventions designed to increase certainty of punishment decrease law violations to the extent that these interventions are publicized and sustained over time. The perceptual studies also point to a likely deterrent effect of certainty of punishment, although this effect is confounded to some extent with past experiences of escaping punishment.

On the other hand, it is also clear that legal punishments are not the only factors influencing decisions to commit law violations. Legal punishments evidently operate in tandem with informal sanctions. Indeed, much of the deterrent effect of legal punishment may be due to the larger ramifications of such punishment for the individual's social life. In addition, anticipated rewards affect behavior, as well as anticipated legal costs. Finally, as suggested by the expanded rational choice models, moral commitments inhibit law violations along with the pains associated with legal sanctions.

SOCIAL POLICY

DETERRENCE

The policy implications of deterrence *theory* are straightforward: Increase the severity, certainty, and celerity of state punishments for law violations. However, the policy implications of deterrence *research* are anything but straightforward. Celerity of punishment, for the most part, has not been the subject of research; and research on the severity of punishment has been unsupportive of deterrence theory. Only research on the certainty of punishment has been consistent with deterrence theory, and the policy implications of even these findings are ambiguous. While deterrence theorists assume that the observed negative relationship between certainty of punishment rates and crime rates comes about through the effect of certainty rates on crime rates, it may also come about through the effects of crime rates on certainty rates (the overload process).

Yet, the lack of clear and consistent research support for deterrence theory has not arrested its implementation in social policy. Indeed, cries for increasing legal punishment have increased since the late 1960s and early 1970s (Wilson 1975; Van den Haag 1975). As we said in Chapter 1, the implementation of policy frequently depends more on feasibility, social values, and social power than on supportive research.

Consider the implications of certainty and severity of punishment for specific agencies within the criminal justice system. Increasing the certainty (or likelihood) of punishment requires increasing certainty at each stage of the criminal justice system: arrest, prosecution, guilty verdict, and sentence. Increasing arrest certainty but not prosecution certainty only results in more people dropping out of the system at a later rather than an earlier stage; increasing prosecution certainty without arrest certainty yields a more likely punishment only for those who make it to the prosecution stage. Increasing severity (the punishment of those found guilty), on the other hand, only requires expanding the final stage of the criminal justice system—the capacity of the prison system.

Clearly, increasing certainty is the more complicated task. It can be done either by making the present criminal justice system more efficient or by expanding it. Efforts to reorganize the criminal justice system have generally not been very successful and have been resisted by criminal justice personnel at both the upper levels and the lower levels. Bureaucratic reorganization can be very disruptive to the careers and lives of criminal justice personnel. Those responsible for planning and administering the criminal justice system generally have vested interests in the present system, and are thus very unlikely to support fundamental changes in it even if they may increase its efficiency. They are much more likely to just expand the system, increasing expenditures and personnel, thereby enhancing their own role and power.

Now, let us examine how the theory has actually been implemented. Starting with the War on Crime program, initiated by the Johnson and Nixon administrations, billions of dollars have been funneled into expanding the criminal justice system. All levels of government (federal, state, and local) spent about $3.3 billion on crime control in 1960, a figure that increased to $13 billion in 1973 (Chapman et al. 1975). The Bureau of Justice Statistics (1990, 1995) reports that the figure had grown to $61 billion in 1988 and $94 billion in 1992.

Where exactly has this money gone? Table 4.2 shows the police size per 100,000 population from 1950 to 1990; and prison inmates per 100,000 population from 1925 to 1995. Note that police size was very stable from 1950 to 1965 (1,900 police per 100,000 population), but then began to increase to 2,300 in 1970, to 2,500 in 1980 to 2,800 in 1990—about a 47

TABLE 4.2 INDICATORS OF THE EXPANSION OF THE CRIMINAL JUSTICE SYSTEM

YEAR	POLICE SIZE[a]	PRISONERS[b]
1925	—	79
1935	—	113
1945	—	98
1955	1.900	112
1965	1.900	108
1975	2.500	111
1985	2.600	200
1993 (95)	2.800	407

[a]*Police Size* refers to the number of police per 100,000 population for all cities over 8,000 population (Uniform Crime Reports).
[b]*Prisoners* refers to the number of state and federal prisoners per 100,000 population (Bureau of Justice Statistics 1997, 1995; Maguire and Pasture 1996).

percent increase from 1965 to 1990. Remember these figures are adjusted for increases in the population. The really dynamic increases have occurred in the prison population. The imprisonment rate was very stable from about 1925 (earliest available year) to 1975, varying around 100 per 100,000 population and ranging from 79 in 1925 to 112 in 1955. Since then the rate has skyrocketed, increasing to about 150 in 1980, to 200 in 1985, to 292 in 1990, and to 407 in 1995—about a 200 percent increase from 1970 to 1990 related to increases in the population.

Clearly, the money is going into one sector of the criminal justice system (the prison) reflecting increases in one dimension of punishment (severity). This increase reflects a significant lengthening of prison sentences and an expansion of the range of offenses that involve a prison sentence. With respect to the latter, the percentage of prison inmates convicted of drug offenses and for less serious crimes has dramatically increased (Blumstein 1988; Zimring and Hawkins 1995).

Increasing the severity of punishment (the length of incarceration) meets with little resistance from any organized group. It is consistent with public sentiment and supported by criminal justice personnel. Initially, it is not even very expensive. If prison space is available, it only requires increasing minimum and maximum penalties. For example, Zimring and Hawkins (1973), in a study of California in the 1970s, reported that with available space (which was the case before the increase in incarceration), the cost of one extra year of imprisonment was only $620 per prisoner per year. Assuming a prison population of twenty thousand, the extra cost of one extra year would be only about $12 million, and the extra cost of five more years would be $60 million—not a bad cost for controlling crime. Unfortunately, the prison space quickly filled and dramatically more space has been needed and built. The total cost (building and maintaining) now seems to run between $20,000 to $40,000 per person per year! The policy has gotten very expensive.

INCAPACITATION

If the imprisonment of some does not deter others or even those punished when they are released, it certainly incapacitates them from committing crime against the general public while they are in prison. No one disputes this; the logic is compelling. The critical question is what proportion of crimes during any time period are committed by repeat offenders? Armed with this information, we could calculate what proportion of the total number of crimes would be reduced, if repeat offenders are identified and not released from prison.

For example, assume that a community experiences one hundred crimes during a year and fifty are committed by repeat offenders convicted of their first offense prior to that year. If all fifty repeat offenders had not been released from prison, their crimes would not have been committed and the number of crimes would have been reduced by 50 percent. Such an indiscriminate or "throw-away the key" policy, one that imprisons for a long time everyone convicted of any crime, is clearly going to imprison a lot of people—some for nonserious crimes and some for serious crimes they may never repeat. Ideally, we want to incapacitate only those first offenders who are most likely to repeat their offenses and to incarcerate them over just that part of their life cycle during which they are most likely to repeat them.

There are two general approaches to identifying repeat offenders. One, we can certainly identify them by their actions; that is, we can incarcerate for a long time only those offenders who have already been convicted of multiple offenses. We are thus assured of not incarcerating for long periods first-time offenders who may never commit another crime. To different degrees this policy is in effect today throughout the United States. How much crime is reduced by such a policy? Again, assume a hypothetical community in which one hundred crimes are committed each year and fifty of them are committed by repeat offenders (twenty-five by second-time offenders, fifteen by third-time offenders, and ten by fourth-time offenders). If a policy incarcerates all of these offenders and if half of them would have committed a crime in the next year, the policy would reduce next year's crimes by one-half. (We would expect another fifty first-time offenders.) But by committing all first time offenders, the policy would also commit those (the other half) who would never commit another crime. If a policy only incarcerates the fourth-time offenders (ten) and half of them would have committed a crime in the next year, the policy would reduce the next year's crime count by five, while incarcerating five other people who would not commit another crime. See the policy dilemma: The more severe the incarceration policy, the lower the future crime rate but the more people incarcerated who would never commit another crime.

We are assuming these proportions of repeat offenders to illustrate the impact of incapacitating repeat offenders on the overall crime rate. To make sensible policy decisions, we must actually know these proportions. That is, exactly what proportion of crimes during any time period (a year) are committed by repeat offenders (second-time offenders, third-time, fourth-time, etc.)? Remember, we are talking about the lives of people, so it is important to be able to make accurate estimates. Various methodologies have been used to address this issue (Zimring and Hawkins 1995). One is called the retrospective method. In one version of that method, researchers examine the prior criminal records of all persons convicted of a crime during any one year. From these records they can determine whether each offense committed that year was committed by a first-time offender, a second-time offender, etc.; and thus they can calculate the percentage of crimes for that year that are committed by first-time offenders, second-time offenders, etcetera. The researchers then pose hypothetical social policies. For example, of the people who commit a crime that year, if those convicted of any prior felony had been imprisoned for five years, what percent of the current year crimes would have been avoided? The estimates vary substantially from study to study. For example, Van Dine et al. (1977, 1978) reports up to 17 percent; and Petersilia and Greenwood (1978) report 31 percent. There are two problems with this method. One, different studies use different samples composed of people in different stages of their criminal careers, thereby yielding very different estimates. Two, this method bases its estimates of reduction in the crime rate only on crimes that are reported to the police, and it bases its estimates of criminal careers (first- and second-time offenders) only on crimes that lead to a conviction. What about all the crimes not reported and all the offenders not convicted?

To avoid the latter problem, some studies use the self-reports of prisoners about their past criminal acts. A sample of prisoners is asked to report the number of crimes committed over a period of time directly before they were arrested and imprisoned. Based on this information, researchers can estimate the number of crimes the prisoners in the sample committed for a particular year; and based on the sample results, they can estimate the number of crimes committed for all prisoners in a particular year. Comparing that number to the actual number of crimes recorded for that year, they further estimate the proportion of crimes that would not have occurred with different incarceration policies: All people convicted of felonies serve five years, ten years, fifteen years, etcetera. Again, the estimates vary wildly (Zimring and Hawkins 1995). This method, too, has its problems: Respondents tend to forget, lie, and place their crimes in the wrong time period.

In sum, these studies, despite their sophistication, do not provide very reliable estimates of the proportion of crimes during any time period that are committed by repeat offenders and thus the proportion of crimes that would not have occurred had those offenders been incarcerated. Yet, even if we know this proportion, we still have to identify the repeat offenders before they become repeat offenders. Presently, most states punish repeat offenders more harshly than first offenders. Note the "three strikes and you're out" policy. By the time we identify three time offenders, they have already committed two crimes and most are already out of their crime-prone years. This policy, in effect, puts them away at a time in their life cycle when they are about to retire. After a few generations of "three strikes and you're out" our prisons may turn into old-age homes.

Identifying repeat offenders before they become repeat offenders is not only technically difficult, it also raises moral and ethical issues. Assume, for example, that specific social factors (e.g., broken home, low family income, and high family unemployment) predict very well which first-time offenders will violate the law again and again. Greenwood and associates (1982, 1987) have developed a scale to predict repeat offenders that includes unemployment. What should be done? If two teenagers are convicted of burglary should society impose different sentences on them based on their social background? Should the one from an intact home with employed parents be returned to them because research gives us reason to believe that the offense will not be repeated? And should the one from a broken home with unemployed parents be incarcerated for the next ten to fifteen years because research gives us good reason to believe that the offense will be repeated again and again over the next fifteen years? Using first-time teenager offenders highlights the moral dilemma; but should the dilemma be any different for second-time teenage offenders or first-time adult offenders? Our system of justice is based on what people have done now and in the past, not on what their social characteristics suggest they are likely to do in the future. Hence, even if we find that repeat offenders commit a high proportion of the total number of crimes in any one year and even if we can identify them based on their psychological and social characteristics before they become repeat offenders, our system of justice prohibits using this knowledge to incapacitate them.

Certainly, incarcerating likely recidivists—if they could be identified—stops them from victimizing the general public in the future; but would it alter the overall crime rate? The projected decreases in the crime rate based on various incarceration polices are based on the assumption that the causes of crime reside in the characteristics of people who commit them; thus, if present offenders are incarcerated, crimes will decrease. This assumption ignores research showing that crime rates are also affected by the structure of social life. For example, some research shows that crime rates respond as much to the routine activities of potential victims (unlocked cars and unoccupied houses during various times of day) as to the population of motivated offenders. Research shows that some crimes respond more to economic market conditions than to the characteristics of offenders. For example, the number of drug sellers seems to be sensitive to the demand for drugs. Incarcerating some sellers may temporarily disrupt the market, increasing the price of drugs; but it also opens market opportunities for others. While price increases may discourage some buyers, it also encourages others to become sellers. If the demand for drugs is relatively insensitive to their price, then strict enforcement will do nothing more than change the characteristics of sellers to people tolerant of high risks.

While considerable research and controversy have emerged over the extent to which different incapacitation policies would reduce the crime rate, few researchers have examined other consequences of incapacitation. One, the economic cost of long-term incarceration (of just a small percent of the criminal population) may be staggering—in some cases far more than the cost of their crimes. We are now paying the cost of a massive prison construction program that began in the 1980s. Two, a long-term incarceration policy can have considerable effects on local communities. Offenders are not a random sample of the population. They tend to be males; indeed, in 1995 males constituted 94 percent of all people under federal and state correctional authorities (Bureau of Justice Statistics Bulletin 1996). Clearly, then, an extensive incapacitation policy will change the sex ratio in communities, affecting family structure. This is particularly true if those imprisoned are in the marrying age (which they tend to be), and it will be particularly true for minorities who constitute a large percent of the prison population. The Bureau of Justice (1996) reports that in 1994 1.88 percent of white adults and 9.12 percent of black adults were on probation, parole, or in jail or prison. Given that about 90 percent of these were male, we can roughly double these figures to estimate the proportion of white males and black males under the supervision of the criminal justice system (about 18 percent of all black males). As high as this figure is, it is substantially higher for young black males (age 18–30) living in urban areas. Estimates vary widely from 25 to 40 percent (Zimring and Hawkins 1995; Messner and Rosenfeld 1997, 5). Whatever the exact figure within this estimated range, its size is astonishing and must have a dramatic effect on the life of urban black communities, altering marriage markets and the structure of black families.

To summarize, while the policy implications of deterrence theory are reasonably clear, the supporting research suggests caution. For the most part, little research has been reported on the celerity of punishment effect; research has not supported a severity of punishment effect; and while research appears to be consistent with a certainty of punishment effect, many questions remain. This, however, has not inhibited efforts at implementing the policy implications of deterrence theory. Since the early 1980s the criminal justice system has dramatically expanded. Lacking supportive deterrence research, this expansion has been justified in terms of its immediate incapacitation effects without seriously considering its long-range consequences.

CRITIQUE
○

THEORY

Perceptions and Objective Levels of Punishment Deterrence theory assumes that objective levels of legal punishment affect criminal behavior through individual perceptions. If the relationship between subjective perceptions and objective punishment is weak (if people are unaware of the laws on the books and the risks of apprehension), according to the logic of deterrence theory the relationship between objective punishment and the crime rate should be weak (Cook 1980). Unfortunately, the relationship between objective levels of punishment and perceptions has not been the subject of much theoretical discussion and research. The relationship may be stronger for some types of crime and persons than others and may be shaped by the mass media. In some cities the mass media may publicize reported crimes without publicizing the level of enforcement creating an image of low punishment certainty; and in other cities it may do the opposite, creating an image of high certainty. An important task for future research is to explain and document the processes through which citizens become aware of legal sanctions.

The Scope of Rational Choice Theory The deterrence/rational choice perspective is intended to apply to all forms of crime (Cornish and Clarke 1986, 6). However, the applicability of the approach is more readily apparent for "instrumental" crimes than for "expressive" crimes. Instrumental crimes refer to illegal acts that involve rational calculation of benefits and costs (such as tax evasion) and that are committed in an atmosphere in which the careful weighing of alternatives is feasible. Expressive crimes refer to illegal acts that are less subject to rational calculation and that tend to be committed in an atmosphere in which the weighing of alternatives is difficult (e.g., crimes of passion). Many assaults, rapes, and homicides occur in an emotional, a social, and a psychological atmosphere in which decisions must be made quickly, if not instantaneously. In a barroom brawl or a lovers' bedroom quarrel, there is little time to calculate the costs and benefits of behavioral alternatives. Actions occur quickly in response to a rapidly changing situation.

Proponents of deterrence/rational choice theories have recognized that the criminal decision-making process varies markedly in different types of situations and have relaxed the notion of rationality to enhance the general applicability of the perspective. For example, Tedeschi and Felson (1994) acknowledge that acts of criminal violence (what they refer to as "coercive actions") typically entail little prior planning and are the result of quick decisions made under emotionally charged circumstances, with only a limited consideration of alternatives. Nevertheless, they maintain that violent criminals still make choices (some individuals inhibit violent impulses) and thus a "weak form of rationality" is relevant in these situations (1994, 350). Expanding the concept of rationality in this way certainly makes it easier to characterize a wider range of crimes as "rational" acts. However, if the concept of "rationality" is stretched too far, it loses any distinctive meaning; and then to claim that a crime involved rational decision-making is simply another way of saying that a crime actually occurred.

A similar difficulty arises from efforts to expand the scope of deterrence/rational choice theory by including a wide range of costs beyond those of the legal system, such as disruption of social relationships, disapproval from significant others, and painful emotions generated by the violation of moral commitments. Including these kinds of factors is likely to increase the explanatory power of rational choice models, but these models then begin to resemble those of other theories. Indeed, as Akers (1994, 60) has observed, some of the expanded formulations of rational choice theory are indistinguishable from other criminological theories.

RESEARCH

Temporal Order A vexing problem in the research on general deterrence is determining cause and effect. For example, various cross-sectional or comparative studies show that the certainty of punishment is negatively correlated with the crime rate, suggesting that high certainty causes a low crime rate. Yet it is also reasonable to argue that a low crime rate increases the likelihood of punishment. As the crime rate decreases, the level of police resources devoted to each crime increases, which raises the probability of solving each crime. The observed negative correlation between certainty of punishment and the crime rate probably reflects both the negative effect of certainty on the crime rate and the negative effect of the crime rate on the certainty of punishment. A somewhat similar process may affect efforts to estimate the effect of severity of punishment. While high severity of punishment may reduce the crime rate (producing a negative relationship), a high crime rate may stimulate legislators to increase the severity of punishment (producing a positive relationship). These two processes might counterbalance one another, thereby producing the often observed negligible relationship between severity and the crime rate. Researchers have recently introduced highly sophisticated statistics to disentangle the causal effects of legal variables and crime rates, but these efforts have just begun (see, for example, Marvell and Moody 1996).

Controlling for the Effect of Other Factors Various social conditions correlate with the level of punishment, and as a result, their effect on the crime rate may obscure the effect of punishment. In states and cities where a particular act (e.g., rape) violates the moral conscience with exceptional force, official punishments are likely to be very severe, and processes of socialization and informal social control are probably intense and rigorous. A corresponding low crime rate may then be a result of both official punishment and these other, nonlegal social control processes. Few studies have systematically partitioned the observed relationships between certainty/severity of punishment and crime rates into the underlying causal dynamics.

SOCIAL POLICY

The deterrence/rational choice perspective is frequently praised for its clear policy implications. Deterrence theory proclaims that crime can be reduced by governmental efforts. If legal punishments are increased, the level of crime should decrease. The more general, rational choice theory points to a host of additional, nongovernmental strategies for reducing crime. For example, if potential crime situations are made less attractive to potential criminals (e.g., if persons carry less property on themselves), fewer crimes will occur.

The case for adopting a deterrence approach to crime control has been argued by James Q. Wilson (1975). The essence of his argument is that deterrence theory, unlike most other theories, directs attention to variables that are tractable to policy manipulations. It is difficult to manipulate factors such as social cohesion, illegitimate opportunity structures, social attitudes, and family ties. Agreed, these social and psychological conditions are not easily altered, but it is also not easy to change the level of punishment. Significant changes in the celerity and certainty of punishment would require nothing less than a reorganization of the criminal justice system. The cost and difficulties of such changes are staggering. Minor changes, such as increasing police expenditures and deployment patterns, are likely to have modest effects at best (Bayley 1994). Only the severity of punishment is subject to simple change—by legislative fiat; yet there is little research support for severity as a strong deterrent. Moreover, as discussed above, the incapacitation effects associated with severe legal punishments entail very serious social costs, especially for those groups in the population who are most vulnerable to arrests (Tonry 1995).

What is perhaps most troubling about state punishment as a social policy (justified according to deterrence or incapacitation) is its political nature. It is most often viewed as the appropriate response to lower-class crimes (murder, assault, rape, burglary, robbery, auto theft). Either by omission or commission, it is rarely discussed or studied as a social response to middle- and upper-class crimes, such as fee splitting between doctors, plagiarism of professors, embezzlement, false advertising, and restraint of trade. The president of a major corporation can be stopped from violating pollution laws just as easily as a lower-class youth can be stopped from stealing automobiles by incapacitation. In terms of deterrence theory it may even be more logical to use state punishments to control corporate offenses than to control lower-class economic offenses, because the former are probably more subject to rational calculation than are the latter. Ironically, social policy informed by the deterrence theory focuses primarily on groups that are least likely to be susceptible to the threat of legal penalties and to the dimension of punishment (severity) that is least likely to yield an appreciable deterrent effect.

Finally, an important aspect of the general rational choice model has been largely neglected in social policy discussions. The decision to commit a crime is presumably the result of a calculation of the costs and benefits of law-violating behavior in comparison with those of law-abiding alternatives. For the most part, crime prevention strategies have focused on increasing the costs and reducing the benefits of illegal acts. An alternative approach, however, is to increase the rewards of law-abiding behavior. If potential criminals can anticipate well-paying earnings from conventional employment, if they are confident that "playing by the rules" will ensure them access to important social resources (e.g., health care), crime is thereby rendered a much less attractive choice.

5 THE LABELING PERSPECTIVE

THEORY

The traditional norm-violation approach to deviance assumes normative stability and consensus. This normative framework constitutes a reference point from which behavior is judged as deviant or nondeviant. When the norms of different segments of society conflict (lower versus middle class; black versus white; young versus old), the norms of the more powerful segments tend to be accepted as the reference point. Even the Chicago socialization researchers who acknowledged normative pluralism implicitly assumed a dominant culture. They chose to focus on the processes by which people are socialized into subcultures that are deviant when judged by the dominant culture.

During the 1960s, numerous social scientists (Gouldner 1970) questioned the assumptions of normative consensus and stability and thus, by implication, the viability of theoretical perspectives built upon them. Instead, they emphasized the emerging, changing, and conflicting character of social norms, thereby stimulating a reconceptualization of the subject matter of the sociology of deviance. Without a clear and stable reference point for judging behavior, the very definition of normative violations is problematic. Hence, since the 1960s, many scholars have conceptualized deviance as a social definition that some groups and people use to describe or judge the behavior of others. Theory and research informed by this perspective have focused on two general questions: What is defined as deviance? Who is defined as deviant?

The first question has directed theory and research toward the emergence of social norms and social categories for labeling people as deviant.

Some social scientists have focused on the historical emergence of general societal norms of behavior. They ask such questions as, Why are the norms of alcohol consumption in Russia different from those in the United States? Why are the norms of sexual behavior in Mexico different from those in the United States? Others (e.g., ethnomethodologists) have directed their attention to studying how social norms, and consequently what is defined as deviance, depend on specific social situations. They argue that general societal norms of behavior are frequently very ambiguous as behavioral directives in specific situations. For example, the norms that govern alcohol consumption vary not only from country to country and from region to region within a country but from situation to situation. The norms of proper drinking depend on the day (weekend or weekday), the time (morning or evening), and even the duration of time that has elapsed at a party. Greater freedom is frequently permitted as a party goes on.

Social scientists have also examined the emergence of the social labels or categories used to describe and define norm violations and violators. This is not a question of semantics but involves the issue of how norm violations and violators are socially treated. The category of mental illness is an instructive example. Today, people who experience emotional problems and cognitive distortions are treated in many ways like people with a physical illness (Scheff 1984; Conrad and Schneider 1992). They are examined by experts trained in medicine (psychiatrists) and are frequently admitted to hospitals. This type of social treatment was not always the case in the United States and is not now the case in all parts of the world. In the United States, at one time or another, such people were labeled as evil, lazy, and as witches and, accordingly, experienced a very different societal treatment. Why? How can we explain the emergence of mental illness as a social category? Generally, then, the question—What is defined as deviance?—refers to the study of the emergence of social norms and social categories for describing norm violations and violators.

The study of legal norms (laws) and the categories used to describe law violations and violators is a special case of the above question. Why are some norms transformed into laws, thus making some norm violators law violators? For example, prostitution is illegal in most but not all states and cities. Why? It is also important to study the emergence of categories for describing law violations and violators. Juvenile norm violators, for example, are treated differently not only by the public but by legal authorities. They constitute a formal legal category in the United States and, consequently, are treated under a specific set of legal procedures (juvenile court) and are subject to a specific set of court dispositions. Why? How can the emergence of this legal category of law violators be explained?

The second major question—Who is defined as deviant?—refers to the study of the process by which existing categories for describing norm violators and violations are applied in specific situations. Of all individuals who violate norms only some are socially identified and labeled by family, friends, colleagues, the public, and authorities. Others somehow escape the social label. Their norm violations remain socially unnoticed. Why? On the other hand, some conformists are falsely identified as norm violators. Why? Under what circumstances are people identified (correctly or incorrectly) as norm violators (drug addicts, witches, mentally ill)? These concerns are important because being publicly identified—correctly or incorrectly—as a norm violator can have serious psychological and social consequences. Social scientists have studied the extent to which being publicly labeled as a norm violator affects social relationships, such as family relations, friendship patterns, and economic opportunities, and the extent to which these in turn influence future norm violations.

As a special case of this question, some scholars have examined how legal categories are applied to individuals and the consequences of such applications (Paternoster and Iovanni 1989). Like norm violators, only some law violators are publicly identified. Of those who violate laws, only some are arrested; of those arrested, only some are prosecuted; and of those prosecuted, only some are sentenced. What affects the degree to which law violators become involved in the legal process, and what are the consequences of different levels of involvement? To what extent does imprisonment or prosecution affect psychological dispositions and social relationships, and to what extent do the latter in turn affect future law violations?

To summarize, the study of deviance as a social definition focuses on the following questions:

I. What is defined as deviance?
    A. What are the general and situational social norms; what are the social categories and labels for describing norm violators and norm violations; and how have these norms and labels emerged?
    B. What are the consequences of these social norms and social labels for society?
    C. As a special case of the above, what are the legal norms (laws) and legal categories for describing law violators and violations; how have they emerged; and what are their social consequences?
II. Who is defined as deviant?
    A. Who is socially labeled a norm violator?
    B. What are the consequences of being labeled a norm violator?
    C. As a special case of the above, who is labeled a law violator, and what are the consequences of being so labeled?

These questions are of primary concern in three general perspectives: the labeling perspective (the subject of this chapter), the social constructionist perspective (the subject of Chapter 6), and the conflict perspective (the subject of Chapter 7).

Labeling theory is identified with the work of social scientists concerned with the study of social process rather than structure and with the study of microphenomena (social psychology) rather than macrophenomena. It has its intellectual roots in symbolic interactionist theory (Turner 1978). Symbolic interactionism emphasizes the role of symbols in communication and the interplay between symbols and the construction of personal identities or "selves." In the course of social interaction, a person anticipates the reactions of others and considers how these others will view himself or herself. In so doing a person develops his or her own identity and takes on roles that are compatible with this identity. Symbolic interactionism thus calls attention to the importance of societal reactions in social life. Applying this insight to the study of deviance, labeling theorists focus on a particular kind of reaction of others—the assignment of a deviant label—and examine the consequences of such a reaction for the person so labeled. Edwin M. Lemert's work provides an exemplary statement of this general theoretical orientation.

DEVIANCE AS A SOCIAL LABEL

According to Lemert (1951, 1967), modern society is pluralistic. Norms and laws are temporary and emergent products of a social process whereby different interest groups compete and struggle for social power and dominance. In this continuing process some groups' norms become defined as society's norms and some as society's laws; consequently, some people become defined as norm violators (deviants) and some as law violators (criminals). While noting the fluid nature of society, Lemert assumed that at any time some standards prevail over others and that behavior can be judged by these standards. He did not, however, assume any necessary relationship between the violation of these standards and being labeled as a deviant or criminal. This is a subject for research.

The terms *primary* and *secondary* deviance are central to Lemert's theory. Primary deviance is defined as behavior that violates a social norm but that does not affect an individual's psychological structure and performance of social roles. It is transitory and caused by a variety of conditions—social, cultural, psychological, and physiological. Secondary deviance, in contrast, is defined as deviance (norm violation) that is a response to the problems or conditions caused by the societal reaction to primary deviance. It is generally prolonged and affects psychological structure and the performance of social roles. Lemert suggested that being publicly labeled a deviant is socially stigmatizing, adversely affecting social relationships and opportunities. It alters informal social relationships because conventional people are reluctant to associate with known deviants; and it decreases job opportunities because employers are reluctant to hire known deviants. Hence, if a reduction in economic opportunities and involvement in conventional social relationships increase the probability of deviance (see Chapters 2 and 3), being publicly labeled a deviant should increase the probability of future deviance. Also, consistent with symbolic interactionism, Lemert argued that people tend to see themselves as others see them and that people tend to act on their self-definitions. Hence, if people are socially labeled as deviant, they come to see themselves as deviant and behave accordingly. In sum, Lemert's formulation of labeling theory postulates that the societal reaction to primary deviance initiates social and psychological processes that sustain deviance and make it more central in people's lives. In studying secondary deviance, we must focus on these processes rather than on the conditions that cause primary deviance.

Lemert's theory may be succinctly conceptualized as asserting that primary deviance and "other" factors frequently lead to societal reaction, which in turn leads to secondary deviance. The term *other factors* refers to a variety of situational contingencies (such as demeanor) and social statuses (race and sex). These other factors operate in combination with, or even without, primary deviance to lead to the labeling of an individual as deviant. (These "other" factors will be discussed in the next two chapters.)

Lemert's analysis of deviance as a social label provided a general orientation in the early formulation of labeling theory. Subsequent work has elaborated two related themes: deviance as a social status and deviance as a self-concept.

DEVIANCE AS A SOCIAL STATUS

Howard S. Becker formulated the classic statement of the labeling conception of deviance. He wrote:

> From this point of view, deviance is not a quality of the act the person commits, but rather a consequence of the application by others of the rules and sanctions to an "offender." The deviant is one to whom that label has successfully been applied; deviant behavior is behavior that people so label. (1963, 9)

Becker further emphasized that a deviant label or definition operates like a social status and that the process by which labeling produces systematic deviance is comparable to that which underlies a conventional career.

Social statuses refer to positions in the social order linked to regular patterns of social interaction (e.g., female, African American, physician). They affect the course and nature of social interaction. In analyzing social statuses, the concepts *master status* and *career* have proven useful (Hughes 1958). *Master statuses* are those that generally override other statuses in affecting interaction. Race, for example, is a master status. African Americans in the United States can experience discrimination somewhat independent of income, education, occupation, and age. *Career* refers to a set of statuses that are arranged in an orderly sequence. In the occupational world, for example, people frequently proceed through an orderly sequence of statuses (apprentice, journeyman, master, retiree).

Becker argued that a public identity as a deviant operates similarly to a social status in that it structures the course of social interaction. For example, people who acquire the label of sex offender, alcoholic, or mental patient because of their behavior or for other reasons may experience difficulty in gaining employment and in maintaining conventional social relationships. A public deviant identity may function as a master status in that it may override other statuses in affecting social interaction. An alcoholic physician and an alcoholic carpenter, for example, may be extremely different in many respects, including the manner in which they imbibe; yet because of their identity as alcoholics, they may be treated similarly in social interaction. Becker proposed that, just as in the study of conventional careers, social scientists should study the contingencies by which deviants move from one stage of the deviant career to the next. Becker also claimed that being publicly labeled as a deviant is the crucial contingency propelling an individual through a deviant career.

Becker's conceptualization of deviance as a social definition emphasizes the orderliness and stability in the process by which labeling transforms someone into a systematic norm violator. While deviance may not always function as a master status and may not always take on the appearance of an orderly career, the analogy sensitizes us to certain social processes by which public labeling affects the course and pattern of deviance.

DEVIANCE AS A SELF-CONCEPT

Whereas some scholars, such as Becker, have examined the orderly aspects of the labeling process, emphasizing the external restrictions and patterning of opportunities for interaction, others have viewed the labeling process as less orderly, emphasizing its emergent and negotiated character and the importance of self-concepts or definitions (Schur 1971; Thoits 1985; Matza 1969). Edwin M. Schur (1971, 1979) argued that people are not automatically labeled as deviant because of what they have done (norm violations) or because of who they are (minority-group member) and that the process of becoming a secondary deviant does not necessarily take on the character of an orderly career. It is more like a protracted, meandering negotiation. Some people are accused and are stigmatized, while others may successfully negotiate a nonstigmatized social label; others accused may successfully defend themselves and even successfully label the original accusers, as in some mental commitment proceedings; and still others may label themselves without any community initiation. To explain the latter phenomenon—persistent deviance in the absence of public labeling, Schur emphasized self-labels, or self-concepts, and self-imposed limits on social interaction (see also Thoits 1985). He argued that secondary deviance is less a function of imposed external restrictions on interaction accompanying a public label than an expression of a deviant self-concept or identity.

To summarize, labeling theory implicitly assumes some minimal level of consensus as a reference point for defining norm violations. However, the thrust of the theory is directed not toward the study of norm violations but toward the study of deviance as a social definition. The theory asks, Why are some people publicly labeled as deviants whereas others are not? and What are the consequences of being labeled, particularly in respect to the level and patterning of future norm violations? Lemert was one of the first to examine deviance as a social definition, and his work provides a general orientation for research. Within this general orientation, some scholars such as Becker have emphasized the orderly aspects of the process by which labeling affects secondary deviance, noting external restrictions on social interaction imposed by a public label. Others such as Schur have emphasized the negotiated character of the process by which labeling affects secondary deviance, noting the importance of self-labels and identities. These are not distinct schools, however. Becker also discussed self-concept, and Schur also discussed external restrictions on interaction; both also examined deviance as a social definition and were concerned with the process by which labeling leads to secondary deviance. Rather than different schools, the themes developed by Becker and Schur constitute different thrusts in labeling theory.

LABELING AND MENTAL ILLNESS

One of the more provocative applications of labeling theory has been to raise questions about the medical model of mental disorders. The medical model of physical illness is based on several assumptions: that physical states of the body can be classified as healthy or ill; that illness or disease can be correctly diagnosed by observations of the body (temperature, appetite, and so on); that effective treatments are available; and that illness tends to worsen if not treated. Most traditional theories of mental illness assume that the mind functions in much the same manner, that is, that mental or psychic states can be defined and classified as healthy or ill, that mental illness can be diagnosed by observable mental states (nervousness, delusions, and the like), that effective treatments are available, and that, if not treated, mental illness tends to worsen. Some theories assume the cause of mental illness to be biological (genetic defects); some assume the cause to be psychological (defective ego); and some assume the cause to be social (a demanding social environment).

Labeling theorists have vigorously criticized this model on several counts (Szasz 1960; Goffman 1961; Scheff 1984): (1) They argue that, unlike physical states, mental states cannot be easily classified into those that are healthy and those that are diseased. Practitioners (psychiatrists and clinical psychologists) frequently disagree as to the criteria to be used in deciding what constitutes mental illness. Moral judgments and cultural values affect these decisions, which is generally not the case for physical illness, where there is considerable consensus among practitioners as to what states of the body are healthy and what states are diseased. (2) These labeling theorists argue that, unlike physical disease, diagnosing mental disease is generally difficult. Mental-health practitioners frequently disagree as to the observable mental states that should be used to infer types of mental abnormalities (schizophrenia, neurosis). While physicians may disagree from time to time over what observations should be used to infer particular diseases, there is considerable agreement as to what observations are necessary and sufficient to infer the presence of a large number of diseases like cancer or pneumonia. Disagreement exists within a general context of consensus. (3) Labeling theorists argue that, unlike physical medicine, effective treatments for mental diseases do not exist; people treated do not necessarily recover significantly faster than those not treated. (4) Labeling theorists argue that, unlike physical diseases, mental states diagnosed as abnormal do not always worsen when not treated; they frequently improve.

Note the similarity between this critique of traditional approaches to mental illness and the general critique of traditional approaches to social deviance. Because of a low level of social consensus, norm violations are frequently difficult to define, and norm violations from the perspective of one group are often acts of conformity from the perspective of another group. Essentially the same argument is made about mental illness. Because of a low level of consensus about mental health, even among psychiatrists, mental illness is difficult to define, and mental illness from the viewpoint of one social group or one psychiatrist is mental health from the viewpoint of another social group or psychiatrist. Thus, like social deviance in general, mental illness may be fruitfully studied as a social definition or label that is applied by some people to the behavior of others. Labeling theorists thus focus our attention on two specific questions: Who is labeled mentally ill? and What are the psychological and social consequences of being so labeled? Of the many labeling theories that have been constructed, Thomas Scheff's (1984) theory is the most significant and well known.

Scheff proposed that mental disorders be understood as "residual deviance." He argued that most norm violations are named or socially categorized: crime, delinquency, drunkenness, drug addiction, bad manners, and the like. When these categories are exhausted, there remains a residue of norm violations for which no clear names or social categories exist—everyone just knows that the behavior is not right. For example, while carrying on a conversation, people are expected to face their conversational partner rather than look away, gaze toward his or her eyes rather than elsewhere, and stand at a proper distance, neither two inches apart nor across the room. How do we categorize someone who violates these norms? There are no specific terms to describe these norm violators although they are frequently thought of as strange, unusual, bizarre, perhaps even frightening. In this sense they are residual deviants.

Scheff also claimed that residual deviance is commonplace. Who amongst us has not at one time or another engaged in behavior that might be viewed as strange, unusual, or bizarre? In most instances, these episodes of residual deviance are of transitory significance. They go unnoticed or are explained away on the basis of extenuating circumstances. Sometimes, however, persons begin to exhibit sustained, patterned residual deviance; they begin to enact the culturally defined role of being insane.

Why would anyone take on such a role? Scheff maintained that the experience of being labeled "mentally ill" provides the impetus for assuming the role of the insane. Labeled deviants are often rewarded for conforming to stereotypes of mental illness and punished when they attempt to assume other roles. For example, mental patients who accept their illness are often thought of as manifesting insight into their problems, and those who show the "right" signs may get more attention from hospital personnel, who find it more pleasing to treat people who fit into standard disease patterns than those who do not. Additionally, patients often find it difficult to return to conventional roles—their jobs may have been filled; their spouses may have found another life. The role of mental patient may thus be relatively rewarding. Furthermore, the experience of being publicly labeled is likely to alter one's self-concept. As others define and react to the person as mentally ill, he or she begins to accept this definition. In sum, Scheff proposed that it is ultimately the labeling of mental illness that causes persistent, patterned careers of residual deviance.

Scheff's theory represents a radical challenge to the medical model of mental disorders. It implies that the kinds of "risk factors" commonly cited in the psychiatric literature are not particularly important for understanding stable patterns of mental disorder. A less radical formulation of the labeling approach to mental illness has been proposed by Link et al. (1989), which suggests that labeling processes can operate in combination with other, more conventional causes in producing chronic mental disorder.

According to the "modified labeling theory" advanced by Link et al., people learn negative conceptions of what it means to be a mental patient during the course of normal socialization. When someone begins to undergo treatment for a mental disorder, these negative conceptions become relevant to him or her. The person worries about whether others will devalue and discriminate against him or her. These worries prompt the person to engage in strategies to minimize stigmatization, such as secrecy (concealing treatment history), withdrawal (limiting social interaction), and education ("enlightening" others to ward off negative attitudes). Although the responses of secrecy, withdrawal, and education represent efforts to protect the patient from the negative consequences of labeling, they are likely to produce negative outcomes themselves. Withdrawal may lead to more constricted social networks and fewer efforts to find well-paying jobs. Preoccupation with concealing one's personal history may undermine self-esteem. These negative outcomes of societal reaction processes—lowered self-esteem, constricted social networks, and lowered earning power—are precisely the kinds of social and psychological conditions that have been identified as risk factors for the development of psychopathology. In sum, according to Link et al., labeling processes operate in combination with other risk factors to increase vulnerability to new disorders and to stabilize existing disorders into chronic conditions.

THE SOCIAL CONTEXT OF LABELING: REINTEGRATIVE SHAMING

In their analyses of secondary deviance, labeling theorists have traditionally been concerned with microlevel dynamics and have largely ignored the social structural context. John Braithwaite (1989, 1995) attempted to overcome this limitation in his theory of reintegration and crime. Braithwaite identified the structural conditions under which labeling processes are more or less likely to contribute to further deviance. The key concept in Braithwaite's theory is that of *shaming*. Shaming refers to "all social processes of expressing disapproval which have the intention or effect of invoking remorse in the person being shamed and/or condemnation by others who become aware of the shaming" (1989, 100). Shaming is essentially a form of moral education; it communicates the "wrongfulness" of crime (Braithwaite 1995, 192).

Braithwaite argued that two different types of shaming can be distinguished: reintegrative shaming and disintegrative shaming (or stigmatization). Reintegrative shaming involves moral disapproval and condemnation followed by efforts to bring the offender back into the community through gestures of forgiveness and ceremonies that decertify the deviant status of the offender. The criminal act is condemned but not the criminal actor. Through reintegrative shaming, offenders are publicly punished without activating the labeling processes that lead to secondary deviance. Reintegrative shaming is an effective form of social control that produces low levels of crime and deviance. In contrast to this type of shaming, disintegrative shaming involves disrespectful disapproval and humiliation. There are numerous ceremonies to certify deviance but few to decertify it. Hence, the offender and not merely the offense is labeled as deviant. This kind of shaming leads to stigmatization, secondary deviance, and high rates of crime.

Braithwaite maintained that the kind of social structure conducive to reintegrative shaming is *communitarianism*. Communitarian societies are characterized by dense interdependencies among the citizenry and strong sentiments of trust. The cultural emphasis is on group loyalties and collective bonds. An example of a communitarian society that relies heavily on reintegrative shaming and that exhibits low levels of crime is Japan. Highly individualistic societies, on the other hand, usually rely on disintegrative forms of shaming. These societies lack the social connectedness and the cultural commitments to collective obligation required for reintegrative forms of shaming. Because they rely on stigmatizing forms of punishment, individualistic societies are characterized by high levels of crime. In sum, Braithwaite's theory stipulates that the consequences of public labeling vary depending on the larger social structural context. Labeling processes leading to further deviance are most likely to be activated in highly individualistic societies (i.e., societies like the United States).

COMMONALITIES

Although the works of Lemert, Becker, Schur, Scheff, Link et al., and Braithwaite develop a number of different themes, there are several noteworthy commonalities. All of these scholars were relatively unconcerned with unorganized, casual, occasional, or sporadic norm violations. Lemert used the term primary deviance, while Scheff used the term transitory deviance to describe these kinds of violations. Instead, all focused on organized or systematic deviance that persists over a prolonged period of time. Lemert referred to secondary deviance; Becker referred to career deviance; Schur referred to role engulfment; Scheff referred to stabilized deviance; Link et al. referred to chronic disorder; and Braithwaite described how the social processes that lead to systematic deviance depend on the collective context. All were concerned with processual or sequential theories, which emphasize the role of social definitions or labeling in transforming primary deviance into secondary deviance. The general thrust of these works, as represented in the causal diagram in Figure 5.1, suggests that the effect of societal reaction on secondary deviance is mediated by interpersonal networks, self-concept, and structural opportunities.

As to structured opportunities, it seems reasonable to argue that being labeled a deviant reduces legitimate economic opportunities. Employers may be very cautious about hiring known ex-deviants. Blocked access to legitimate opportunities is likely, in turn, to increase the likelihood of fur-

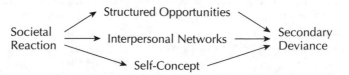

**FIGURE 5.1   CAUSAL PROCESSES UNDERLYING
THE EFFECT OF SOCIETAL REACTION ON SECONDARY DEVIANCE**

The diagram shows that societal reaction (labeling) affects structured opportunities, interpersonal networks, and self-concept, which in turn affect secondary deviance.

ther deviance. Labeling may also alter interpersonal relationships. Conventional persons may not wish to associate with publicly known deviants, fearing that the social stigma may rub off; thus, labeled deviants may seek each other out for assistance or companionship, which facilitates the learning of deviant attitudes and values, and reinforces previously held deviant attitudes and values. Labeling also affects self-definitions. People who are socially labeled as deviants may come to view themselves that way. If people tend to act consistently with their self-concepts, labeling people as deviant should increase their level of future deviance.

RESEARCH

The research section is organized into two major subsections: delinquency/crime and mental illness.

SECONDARY DEVIANCE: DELINQUENCY AND CRIME

Labeling research on crime and delinquency addresses two questions: Who is labeled? and What are the consequences of the label? Following the theory section, this section focuses on the latter question. The organization follows the causal diagram in Figure 5.1. The first set of studies examines the link between labeling and the mediators (structural opportunities, interpersonal networks, and self-concept). The second set examines the link between labeling and secondary deviance.

Labeling and the Mediators Richard D. Schwartz and Jerome H. Skolnick (1962) used a clever field experiment to study the link between being labeled a deviant and future economic opportunities. Four sets of employment credentials were prepared. In all sets, the applicant was described as thirty-two years old, single, male, high school trained in a trade, with a record of successful employment in unskilled jobs—the normal characteristics of applicants for the specific job. The four sets of credentials differed only in the following respect: One indicated that the applicant had been sentenced for assault; one indicated that the applicant had been tried for assault but acquitted; one indicated that the applicant had been tried for assault and acquitted and included a letter by the presiding judge affirming the applicant's innocence; and one did not mention anything about a criminal record. A sample of one hundred employers was selected. The employers were not told that they were participating in a field experiment. Each employer was presented with only one of the four sets of employment credentials. Representing themselves as agents of an employment agency, the researchers simply asked each employer if he or she could use the person in question, and categorized his or her response as positive or negative.

The top panel of Table 5.1 shows the relationship between the level of involvement in the criminal justice system (degree of labeling) and the level of employment. For those with no record, 36 percent of the employers gave a positive response (the baseline); for those acquitted with a letter, 24 percent gave a positive response; for those acquitted with no letter, 12 percent gave a positive response; and for those convicted, only 4 percent gave a positive response. Note the relatively low rate of positive response (12 percent) for those accused and acquitted. Being found innocent does not appear to allow the labeled person to escape the social consequences of being accused and prosecuted. At least to the employers in this study, a person is not "innocent until proven guilty."

Wouter Buikhuisen and P. H. Dijksterhuis (1971) conducted a similar study in the Netherlands. They constructed three sets of credentials: One included a conviction for theft; a second included the temporary loss of a driver's license for drunken driving; and a third made no mention of a criminal record. Employment applications were sent to seventy-five large companies. As in Schwartz and Skolnick's study, the companies did not know that they were participating in a field experiment, and their responses were simply categorized as positive or negative. The results, given in the bottom panel of Table 5.1, show that 52 percent of the applicants with no record received a positive response, while only 32 percent and 26 percent of those

TABLE 5.1   CONSEQUENCES OF LABELING

SCHWARTZ AND SKOLNICK STUDY

	NO RECORD	ACQUITTED WITH LETTER	ACQUITTED	CONVICTED	TOTAL
	(N=25)	(N=25)	(N=25)	(N=25)	(N=100)
Positive	36%	24%	12%	4%	19%
Negative	64%	76%	88%	96%	81%
	100%	100%	100%	100%	100%

BUIKHUISEN AND DIJKSTERHUIS STUDY

	NO RECORD	CONVICTED THEFT	CONVICTED DRUNKEN DRIVING	TOTAL
	(N=50)	(N=50)	(N=50)	(N=150)
Positive	52%	32%	26%	37%
Negative	48%	68%	74%	63%
	100%	100%	100%	100%

Sources: Richard D. Schwartz and Jerome H. Skolnick, "Two Studies of Legal Stigma." Social Problems 10:2 (Fall 1992), p. 137. © 1962 by The Society for the Study of Social Problems. Reprinted by permission of the publisher; Wouter Buikhuisen and P. H. Dijksterhuis, "Delinquency and Stigmatization." British Journal of Criminology 11 (April 1971), p. 186. © 1971 by the British Journal of Criminology. Reprinted by permission of the publisher.

with records of theft and drunken driving, respectively, received a positive response. These two studies suggest a direct link between criminal labeling and subsequent economic opportunities.

Research by Christine Bowditch (1993) indicates how deviant labeling of youths in school might affect economic opportunities indirectly by altering prospects for educational attainment. Bowditch conducted a qualitative case study of a high school in a poor, inner-city neighborhood in a northern city. She observed the interactions between students, teachers, and administrators, focusing on the processes used by school officials to deal with disciplinary problems. She found that rule violations were actually quite common—most students occasionally violated school rules. Only some students, however, were likely to receive formal punishments. The students formally punished were typically those judged to be "troublemakers" by virtue of their general academic profiles (their grades, attendance history, and plans for the future). School officials viewed troublemakers as undeserving of the school's services, and they employed various strategies to "get rid" of them, such as suspensions and transfers. Being suspended from school and being transferred to another school often lead to dropping-out of school. Bowditch's research thus suggests that the label of troublemaker facilitates the termination of the youth's academic career, thereby restricting opportunities for economic achievement later in life.

Labeling theory also asserts that being labeled a deviant affects interpersonal networks and attitudes. Research has examined different aspects of this process. For example, Jack D. Foster et al. (1972) studied juveniles' subjective impressions of how their involvement with police and courts influenced their relationships with peers, teachers, and parents. They interviewed 196 boys whose behavior had brought them into contact with the police and courts; the interviews occurred no later than twenty days after the final disposition. While the majority did not feel any stigma or change in their relationships with their parents, peers, and teachers, a substantial proportion did experience such consequences. For example, 27 percent thought that their parents' attitudes toward them had changed as a result of their involvement with legal authorities. In addition, they felt that their involvement with the law would affect their future economic opportunities. Of those incarcerated, 73 percent felt that future employers would hold that imprisonment against them.

Zhang and Messner (1994) conducted a related study in the Chinese city of Tianjin. They selected a sample of youthful offenders in correctional facilities who had committed prior offenses ("recidivists") and had received official punishment for those offenses. These recidivists were asked questions about the consequences of their earlier punishments for their relationships with parents, relatives, friends, and neighbors. Specifically, respondents were asked whether or not their relationships with these "significant others" had become more estranged (more distant, cold) after the imposition of official legal sanctions. Zhang and Messner found that there were, indeed, negative consequences of official punishment for interpersonal relationships, consistent with labeling theory, and that the likelihood of such consequences varied for the different types of relationships. Only 9.8 percent reported estrangement from parents, whereas 33.7 percent reported estrangement from neighbors (estrangement from relatives and friends was in between). In addition, Zhang and Messner discovered that the *severity* of official sanctioning was related to the likelihood of estrangement from friends and neighbors. Youths who received a more severe sanction (a court-imposed punishment) were more likely to become estranged from friends and neighbors than were those who received a milder punishment (an administrative disposition by the police).

Labeling theory also suggests that people who are labeled deviants come to view themselves as deviants, consequently lowering their self-esteem. In a pioneering study, Gary F. Jensen (1972a) examined this relationship using a large sample of juveniles from eleven junior and senior high schools in California. The survey collected information on officially recorded delinquency, self-reported delinquency, perception of self as a delinquent, and self-esteem. Jensen found a moderate-to-strong relationship between having an official record and viewing oneself as a delinquent, which was accentuated for whites. To explain the racial difference, Jensen argued that being labeled a delinquent is more meaningful for whites than blacks. Blacks occupy a negative social status irrespective of their social behavior and official reactions to it. As outsiders they may be less sensitive to official reactions. Whites, on the other hand, are more tied to conventional institutions; thus, their self-concepts are affected more directly by official actions. A similar racial difference in the effects of labeling on self-concept has been observed in other studies as well (Ageton and Elliot 1974; see also Harris 1975, 1976; Paternoster and Iovanni 1989).

To summarize, studies suggest that being labeled a criminal or delinquent reduces economic and educational opportunities, disrupts interpersonal networks, and alters self-concepts, particularly for whites.

Effects of Labeling on Future Deviance   If labeling decreases economic opportunities, conventional associations, and self-esteem, then it follows that labeling should increase future deviance. Note that this proposition is contrary to deterrence theory (Chapter 4), which asserts that state punishment (a special case of labeling) should decrease future law violations of those punished (labeled) through special deterrence. This section examines state punishment studies as a crucial test of both labeling and deterrence theories (see Figure 5.2).

One of the major areas of interest in research on state punishment has been the effect of imprisonment on the likelihood of future criminal activity, or on "recidivism." At first glance, the data would seem to contradict

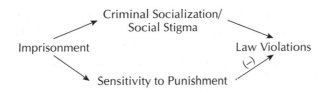

FIGURE 5.2   CAUSAL PROCESSES MEDIATING THE EFFECT
OF IMPRISONMENT ON FUTURE LAW VIOLATIONS

Imprisonment affects criminal socialization and social stigma, which are assumed to increase future violations; imprisonment also affects sensitivity to punishment, which is assumed to decrease future violations. Thus, the size and direction of the effect of imprisonment on law violations are functions of the relative strengths of these two causal processes.

deterrence theory and support the labeling approach. Research indicates that the majority of inmates serving time in state prisons in the United States have been previously incarcerated (Beck et al. 1993), and large proportions of convicted felons are re-arrested within a few years following their release (Beck and Shipley 1989). These data do not allow for a definite test of labeling theory versus the specific deterrence theory, however, because they do not reveal the percentage of *unpunished* law violators who commit subsequent law violations. A crucial test of the two theories requires a comparison of the subsequent law violations of those who have committed law violations and have escaped punishment with those who have committed law violations and have been punished. In addition, it seems likely that those who are most severely punished and labeled (e.g., receive the longest sentences) have probably committed the most numerous and serious violations; hence, if they show a high level of future law violations, this could be an effect of labeling, but it could also be just a continuation of prior behavior. To address this issue, researchers must examine the future violations of people who are differentially labeled (punished) for comparable law violations and who have histories of similar prior violations.

Terence P. Thornberry (1973) conducted one of the first rigorous attempts to isolate the distinctive effects of official punishment on future law violation. Thornberry's study was based on data collected on all boys born in 1945 who lived in Philadelphia between the ages of ten and seventeen. Their police records were examined and classified into four official dispositions: remedial arrest (the boy was released by the police with no further action); adjustment (the boy was referred to the probation department and warned to stay out of trouble); probation (the boy was given a court hearing and placed under supervision); and institutionalization (the boy was incarcerated). Thornberry examined both the number and seriousness of future offenses. The results were complex, and few clear patterns could be discerned. Consistent with labeling theory, as involvement in the juvenile justice system increased up to institutionalization, the volume of future delinquency increased, but only for whites, upper-social-class youths, and boys apprehended for less serious crimes; however, consistent with deterrence theory, the institutionalized youths showed fewer future offenses and less serious offenses upon release than did the noninstitutionalized youths.

While Thornberry's findings offered some support for labeling theory, a subsequent study by Brown et al. (1991) yielded results directly counter to the labeling perspective. Brown and colleagues randomly sampled five hundred juvenile delinquents from the files of the juvenile probation department of Dauphin County, Pennsylvania, for the years 1960–75. They divided the youths into two groups: those who had been formally adjudicated at their first referral and those who were "given another chance" (i.e., those who were not adjudicated at their first referral but rather were adjudicated at a later referral). They also collected follow-up data on adult imprisonment to assess the consequences of differential treatment at first referral. Labeling theory predicts that formal processing by the criminal justice system should increase the likelihood of subsequent offending. Hence, the early adjudication group should exhibit higher rates of imprisonment later on in life. Brown et al. found that, contrary to the labeling hypothesis, 20.1 percent of those adjudicated on first referral went on to adult prison, whereas 42.5 percent of those not adjudicated on first referral went on to prison. The researchers concluded that there is a human cost of "giving the kid another chance": The risk of imprisonment is roughly doubled.

In general, research on the impact of processing offenders through formal court sanctioning in comparison with other, presumably less stigmatizing procedures is mixed. Some studies suggest that alternatives to using the criminal justice system might result in less recidivism, while others suggest just the opposite. This issue is likely to remain a matter of considerable controversy within the field in the years ahead (see Gibbons and Krohn 1991).

In addition to the work on differential punishment and recidivism, researchers have considered the consequences of the initial phase of state punishment or labeling—being arrested. For example, a series of studies by Richard A. Berk, Lawrence W. Sherman, and colleagues has examined the effect of arrest for domestic violence. The first of these studies (Sherman and Berk 1984) involved a field experiment conducted by the Police Foundation and the Minneapolis Police Department. Over an eighteen-month period police implemented one of three strategies (arrest, order the suspect to leave the house for eight hours, or informally mediate the dispute) in response to a sample of on-going family disputes. The design called for the intervention strategies to be applied randomly to cases that met the criteria for involvement in the study. The suspect was then followed for six months, using both official police reports and self-reports. Of the three strategies, arrest is the most punishing and labeling. Thus, deterrence theory predicts that those arrested should have the lowest subsequent level of domestic violence; and labeling theory, of course, predicts the exact opposite. The findings supported deterrence theory. According to official police reports, 18 percent of all households showed a repeat assault, but of those arrested only 13 percent showed a repeat assault; and according to self-reports, 28 percent of all households exhibited a repeat assault, but of those arrested only 19 percent exhibited a repeat assault.

A follow-up study in Milwaukee by Sherman et al. (1991) yielded somewhat different results. This research examined cases of misdemeanor domestic assault in four districts of the city with the greatest concentration of poor, minority residents. The researchers introduced two refinements to the earlier study design: (1) They compared the effects of short-term arrests, in which the assailant was in police custody for about three hours on average, with long-term arrests, in which the assailant was in police custody for approximately twelve hours. (2) They extended the time frame for evaluating outcomes for a period up to thirty-three months. This enabled them to distinguish any "initial" deterrent effect of arrest from any "long-term" effect. As in the Minneapolis study, the research involved a field experiment where police responses were randomly assigned to three treatment modes—in this instance, short-term arrest, long-term arrest, and no arrest (a warning only).

The results were quite surprising. There was modest evidence of an initial deterrent effect of full-term arrest and strong evidence of an initial deterrent effect of short-custody arrest. However, over a longer period, the deterrent effect of full arrest disappeared, while the effect of short-term arrest was actually reversed. Suspects in this latter group exhibited higher rates of future involvement in domestic violence than did those who had not been arrested. Sherman et al. speculated that, under certain circumstances, the short arrest might increase anger at society without increasing fear of arrest; they thus cautioned that "a little jail time can be worse than none" (1991, 846).

How can the discrepancies across studies be explained? Further analyses by Berk et al. (1992) of the Milwaukee data along with data from three other field studies in Omaha, Dade County, Florida, and Colorado Springs point to a possible answer. These analyses indicate that the impact of arrest depends upon background characteristics of the offender. For example, arrest seems to be more likely to deter future episodes of domestic violence for the employed than for the unemployed. Simply, it is the employed who have the most to lose. Being arrested may well remind them of that. Studies in different communities will thus yield different estimates of the overall impact of arrest on future domestic assault depending on the particular "mix" of background characteristics of those who happen to be part of the research. While resolving the puzzle about different research findings in the field studies on domestic violence, the analyses of Berk et al. raise difficult policy issues. Should the decision of the police to make an arrest when called to the scene of a domestic violence be based on background characteristics of the offender? Is this very practical, and is it fair?

Reintegrative Shaming   Braithwaite's theory of reintegrative shaming offers an explanation for varying labeling effects in different social contexts. The theory stipulates that the net effect of labeling on crime depends on the extent to which labeling leads either to stigmatization, and attempts to exclude the offender, or to reintegrative shaming, and efforts to bring the offender back into the fold. At present there is little systematic research testing this theory. However, one such test was conducted by Makkai and Braithwaite (1994) in Australia. They examined compliance with quality of care regulations for nursing homes. In 1987, the Australian government assumed the responsibility for regulating nursing homes throughout the country. The government commissioned an evaluation of the effectiveness of the new government regulations and sent teams of inspectors to 242 nursing homes over a twenty-month period. The inspecting teams rated the compliance of the nursing homes with government regulations at an initial inspection and at a follow-up inspection. Makkai and Braithwaite classified the inspection teams as having an enforcement ideology supportive of reintegrative shaming or having an ideology more consistent with stigmatizing attitudes. They then assessed the effect of enforcement ideology on change in compliance with regulations between the two inspections. Their results offered mixed support for the theory. Reintegrative shaming had a positive effect on improving compliance but only when the director of nursing at the nursing home knew one or more members of the inspection team before the inspection. Makkai and Braithwaite concluded that reintegrative shaming is most likely to occur in situations of interdependency between offenders and those imposing sanctions.

Zhang et al. (1996) have applied the theory of reintegrative shaming to explain low recidivism in China. They studied a social arrangement called "Bang-jiao," a community-based organization comprising parents, relatives, friends, and neighbors. These groups attempt to provide help and guidance to publicly identified offenders and to facilitate their reintegration into the community. Zhang et al. assessed the impact of Bang-jiao with a sample of inmates in the city of Tianjin. Inmates were asked whether or not Bang-jiao groups had been established in their communities. Inmates were also asked about their history of prior offenses, allowing the researchers to distinguish first-time offenders from recidivists. Zhang et al. examined the relationship between presence of Bang-jiao in the inmate's community and their recidivism. Consistent with the theory of reintegrative shaming, inmates from communities with Bang-jiao were significantly less likely to be recidivists than those from communities with no such organizations, controlling for other characteristics of inmates and their neighborhoods. Zhang et al. concluded that Bang-jaio appears to be an effective structural mechanism for implementing reintegrative shaming as a mechanism of social control.

To summarize, research on the effects of punishment/labeling on those punished/labeled is ambiguous and subject to various interpretations. Findings are frequently inconsistent from study to study. The safest conclusion to draw is that official punishment activates multiple social processes (labeling and deterrence), which operate in opposing directions, and the outcome depends on specific circumstances of the labeled person (e.g., employment) and on the larger social context (e.g., cultural attitudes toward deviance and social interdependencies).

SECONDARY DEVIANCE: LABELING AND MENTAL ILLNESS

Research focuses on two questions: Who is labeled mentally ill? and What are the consequences of being so labeled? Like the previous section, this section examines only the latter question. Following the diagram in Figure 5.1, we review studies which examine the effect of labeling on the mediating conditions and on persistent or chronic mental disorder.

Labeling and the Mediators In Scheff's theory, social stigma is an important concept. Stigma makes conventional roles inaccessible, thereby increasing the relative rewards of the mental-illness role. Stigma also generates stress, thereby increasing susceptibility to social influence.

Derek Phillips (1963) developed a pioneering design for studying the relative effects of psychological behavior symptoms and involvement with mental-illness practitioners on social rejection (social stigma). He constructed case abstracts describing a paranoid schizophrenic, a simple schizophrenic, a depressed-neurotic, a phobic-compulsive, and a normal individual. Five versions of each case were constructed, differing only by the level of involvement with mental-illness practitioners. For example, in one version of the paranoid-schizophrenic case the phrase was added, "He has been in a mental hospital because of the way he was getting along." In a second version the person was said to be seeing a psychiatrist; in a third the person was said to be seeing a physician; in a fourth the person was said to be seeing a clergyman; and in a fifth there was no mention of professional help. Through this procedure twenty-five case studies were generated, five illnesses times five sources of professional help. (See Table 5.2.)

Each of three hundred respondents from a small New England town was presented with five of the twenty-five cases. Combinations of five were selected so that each respondent was presented only once with each set of symptoms (illness) and each help source. The following questions were then asked to permit the construction of a social distance scale that mea-

TABLE 5.2   REJECTION SCORES FOR EACH HELP SOURCE AND EACH SET OF BEHAVIOR SYMPTOMS

		HELP SOURCE UTILIZED				
BEHAVIOR	NO HELP	CLERGY-MAN	PHYSI-CIAN	PSYCHIA-TRIST	MENTAL HOSPITAL	AVERAGE
Paranoid schizophrenic	3.65	3.33	3.77	4.12	4.33	**3.84**
Simple schizophrenic	1.10	1.57	1.83	2.85	3.68	**2.21**
Depressed-neurotic	1.45	1.62	2.07	2.70	3.28	**2.22**
Phobic-compulsive	.53	1.12	1.18	1.87	2.27	**1.39**
Normal individual	.02	.22	.50	1.25	1.63	**.72**
AVERAGE	**1.35**	**1.57**	**1.87**	**2.56**	**3.04**	—

Note: Scores refer to the mean number of items rejected on the Social Distance Scale.

sured the level of rejection of the hypothetical person described in the vignette:

> Would you discourage your children from marrying someone like this?
> If you had a room to rent in your home, would you be willing to rent it to someone like this?
> Would you be willing to work on a job with someone like this?
> Would you be willing to have someone like this join a favorite club organization of yours?
> Would you object to having a person like this as a neighbor?

The answers were scored as either rejection (1) or acceptance (0), yielding composite scores ranging from zero (no items rejected) to five (all items rejected).

Each cell in Table 5.2 shows the mean rejection score for all respondents presented with that case. For example, the depressed-neurotic seeking no help received a mean rejection score of 1.45, and the simple schizophrenic seeing a psychiatrist received a mean rejection score of 2.85. Generally, rejection scores increased as the severity of symptoms and the level of involvement with the help-source increased. Hence, the highest level of rejection was received by the hospitalized paranoid schizophrenic (4.33) and lowest by the normal person involved with no help source (.02).

Clearly, both the level of symptoms and the help source made a difference. Which was more important? The effect of the help source can be estimated by comparing the average rejection scores for each type of help source (given at the bottom of each column). For those seeking no help, the average rejection score was 1.35, and for those hospitalized, the average rejection score was 3.04, a difference of 1.69. In terms of symptoms, the average rejection score was 0.72 for normal individuals and 3.84 for paranoid schizophrenics, a difference of 3.12. Clearly, symptoms were more important than help source. Phillips' work nevertheless suggests that the help source might also be very important. Consistent with labeling theory, people may learn who is mentally ill in part by who is seeking professional help. Phillips' work led to a number of studies using the same or a similar research design. These studies have been reviewed by Link and Cullen (1990), on whom we rely in the discussion below.

Critics of the labeling perspective have questioned this study and others like it as hypothetical. They have argued that mental patients and former patients do not, in fact, experience severe rejection by the general public. Some contend that people are generally willing to maintain contacts with former patients; others report that patients do not feel uniformly stigmatized; and still others maintain that whatever negative stereotypes exist do not get translated into rejecting behavior (Link and Cullen 1990, 92). In addition, several studies indicate that any rejection associated with the label of mental patient is accounted for by disturbed behavior of the labeled patient and not by the label itself. This body of research has led critics to question the claims of labeling theory about the negative consequences of labels of mental illness.

Over the past fifteen years, however, another series of studies has once again revived interest in the potentially harmful consequences of the labels associated with mental illness. Link and Cullen (1983) challenged the methodological foundations of the research purporting to show no relationship between labeling and rejection. They argued that measures of social distance are often affected by social desirability bias—people have learned that they "should be" accepting of mental patients. Consistent with their argument, Link and Cullen found that respondents whose answers to social distance questions represented their own personal attitudes were more rejecting of labeled deviants than those who answered questions with reference to the attitudes of an "ideal" person or of "most people."

Link and colleagues (Link et al. 1987) addressed the issue of whether any rejection associated with mental patient status is due to labeling or simply to the disturbed behavior of the person. They hypothesized that labeling processes "activate" beliefs about the dangerousness of the mentally disturbed, which then leads to social rejection of those who have been labeled. To test this hypothesis, Link et al. used a vignette experiment similar to that of Phillips', where they varied labeling (past mental hospitalization) and disturbed behavior, and measured beliefs about the dangerousness of the mentally ill. Their results supported their hypothesis. When the subject in the vignette was not labeled a mental patient, beliefs about the dangerousness of the mentally ill had no effect on social distance. When the subject in the vignette was labeled a mental patient, in contrast, these beliefs had a strong effect on social distance, and this effect emerged regardless of the degree of disturbed behavior. These findings suggest that the fear of stigmatization expressed by former mental patients is not irrational. The label of mental illness leads to social rejection by people who hold unfavorable beliefs about the mentally ill.

Finally, research by Link and colleagues on samples of community residents and psychiatric patients in New York City indicates that the fear of stigmatization can lead to a variety of negative outcomes for the person labeled mentally ill. In one study, Link (1987) found that expectation of social rejection was related to demoralization, income loss, and unemployment for persons labeled mentally ill, but not for those unlabeled. In another, Link et al. (1989) discovered that former mental patients who anticipated rejection from others withdrew from social life in general. This left them with insular social support networks limited mainly to family members.

In sum, the research on labeling someone as mentally ill and the mediators (see Figure 5.1) has progressed through different phases. The early evidence suggested that labels have devastating consequences for persons with the status of mental patient or former patient. Subsequent studies challenged much of this evidence and suggested that labeling theorists had exaggerated the stigmatization associated with labels of mental disorders and had failed to take into account the effects of the disturbed behavior of those receiving labels. More recent research has suggested that labels are potentially harmful, but that labeling processes are complex and their effects depend on other factors. Labeling processes apparently operate in combination with other factors, such as the nature of beliefs about the mentally ill, to produce social rejection.

Effects of Labeling on Mental Illness   The original labeling theorists raised serious questions about the efficacy of professional treatment for mental illness. Such treatment presupposes identification of disorders, which in turn implies labeling. If labeling leads to negative consequences, treatment might not only fail to help people; it might ultimately make them worse.

The early research on the effectiveness of various forms of psychotherapy was generally pessimistic. Studies in the 1960s (Goffman 1961; Wing 1962) examined the relationship between hospitalization and the subsequent level of mental illness. These studies indicated that the level of mental symptoms was positively related to the duration of hospitalization: the longer the duration of the stay, the more severe the psychological symptoms of the patient. They were thus critical of long term hospitalization.

More recent research offers a much more positive assessment of treatment effects. In one review of over 1,700 comparisons of patients in therapy with comparable controls not in therapy, the treated patients scored better than 80 percent of the controls on a wide range of psychological outcome measures (Link and Cullen 1990, 87). This general pattern has been reported with different populations (inmates, students, patients) in both experiments and quasi-experiments. Although most studies involve relatively short follow-up periods, which raises questions about long-term effects, the evidence clearly indicates that psychotherapeutic interventions can have beneficial consequences.

Similarly, evidence documenting the effectiveness of pharmacological interventions has accumulated over recent years. These studies typically employ *double blind randomized* experiments. These are rigorous research designs in which neither the subjects nor the researchers know who is receiving the experimental treatment and who is receiving an inert substance or *placebo*. The results of these studies indicate that various types of mental disorder, such as depression, schizophrenia, and anxiety/panic attacks, are responsive to drugs. In general, the evidence that drug treatment improves the condition of at least some persons diagnosed as mentally ill is persuasive (Link and Cullen 1990, 88–89).

What general conclusions can be drawn from the research on labeling and mental disorders? Clearly, the original labeling theorists overstated their case. Labeling certainly can be debilitating, but it need not be. Also, times have changed. The early studies of Wing (1962) and Goffman (1961) occurred in an era of long-term hospitalization. Today many people are admitted on an outpatient basis or to general hospitals. Hence, while the effects described by Wing and Goffman are quite possible and may have been quite prevalent in the past, today they are the exceptions. Most people simply do not stay long enough for institutionalization effects to occur. On the other hand, the research indicates that labels do matter; they elicit social reactions from others that can set into motion processes with undesirable outcomes for the labeled. The most reasonable conclusion is that labeling for mental illness has both positive and negative consequences. Labeling is often stigmatizing, but it also opens up opportunities for treatment. The net effect of labeling will be determined by the benefits of treatment relative to the costs of stigma. This is likely to depend, in turn, on characteristics of those labeled and the quality of treatment (see Link and Cullen 1990).

SOCIAL POLICY

The implications of labeling theory for social policy are reasonably clear in principle: Reduce labeling and the social stigma attached to it. In practice, this has lead to calls for greater tolerance for behaviors that are currently labeled as deviant and for alternative responses to these behaviors.

DELINQUENCY AND CRIME

While the theoretical implications for social policy with respect to delinquency and crime may be clear, the research implications are not. Most studies do not show a clear and simple link between societal reaction and social stigma and between societal reaction and recidivism. Some studies suggest linkages; others do not; and still others suggest linkages for some segments of the population but not for other segments. The research indicates, for example, that whites are more likely to exhibit decreased self-esteem as a result of an official societal reaction than are blacks. Some evidence also suggests that the employed are more likely to be deterred by arrests than are the unemployed. Hence, a *decrease* in societal reaction may be more effective in reducing secondary deviance for whites than for blacks, whereas an *increase* in societal reaction may be more effective in reducing recidivism for the employed than for the unemployed. Continued analysis might identify additional social categories (class, sex, ethnicity, age) for whom a reduction or increment in societal reaction may be more or less effective in reducing secondary deviance.

What does this mean? Should the imposition of legal sanctions depend on an offender's social category and research findings about the susceptibility of members of this category to labeling or deterrence processes? There are important ethical issues to be considered here. Whatever the ethical concerns, present research is too weak to support any definitive policy recommendations derived from labeling theory.

The scarcity of supporting research has in no way dimmed the fervor of labeling theorists for social policies that reduce or change the present pattern of societal reaction to norm violations. One radical approach is to redefine behavior itself. With respect to delinquency and crime, this entails *decriminalization*. Advocates of decriminalization criticize the over-reach of the law, especially the application of the criminal law to the so-called victimless crimes. These are criminal prohibitions against consensual behavior involving adults. Examples include prostitution, the distribution of pornographic materials, and the sale and possession of illicit drugs. Labeling theorists argue that criminal prohibitions against these behaviors actually do more harm than good. By enforcing these laws, criminal self-conceptions are instilled among many persons who would otherwise lack them. Critics of decriminalization respond that the behaviors to be decriminalized are not truly victimless, that considerable social harm is often associated with them, and that decriminalization would increase levels of involvement (for contrasting positions, see Schur and Bedau 1974; Inciardi 1991). At present, given widespread public support for "get tough" approaches to crime control (Messner and Rosenfeld 1997, 5), it seems unlikely that calls for decriminalization will reach a sympathetic audience.

Another policy recommendation advanced by labeling theorists is to minimize the stigma associated with the response to delinquency and crime. This might involve doing nothing to the offender, a policy sometimes referred to as "radical nonintervention" (Schur 1973). The nonintervention strategy is based on the premise that offenders, especially youthful offenders, are most likely to desist from future offending if they are simply left alone. While this seems to make some sense for the marijuana smoker and perhaps even the juvenile who has committed a minor theft for the first time, what about the first-time offender who commits a serious offense, such as homicide, or the habitual offender?

More commonly, labeling theorists recommend some form of *diversion*, whereby youthful offenders are steered away from the criminal justice system and provided with treatment, counseling, or therapy. For the most part this is what diversion has come to mean in practice (Lundman 1976, 1984). In effect, youths are diverted from the formal justice bureaucracies to the formal "treatment" bureaucracies, generally administered by probationary officers or social-welfare workers.

What is the actual impact of diversion compared with more direct intervention by criminal justice agencies? Numerous studies have attempted to answer this question, with mixed results. Some studies report positive outcomes, such as lower recidivism for divertees in comparison with controls (Gibbons and Krohn 1991, 319), and more positive perceptions of staff among those in diversion programs than among those handled by criminal justice agencies (Osgood and Weichselbaum 1984). On the other hand, the impact of diversion appears to be negligible in other studies (for a review, see Gibbons and Krohn 1991).

The conflicting nature of these results is not surprising given the difficulties associated with efforts to evaluate the success of diversion programs. One problem is that of a "selection artifact" (Smith and Paternoster 1990). Frequently, those in charge of assigning youths to diversionary programs select youths who they feel will benefit most from the program and will fit into the program. These are typically youths least involved in law violations. Hence, differences in postrelease delinquency between youths assigned and youths not assigned to diversionary programs may be a result not of the programs, but of differences between those assigned and those not assigned. To evaluate these programs adequately, youths assigned to them must be similar to youths not assigned.

Various studies have tried to deal with this problem, either by matching the youths assigned and not assigned on such characteristics as prior record and seriousness of present offense, or by randomizing the assignment. In practice, these procedures are difficult to implement fully. Consider the study by Malcolm Klein (1976). Using a sample from a West Coast city, Klein's research design called for the random assignment of 800 youths to the following four conditions: a group counseled and released, a group that received a nondetention petition, a group referred to a community agency with the purchase of social services, and a group referred to a community agency without the purchase of social services. After six months, Klein sent questionnaires to the youths' parents asking about the youths' behavior, obtained self-reports of delinquency from the youths themselves, and examined police statistics. For the most part, the four groups showed few differences on the three delinquency measures. These results, however, must be considered cautiously. While the research was carefully designed, the final study ended up with only 306 youths partially randomized. This occurred because the police frequently assigned youths to the condition that they thought would be best for them, thus making the groups noncomparable. The real world is not like a laboratory where researchers have control over events. In field studies, researchers must deal with agencies that have their own ideas about how things should be done.

Questions might also be raised about a basic premise underlying diversion programs—the notion that diverting youths to "treatment" bureaucracies lessens stigmatization. Do these programs avoid social stigma? They are certainly less stigmatizing than being incarcerated, but are they less stigmatizing than being involved in noncustodial traditional programs, like probation?

Whatever the actual consequences might be, the belief that diversion programs are less stigmatizing and more benign can lead to ironic outcomes. Several researchers have argued that criminal justice personnel are more willing to send juveniles who might otherwise be released to diversion programs (Austin and Krisberg 1981; Lemert 1981). To the extent that this has occurred, such programs have widened the net of juveniles who are officially labeled and brought under state supervision. In the past, by necessity, diversion was informally practiced at different stages of the juvenile justice system. Because of the high ratio of cases to processing facilities, most cases simply had to be dismissed. Now police have an additional option to either prosecution or outright dismissal. They can refer youths for treatment. If this type of social reaction, whether labeled punishment or treatment, is socially stigmatizing, and if social stigma leads to secondary deviance, diversionary programs may have the effect of increasing the number of secondary delinquents!

To summarize, the research on the impact of diversion is inconclusive and is characterized by a host of methodological limitations. It is difficult for researchers to construct comparable groups either by matching or randomization. Sample attrition rates are often very high, the observation of postrelease delinquency is limited to short time intervals, and differences in future delinquency among those assigned to different programs, whether labeled detention, treatment, or diversion, tend to be minor. Nevertheless, in evaluating diversion as a societal response to crime and delinquency, one should remember that, while the research may be ambiguous, such programs are generally more humane and less expensive than most incarceration programs (Lundman 1984).

MENTAL ILLNESS

Labeling theorists working in the area of mental disorders, like those studying crime and delinquency, have proposed two general strategies to reduce the harmful effects of labeling: Redefine the behavior and alter the common ways of responding to it. The former strategy was proposed in the 1960s by the psychiatrist Thomas Szasz (1960, 1970). Szasz vigorously attacked the medical model of mental disorder and proclaimed that "mental illness" is a "myth." He did not deny the reality of bizarre behavior; rather, he argued that this behavior represents inevitable problems of living associated with forming and maintaining human relationships. Treating these problems as an illness analogous to physical illness disguises the moral and ethical conflicts inherent in social life. Szasz proposed that personal responsibility and freedom would be advanced if the label of mental illness were to be eliminated, and if the associated disorders were to be regarded as social and ethical problems rather than medical conditions.

Most proponents of the labeling perspective adopt a more moderate view about how to reduce the negative consequences associated with the "mentally ill" label and advocate alternatives to hospitalization in mental institutions. These alternatives include outpatient care, community psychiatry, drug therapy, and home care. In evaluating the success of these alternatives to hospitalization, David Mechanic (1969) suggested the following three criteria: psychological symptoms of the patients, performance in normal social roles, and economic and social costs.

During the 1960s and 1970s a number of studies attempted to evaluate the consequences of treatment alternatives. One of the first comprehensive efforts to compare hospitalization and various alternatives was a study by Benjamin F. Pasamanick and colleagues (Pasamanick et al. 1967). One hundred and fifty-two schizophrenics referred to a state hospital were randomized into three groups: a hospital group, a home-care drug group, and a home-care placebo group. Those receiving home care were seen frequently by a nurse and occasionally by a psychologist, a social worker, and a psychiatrist; they were further divided into those treated with drugs and those led to believe they were being treated with drugs but were not (a placebo group). Patients were involved in the study from six to thirty months.

Economic costs were estimated in terms of the number of hospital days saved by home care. Over the duration of the study, 77 percent of the home-care drug group required no hospitalization; home care resulted in a savings of 4,800 hospital days for the drug group and 1,150 for the placebo group. This savings must be balanced by the problems the patients caused for their families, although after six months of home care such problems abated. In terms of psychological symptoms and role functioning, all three groups were evaluated after six, eighteen, and twenty-four months. All three groups improved after the first six months but did not improve much after that; more significantly, there was little difference in improvement between the home-care and hospitalized groups. Also, the level of rehospitalization required of the hospitalized group was actually higher than the level of initial hospitalization required of the patients treated at home.

Generally, the data indicated that home care is significantly less costly than hospitalization, and that it is as effective as hospitalization in improving psychological symptoms and role functioning and in reducing future hospitalization.

Five years later, Davis, Dinitz, and Pasamanick (1972) located and studied 92 percent of the original sample. They interviewed the patients and their significant others and surveyed clinic and hospital records over the five years to identify patients receiving hospital and clinical care. They found few statistically significant differences between the three groups in terms of hospitalization, psychological symptoms, and social adjustment. For example, during the five-year period, 61 percent of the previously hospitalized and the home-care drug patients and 57 percent of the home-care placebo patients were hospitalized, and approximately 27 percent of all three groups were employed. Generally, while the follow-up study showed that without any care at all patients diagnosed as schizophrenic deteriorate, it also showed that hospitalization is no more effective than home care coupled with community services. Other studies in the 1960s and 1970s also indicated that benefits for patients over the short term are usually no greater from hospitalization than from a variety of alternatives (Townsend 1976).

Perhaps because of this research, the use of hospitalization to deal with mental disorders has fallen dramatically since the 1960s, a trend that is commonly referred to as *deinstitutionalization*. Capacity rates of mental hospitals have dropped sharply, admission rates to mental hospitals have declined steadily, and the typical length of stay in hospitals has dropped markedly. For example, the capacity per capita of public mental hospitals (beds per 100,000 population) peaked at 356 in 1950. By 1960 it dropped to 314, by 1970 to 213, by 1980 to 65 and by 1990 to 40. Since then the rate has remained stable (Morrissey 1982; Morrissey et al. 1986; Manderscheid and Sonnerschein 1994). This is a dramatic change—rarely seen in any control institution. This change in capacity has led to an equally dramatic drop in the length of stay and in admission rates. The result has been much less reliance on treatment in hospitals and much more reliance on community- and home-based treatment. While the above cited research informed by labeling theory may have contributed to this development, other factors have been cited as well. These include the development of psychotropic drugs, new forms of psychotherapy, court decisions enhancing patients' rights and restricting involuntary confinement, and fiscal concerns of state governments (Weinstein 1990).

Has deinstitutionalization brought about the benefits one would anticipate from a labeling perspective? The evidence is once again mixed. On the one hand, several demonstration projects have shown that modern community care can be more effective than hospitalization in treating mental patients (Wegner 1990). This suggests that many persons with mental disorders can continue to function in the community when treatment is available. On the other hand, research also indicates that effective aftercare programs are often not provided to those discharged from mental hospitals. Studies indicate that somewhere between 30 and 70 percent of former patients receive no aftercare, and many others participate in aftercare programs for brief periods of time and then drop out (Wegner 1990, 308). In the words of one critic of contemporary practices, "community-based care for the chronically ill is often little more than rhetoric" (Wegner 1990, 318).

In sum, the policy implications of labeling theory are relatively clear: Reduce the level of negative social labeling. Reduce involvement in the criminal justice system for those accused or convicted of law violations, and reduce hospitalization for those showing signs of mental disorder. Social policies vary from radical nonintervention (community tolerance) to various alternatives to incarceration, such as diversion and community-based and home-care programs. Because of program selection and attrition, evaluation of these programs is difficult. Generally, the data suggest that while labeling theorists have correctly alerted us to the negative consequences of various forms of societal reaction, they have overstated their case. For crime and delinquency there is little evidence showing that present diversionary programs are more successful at reducing future violations than are traditional forms of societal reaction; and for mental illness there is little evidence showing that the available alternatives to hospitalization are more effective than short-term hospitalization. On the other hand, even though research does not show major differences in effectiveness between forms of societal reaction, a good case may still be made for many of the policies advocated by labeling theorists, as they are often economically less costly and more humane to those involved.

CRITIQUE

Labeling theory was a dominant theoretical perspective in the mid- and late-1960s. It generated considerable research at that time, but it was subsequently subjected to severe attacks and was "pronounced dead" by segments of the scholarly community by the mid-1980s (Paternoster and Iovanni 1989). More recently, researchers have attempted to revitalize the approach by responding to the criticisms of its original formulation. This section reviews some of the more prominent criticisms that have been leveled at the labeling perspective.

THEORY

Primary Deviance By focusing on secondary deviance, labeling theory tends to neglect the study of primary deviance and the deviance of the powerful. The classical labeling theorists—Lemert, Becker, and Scheff—argued that primary deviance is episodic and widespread; therefore, it is of minimal importance for the deviant and for society. This claim is difficult to accept. Primary deviance may frequently be of considerable importance to both the deviant and society. Consider suicide, domestic assault, rape, murder, and child molesting (to mention only a few). Are these actions unimportant when committed by primary deviants? Additionally, the emphasis on secondary deviance subtly directs research away from the deviance of the powerful who possess the resources to resist societal reaction. Because they frequently commit norm and law violations without prosecution and even without detection, their violations tend to be ignored by labeling theorists. The powerless, lacking the resources to avoid labeling, are thus the objects of study.

Labeling and Secondary Deviance   While most scholars agree that labeling is important, many have questioned the very strong claim that labeling is the sole cause of secondary deviance. If this were true, labeling would be both a necessary and sufficient causal condition (Mankoff 1971). A "necessary" condition is one that must be present before deviance occurs, and a "sufficient" condition refers to one that always produces deviance. Research indicates that labeling is neither necessary nor sufficient to produce secondary deviance. Secondary deviance does not automatically follow from labeling; sometimes labeling (official punishment) functions as a deterrent (see Chapter 4). Concerning the necessity of labeling, people may be involved in persistent deviance despite never having been formally or informally labeled; there are certainly some "secret" deviants in society. These persons become career deviants because of persistent exposure to social situations that cause deviance. For example, secondary deviance may be a persistent response to a continuing lack of legitimate opportunities, as specified in Merton's anomie theory.

Delimiting the Application of Labeling Theory   Labeling theory, like most theories of behavior, may be limited in its scope of application. For the most part labeling theorists and researchers have not taken this issue seriously. They have applied labeling theory to all patterns of norm violations and people. Yet labeling theory may be more useful, for example, in explaining the secondary deviance of those who commit relatively minor acts while young and impressionable than of those who are involved in serious violations of social norms at mature ages.

Contemporary formulations of labeling theory are less extreme and more flexible than the original formulations. Labeling is not typically cited as the sole cause of persistent deviance; it is considered one causal factor among many. Also, most contemporary proponents of labeling theory acknowledge that societal reactions to labeling are variable. The labeled person is sometimes excluded but sometimes is welcomed back into the fold. The challenge for labeling theorists in the future is to specify the relative importance of labeling in comparison with other causes of deviance and to identify the conditions under which the alternative reactions to labeling are more or less likely to occur.

RESEARCH

Selection People are not randomly labeled. Those who most frequently commit the most serious violations of social norms are most likely to be labeled. Thus, more frequent future violations by those labeled than those not labeled may simply reflect behavioral continuity over time, not social labeling. While researchers have tried to deal with this problem, their efforts have not always been successful. Some researchers have attempted to randomize the labeling process; hence, those labeled are initially no different socially and psychologically from those not labeled except for chance differences, which can be statistically adjusted. Such studies generally require the cooperation of official agencies legally charged with the responsibility for processing people accused of norm and law violations. These agencies are not always cooperative. They may agree to randomize but in practice may assign people to the program they believe to be most helpful for them. As a consequence, it is very difficult to isolate labeling effects.

Critical Tests of Mediators Most research has examined the relationship between labeling and future norm violations. Yet research on the hypothesized mediating conditions, such as structured opportunities, interpersonal relationships, and self-concept, may be more useful in understanding why labeling is found to increase future norm violations in some studies, decrease it in others, and have no effect in still others. A few studies have addressed this issue, but researchers have yet to generate a body of literature with widely replicated and consistent findings.

SOCIAL POLICY

The social policy implications and implementations of labeling theory can be divided into two broad categories: social tolerance (or radical nonintervention) and treatment programs. The former has never attracted widespread popular support; people generally feel that "something must be done" about deviance. Hence, most efforts to implement labeling theory have involved some form of treatment. For crime and delinquency these programs have been termed diversionary, and for mental illness they have been called community and home care. The problem with these programs is that those involved are frequently still labeled by agents of the programs and by acquaintances. In fact, many diversionary programs are not too different from traditional probationary programs. Although diversionary programs may be somewhat·more flexible and entail somewhat less supervision, the accused norm violator is still under some form of agency supervision. Can this be avoided? It is difficult for people (agents of social control bureaucracies or friends) to suspend their moral judgments when dealing with norm violators. Some form of labeling may be inevitable. The challenge for social researchers is to discover how primary deviance can be responded to, in some cases even deterred, without increasing secondary deviance.

THE CONSTRUCTIONIST
PERSPECTIVE

6

THEORY

The constructionist perspective has its philosophical roots in phenomenology, which emphasizes two themes: "going back to the phenomenon" and "showing how the phenomenon is built up." The *phenomenon* of interest refers to perceptions, cognitions, and consciousness. Phenomenologists assume that reality can only be experienced through a process of social interpretation. Hence, phenomenologists ignore the objective world. They focus instead on describing people's subjective perceptions and interpretations of the world and the processes by which people "build up," or construct, their worlds. To explain action, phenomenologists argue that we must come to know people's constructions. Theories of action must capture people's constructions or at least be consistent with them.

Much of phenomenology is divorced from the traditional concerns of social science. Nevertheless, constructionists have used insights from phenomenology to address three broad issues relevant to the study of deviance. One issue involves the identification of the underlying rules or principles people use to construct their realities (Schutz 1966). The application of these principles ultimately determines what and who is perceived as deviant and the level of officially recorded deviance. A second issue pertains to contests over symbols and definitions in the construction of widely recognized social problems. The social world can in principle be defined and interpreted in many different ways, and the way in which the social world is defined and interpreted is more or less advantageous to different people. The prevailing shared understandings of social phenomena, including what is regarded to be socially problematic, thus reflect the outcome of conflicts and struggles over meanings. A third issue deals with the "experiential reality" of deviance. Since human action is guided by the meanings and understandings of situations, an adequate explanation of any action, including deviance, requires an appreciation of how the actor himself or herself views the situation in which action takes place.

Before proceeding further, it is necessary to discuss the relationship between the labeling perspective (the subject of the preceding chapter) and the constructionist perspective. These two approaches are similar in many respects, and in the work of some scholars they tend to merge (Schur 1971). Indeed, the terms *labeling* and *constructionist* are sometimes used interchangeably (Woolgar and Pawluch 1985). Both perspectives share the core assumption that deviance is best viewed as a social definition. Nevertheless, the perspectives make different assumptions about reality, and they lead to different theoretical and research questions.

Labeling theory takes a more or less pluralistic view of society, assuming that social norms are in flux and constantly emerging. Deviance, as norm violations, can be defined at any time relative to the dominant norms; however, because norms are conceptualized as shifting and emerging, deviance, as norm violations, is viewed as more relative, situationally contingent, and difficult to identify than in the traditional perspectives. Labeling theorists thus use societal reaction to define deviance. Like constructionists, they view deviance as a social definition or construction, but unlike constructionists, they do not suspend belief in, or ignore, "objective" reality. In discussing social labels and labeling processes, they use terms like discrimination and bias, and ask why only some norm violators and some nonviolators are labeled, and what the consequences are of labeling on the structuring and patterning of future norm violations. These are nonsensical questions if belief in an objective reality is suspended. The use of words like *discrimination* and the posing of questions about norm violations assume some underlying objective condition as a reference point. In suspending belief in reality, constructionists ignore these questions and examine the processes and methods by which deviance is constructed and people are perceived as deviants. Social constructions are not described as "right" or "wrong" or even as "correct" or "incorrect." The constructions are what they are, and the analytic task is to describe them accurately and explain how they emerge.

Our focus in this chapter thus differs from that in the previous chapter. In Chapter 5, we discuss how the labeling perspective is used to examine the extent to which being labeled a deviant affects future levels of norm and law violations. In this chapter, we consider how the constructionist perspective is used to examine the processes by which some behavior is defined as deviance and some people are defined as deviant. We focus on three related topics: the experiential understanding of deviance, rules of social construction, and constructing social problems.

THE EXPERIENTIAL UNDERSTANDING OF DEVIANCE

Following in the tradition of phenomenological sociology, these constructionists emphasize the importance of "getting back to the phenomenon."
The researcher's principal task is to capture the essence of social phenomena as experienced by those involved. This involves probing the subjective
interpretations attached to behaviors and situations.

The work of David Matza (1964, 1969) in the 1960s was largely
responsible for popularizing the phenomenological study of deviance. Matza
criticized what he referred to as the "correctional" perspective on deviance.
Researchers who adopt this perspective are preoccupied with ridding society
of deviance, and as a result, they are unable to empathize with deviants and
fully comprehend them. Matza argued that the correctional perspective
should be replaced with an "appreciative" perspective. In his words:

> Only through appreciation can the texture of social patterns and the
> nuances of human engagement with those patterns be understood and
> analyzed. Without appreciation and empathy we may gather surface
> facts regarding a phenomenon and criticize the enterprise connected
> with it, but we will fail to understand in depth its meaning to the sub-
> jects involved and its place in the wider society. (Matza 1969, 15–16)

Matza (1969) applied this approach in his influential monograph on
the development of deviant identity. He argued that the process of becoming deviant involves a fundamental conversion in consciousness. The person must first decide that deviant behavior is a realistic option for him or
her. This is the stage of "being willing." Being willing does not guarantee
that the individual will commit the act; the process is not deterministic.
However, once the actor engages in deviant behavior, he or she confronts a
new set of circumstances. Deviant behavior is banned, and the person committing such acts consequently tends to become distanced or "disaffiliated"
from conventional society. If this disaffiliation extends beyond a certain
point, the person reaches the final stage of the process of becoming deviant:
the construction of a deviant identity. He or she is no longer simply someone who has happened to commit a deviant act. He or she *is* a deviant. This
construction of a deviant identity typically leads to subsequent deviance
(note the similarity to the arguments of labeling theorists about the transition from primary to secondary deviance). In sum, Matza proposed that the
process of becoming deviant ultimately entails a transformation of consciousness. The actor alters his or her conventional identify and essentially
"becomes" someone else.

A contemporary illustration of the phenomenological approach to the
study of deviance is Jack Katz's (1988) *The Seductions of Crime*. Like Matza,
Katz faulted mainstream theorists for imposing their own interpretations of
the motives and causes of deviance and for failing to probe into the meanings as understood by those involved. As a result, much deviant behavior,

especially crime, appears to be irrational and incomprehensible. Why would someone kill another during altercations over seemingly trivial disputes? Why would anyone engage in robbery or other kinds of thefts when the actual financial returns are typically low and the risks of punishment relatively high? Katz argued that to answer these questions, the researcher must look at the "phenomenal foreground" (i.e., the state of mind of the offender at the time of the offense).

Katz proposed that people commit crimes because they are seduced into doing so. Crime has a seductive appeal to offenders because it enables them to rectify the humiliations of everyday life and transcend the limitations of conventional morality. Katz also suggested that different types of crime are attractive to offenders in different ways. A large proportion of homicides, for example, can be understood as acts of "righteous slaughter." In these incidents, the offender's dignity has in some way been challenged by the victim. As a result of this challenge the offender experiences an acute sense of humiliation, which is transformed into a passionate rage. The expression of this rage in a self-righteous killing allows the offender to avenge the affront, to escape the humiliation, and to demonstrate superiority over the victim.

Adolescent property crimes (e.g., shoplifting, vandalism, joyriding) can also be understood with reference to their sensual appeal to the offender. Consider the following illustration of an incident involving two teenagers who were driving around town in a new car that one of them had just received for his birthday:

> We just happened to drive by the local pizza place and we saw the delivery boy getting into his car.... We could see the pizza boxes in his back seat. When the pizza boy pulled into a high rise apartment complex, we were right behind him. All of a sudden, my neighbor said, "You know, it would be so easy to take a pizza!"... I looked at him, he looked at me, and without saying a word, I was out of the door ... got a pizza and ran back.... (As I remember, neither of us was hungry, but the pizza was the best we'd ever eaten.) (Katz 1988, 52)*

According to Katz, these kinds of crime cannot be understood in terms of the mere acquisition of material goods—"it is not the taste for pizza that leads to the crime; the crime makes the pizza tasty" (Katz 1988, 52). Rather, these crimes are appealing because they give rise to "sneaky thrills." The potential offender recognizes the prohibitions against stealing but anticipates the possibilities of escaping detection. He or she thus initially experiences the excitement of being able to "get away with it." After successfully completing the crime, the offender feels the euphoric thrill of having self-consciously defied the rules that apply to everyone else. Stealing is thus appealing primarily because of its symbolic significance; it enables the offender to transcend the boundaries of the conventional moral order.

---

*From Jack Katz, *The Seductions of Crime*. New York: Basic Books, p. 52. © 1988 by HarperCollins Publishers. Reprinted by permission of the publisher.

In sum, constructionists who draw upon the phenomenological tradition emphasize the importance of subjective factors, especially individual consciousness, in explaining deviance. They argue that understanding deviance requires an appreciation of the ways in which deviants themselves experience their social worlds.

RULES OF SOCIAL CONSTRUCTION

As noted, some constructionists have attempted to uncover the underlying cognitive principles of social constructions. These theorists attempt to abstract from concrete social interactions the methods that people use in everyday life to coordinate the behavior of multiple actors and to make sense out of the world. In the 1960s and 70s, scholars working in this field were referred to as *ethnomethodologists* (Garfinkel 1967; Zimmerman 1978). Although a comprehensive, unified theory of the "methods" of social constructions has yet to be developed, several of the fundamental processes involved have been identified.

Images of Deviance   General categories are a necessary and natural outcome of people's inability to process cognitively the intricate and detailed complexities of the environment; they simplify the environment, thereby making it stable and understandable. Traditionally, social scientists and other observers have been concerned with the extent to which general categories and images (particularly ethnic, racial, and gender images) are accurate and unbiased reflections of the environment. Upon suspending belief in reality, constructionists, of course, ignore this type of question and focus on the role of such images in perceiving and processing information—in constructing reality. Thus, rather than using the traditional term *stereotype*, constructionists prefer the term *typification* to refer to these general categories and images.

The general images of deviance are simply a special case of general cognitive categories (typifications) that people use to describe and order the world. Images of deviance do not exist in isolation but are embodied and have meaning only within general common-sense theories of deviance. Traditionally, these theories have conceptualized deviance in moralistic and legalistic terms, thereby viewing the deviant as responsible for his or her behavior and implying that punishment is the appropriate societal response. More recently these theories have conceptualized certain forms of deviance as mental illness, thereby suggesting minimal personal responsibility and various forms of therapy as the proper societal response. (See Chapter 5 for a discussion of the medical model.)

Contextual Constructions of Deviance   While constructionists are concerned with general collective images of deviance and their historical emergence, much of the work focuses on how such images are applied in spe-

cific situations—contextual constructions. Two cognitive rules are especially important for organizing information to construct social reality: the rule
of consistency and the rule of economy (Sacks 1972). The former suggests
that once people have categorized events and persons, they organize past
information and future perceptions to be consistent with these categories.
For example, upon defining a man as a child molester, people tend to search
for and remember confirming cues. They may note that person's very
"friendly" demeanor toward children, or his active involvement with youth
groups (e.g., the Boy Scouts), which would have been ignored or organized
differently if the person had not been initially categorized as a child molester. The economy rule refers to a tendency to "lock in" categories. That is,
once a general category is selected for interpreting a situation, people tend
not to reorganize situational cues to test the application of alternative categories. Upon deciding that a person is a child molester, for example, people
are not inclined to consider alternative interpretations for a friendly
demeanor toward children.

As a special case of this cognitive process, constructionists have been
particularly interested in *retrospective interpretations*. These are cognitive
processes whereby a person's past behavior is reinterpreted on the basis of
present typifications. For example, upon classifying a man as a child molester, people are likely to reinterpret his past behavior in a consistent manner.
Events that were ignored as meaningless (standing close to children, patting
children on the knee, giving children a hug) take on a new significance. In
the words of Harold Garfinkel, one of the pioneers of the constructionist
perspective:

> The other person becomes in the eyes of his condemners literally a dif-
> ferent person. It is not that the new attributes are added to the old
> "nucleus." He is not changed; he is reconstituted. The former identity,
> at best, receives the accent of mere appearance ... the former identity
> stands as accidental; the new identity is the "basic reality." What he is
> now is what, "after all," he was all along. (1956, 421–422)

People are not always pleased with being labeled a deviant, and they
frequently resist the imposition of labels. The end social product or definition is thus often the culmination of extensive negotiation and bargaining.
A particularly important component of this process is the use of "accounts"
(Scott and Lyman 1968). Accounts are linguistic devices that are invoked
when behavior is susceptible to social evaluation. The most common types
of accounts are "excuses" and "justifications." Excuses are verbalizations
that mitigate responsibility for an action. For example, an individual may
explain his or her wayward action as a manifestation of an uncontrolled
biological drive, as an unintended and unforeseen accident, or as a result of
misinformation. Justifications are verbalizations that emphasize the positive
consequences of an act, particularly under certain situations, while recog-

nizing its negative consequences in principle. For example, a man identified as a rapist may contest the label by excusing the act as the result of drinking, drugs, or emotional problems, or by justifying the act by saying that women instigate sex, that women mean "yes" when they say "no," that women eventually relax and enjoy it, that nice girls don't get raped, and that coerced sex is only a minor wrongdoing (Scully and Marolla 1984).

Significant others may also play a role in the negotiation of labels. Gill and Maynard (1995) provide an example in their research on the complex labeling processes that occur in a children's clinic for developmental disabilities. They found that clinicians proceeded cautiously when delivering "bad news" to parents about disabilities. The clinicians asked for parents' views and invited them to infer diagnoses rather than pronouncing these diagnoses unilaterally. By using these techniques, clinicians were able to strategically involve parents in the labeling process, thereby overcoming parental resistance to labeling and facilitating the emergence of mutual agreements about required remedial action.

To summarize, constructionists study the techniques used by people to categorize deviance and to assign people to deviant categories. Being defined as a deviant is thought to be situationally problematic and the end product of a social process involving typifications, common-sense theories, retrospective interpretation, and negotiation.

Organizational Constructions In modern societies, deviance is commonly defined and processed by formal organizations of social control (police, hospitals). Constructionists have accordingly studied the operation of these organizations. In one influential analysis, Richard Hawkins and Gary Tiedeman (1975) argued that the constructions used by these organizations are shaped by organizational needs for efficiency, perpetuation, and accountability. Efficiency requires a stable and simple categorical system in terms of which the complex world can be organized and described. As the business of social control organizations increases, demands for efficiency cumulate in more general and abstract typifications of deviance. The details and intricacies of individual cases must be ignored if they are to fit into organizational categories and routines. The need for accountability frequently results in esoteric categorical systems (such as the categorical systems of psychiatrists) through which organizations justify their contribution to solving social problems. Organizational categorical systems also reflect the professional and semiprofessional socialization of their members. In law school, future lawyers learn to view the world through a legal model and in medical school future psychiatrists learn to view the world through a medical model.

In applying typifications to specific cases, social control agents function like everyone else, although within organizational constraints. Certain combinations of cues are used to categorize cases. Once categorized, via principles of consistency and economy, perceptions are ordered and information is collected to confirm the original categorization. This process involves "biography building," wherein social control agents search into an individual's past for events that confirm the present label. For example, in constructing the biography of a man classified as paranoid, a psychiatrist might note and record that he always locked the doors of his residence, accused his teachers of unfair grading, and divorced his wife for cheating; and in constructing the biography of a woman identified as a suicide, a psychiatrist might note and record that she was depressed and recently lost her job. These events and actions may be quite normal within various social contexts, yet when compiled selectively, they suggest abnormality. The ultimate outcome of these processes is the creation of official records and rates of deviance. From the constructionist perspective, the statistics of social control organizations (e.g., rates of crime and mental illness) are conceptualized and studied not as indicators of underlying "real" rates but as indicators and reflections of organizational properties and routines. A schematic summary of organizational construction processes is presented in Figure 6.1.

THE SOCIAL CONSTRUCTION OF SOCIAL PROBLEMS

The constructionist perspective is perhaps most influential today in the sociological study of social problems, many of which are associated with deviant behavior. From this perspective, social problems are conceptualized as a process of collective definition (Blumer 1971; Kitsuse and Spector 1973; Schneider 1985). This definitional process entails "claims-making" activities. People make claims that certain putative conditions are troublesome and assert that some type of remedial action is required. The constructionist tries to explain what kinds of claims are generated, who is responsible for making these claims, how the claims are disseminated, and how competing claims fare in the public arena.

Constructionists disagree over just how the "conditions" about which

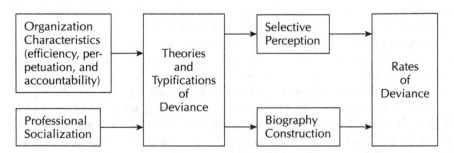

FIGURE 6.1   ORGANIZATIONAL CONSTRUCTION PROCESSES
Organizational characteristics and professional socialization influence organizational typifications and theories of deviance, which influence perception and biography construction, which in turn influence the official rates of deviance.

claims are being made should enter into the analysis (Best 1989; Rafter 1992; Troyer 1992). One position, which has been referred to as "strict constructionism," holds that the analyst should eschew any effort to assess the validity of claims about the conditions themselves. Consistent with phenomenological approaches more generally, the strict constructionist suspends belief in objective reality. The social reality is what people believe it to be, so it is meaningless to ask whether or not claims about social problems are "really" valid. The other position has been referred to as "contextual constructionism" (Rafter 1992). Contextual constructionists believe that knowledge about conditions is attainable and that claims concerning these conditions can be evaluated and their validity assessed with reference to such knowledge. By acknowledging objective conditions, contextual constructionism is similar to the labeling perspective philosophically. The indispensable and distinctive element of any constructionist approach to social problems, however, is the primary analytic focus on the claims-making activities of people and the processes by which social problems are "identified, acknowledged, and translated into action" (Rafter 1992, 18).

Hilgartner and Bosk (1988) used the constructionist perspective to develop a general theory of the rise and fall of social problems. They observed that there are many perceived conditions in society that could possibly attain the status of social problems, but only a limited number actually do. Why is it that claims about some conditions and not others are able to attract widespread attention and gain general acceptance? To answer this question, Hilgartner and Bosk proposed a "public arenas model." This model assumes that public attention is a scarce resource, allocated through competition in public arenas. These public arenas include the media, branches of government, social and political organizations, private foundations, and the research community. Each of these arenas has a limited "carrying capacity." In other words, at any given time, there is only so much public "space" available in each institutional arena that can be devoted to social problems claims. The number of pages is limited in newspapers; only a finite amount of time is available for hearings at congressional committees; budgets of foundations and other organizations are relatively inflexible. The fact that the carrying capacity in the public arena is limited has two important implications. One, the number of social problems is ultimately determined not by the conditions confronting society but rather by the available space in public arenas. Two, competition over this space tends to assume the form of a zero sum game. Unless the overall carrying capacity of the institutional arenas expands, "the ascendance of one social problem will tend to be accompanied by the decline of one or more others" (Hilgartner and Bosk 1988, 61).

Hilgartner and Bosk identified several "principles" that govern the selection of claims in the competition over public attention. One such principle is drama. Social problems claims that are depicted in vivid, dramatic terms are more likely to succeed than those depicted in more mundane terms. Another principle is novelty or saturation. Claims that employ new images and that exploit current events are more likely to attract attention than those that have become repetitive and have "saturated" public discourse. A third principle is that of culture. Social problems claims that are rooted in deep mythic themes or cultural preoccupations have a comparatively high probability of success. Finally, politics governs the competitive selection process. Social problems claims that have powerful "sponsors" from the political and economic elite are advantaged relative to those that lack such sponsorship.

In sum, the constructionist approach to social problems shifts attention away from the allegedly problematic conditions in society to focus on definitional activities. The emergence, persistence, and disappearance of social problems are explained with reference to contests and struggles over different definitions and claims about prevailing conditions. Commonly recognized social problems are conditions that have been successfully "claimed" to be problematic by those who are troubled by them.

In review, social constructionists "suspend" belief in objective reality and focus on people's subjective construction of it. Applied to social deviance, we have discussed three subschools: self-constructions, rules of construction, and constructing social problems.

RESEARCH

Constructionists argue that to understand deviance, researchers must come to know people's methods or tools for reality construction—language, typifications, common-sense theories, and so on. This knowledge usually cannot be obtained through the standard techniques of data collection, such as official records and standardized questionnaires. The latter categorize the constructions of people in terms of the constructions of social scientists; and the former categorize the constructions of people, first in terms of the constructions of social control agencies, and then in terms of the constructions of social scientists. Social scientists are thus two steps removed from people's constructions when using official records. In place of the standard methodological procedures, researchers are implored to experience reality as people experience it—to "go native." Where possible, participant observation is advocated. The participant observer becomes involved with the people studied and experiences what they experience. The researcher thereby comes to construct reality in the subjects' terms. Where participant observation is neither practical nor possible (as with criminal activity or alcoholism), nonparticipant observation is recommended. The nonparticipant observer observes the action firsthand but does not actually become involved. Other techniques are used as needed (such as interviews, questionnaires, content analysis of documents), but in using them constructionists remain sensitive to the problem of imposing their own interpretations on those of the people studied.

This section describes three research areas: methods of construction used by social control agents, organizational products (records), and claims-making activities in the construction of social problems.

CONSTRUCTION METHODS: POLICE AND PSYCHIATRISTS

Police   A major thrust of constructionist research has been the examination of the methods used by social control agents for labeling acts as deviance and actors as deviant. This work shows how cognitive methods (typifications, commonsense theories, retrospective interpretation, and so on) are used by officials to construct everyday reality, thus affecting who is officially processed by formal agencies of social control. A particularly rich research tradition has developed around the activities of the police and the nature of encounters between the police and civilians. This tradition was inspired by two influential studies conducted in the 1960s by Aaron Cicourel (1968) and by Irving Piliavin and Scott Briar (1964). Both studies used field observation methods. Piliavin and Briar's research was based on a nine-month observation study of all juvenile officers (approximately thirty) in one police department. Cicourel's research consisted of a two-year participant observation study of police and probation departments in two cities.

Both studies indicated that police make critical judgments about the underlying character of juveniles when deciding whether or not to take official action. Youths are classified into two broad categories as being either "good" or "bad." In the case of youths classified as "good" kids, the delinquent acts are not viewed by police as evidence of an underlying character flaw; these acts are viewed as a consequence of adverse circumstances. In contrast, for youths who are viewed by the police as basically "bad," their delinquent acts are seen as a sign of immoral character. Consequently, the police feel compelled to take official action when dealing with these "bad" youths; unless something is done, they will continue to get into trouble.

These typifications of "good" and "bad" youths are enmeshed in police theories of delinquency. Cicourel's data suggest that the police view character development as a response to family and neighborhood disorganization or deprivation. Disorganized families (unemployed father, working mother, divorce, separation) and disorganized neighborhoods (widespread unemployment, high crime rate) are thought of as causing troubled and trouble-making youth. Youths who come from disorganized families or neighborhoods are thus likely to be typified as "bad" kids.

Cicourel and Piliavin and Briar also examined the behavioral cues that police use in classifying youths as essentially good or bad. Offense behavior (burglary or truancy) is, of course, important, but it is only one among many cues and not always the most important. Police also scrutinize a youth's demeanor (body motion, facial expression, voice intonation, dress, walk, mannerisms, attitude, grooming). The importance of demeanor is illustrated in the following two cases excerpted from Piliavin and Briar's field notes:*

> *Case One*: The interrogation of "A" (an eighteen-year-old upper-lower-class white male accused of statutory rape) was assigned to a police sergeant with long experience on the force. As I sat in his office while we waited for the youth to arrive for questioning, the sergeant expressed his uncertainty as to what he should do with this young man. On the one hand, he could not ignore the fact that an offense had been committed; he had been informed, in fact, that the youth was prepared to confess to the offense. Nor could he overlook the continued pressure from the girl's father (an important political figure) for the police to take severe action against the youth. On the other hand, the sergeant had formed a low opinion of the girl's moral character, and he considered it unfair to charge "A" with statutory rape when the girl was a willing partner to the offense and might even have been the instigator of it. However, his sense of injustice concerning "A" was tempered by his image of the youth as a "punk," based, he explained, on information he had received that the youth belonged to a certain gang, the members of which were well known to and disliked by the police. Nevertheless, as we prepared to leave his office to interview "A," the sergeant was still in doubt as to what he should do with him. In the interrogation, however, three points quickly emerged that profoundly affected the sergeant's judgment of the youth. First, the youth was polite and cooperative; he consistently addressed the officer as "sir," answered all questions quietly, and signed a statement implicating himself in numerous counts of statutory rape. Second, the youth's intentions toward the girl appeared to have been honorable; for example, he said that he wanted to marry her eventually. Third, the youth was not in fact a member of the gang in question. The sergeant's attitude became increasingly sympathetic, and after we left the interrogation room he announced his intention to "get 'A' off the hook," meaning that he wanted to have the charges against "A" reduced or, if possible, dropped.

> *Case Two*: Officers "X" and "Y" brought into the police station a seventeen-year-old white boy who, along with two older companions, had been found in a home having sex relations with a fifteen-year-old girl. The boy responded to police officers' queries slowly and with obvious disregard. It was apparent that his lack of deference toward the officers and his failure to evidence concern about his situation were irritating his questioners. Finally, one of the officers turned to me and, obviously angry, commented that in his view the boy was simply a "stud" interested only in sex, eating, and sleeping. The policemen conjectured that the boy "probably already had knocked up half a dozen girls." The boy ignored these remarks, except for an occasional impassive stare at the patrolmen. Turning to the boy, the officer remarked, "What the hell am I going to do with you?" And again the boy simply returned the officer's gaze. The latter then said, "Well, I guess we'll just have to put you away for a while." An arrest report was then made out and the boy was taken to Juvenile Hall.

---

*From Irving Piliavin and Scott Briar, "Police Encounters with Juveniles." *American Journal of Sociology* 70 (September 1964), pp. 206–214. © 1964 by University of Chicago Press. Reprinted by permission of the publisher.

Demeanor is likely to be particularly important for decisions made in the field, because the police do not have access to official files to check a youth's past record, and they cannot check a youth's family background or school performance. To assess the impact of demeanor on police officers' field decisions to make arrests, Piliavin and Briar classified youths as cooperative and noncooperative based on their responses to police questions, their respect and deference toward the police, and officers' assessments of them. Of the cooperative youths, only two of forty-five (4.5 percent) were arrested; but of the noncooperative, fourteen of twenty-one (67 percent) were arrested. Piliavin and Briar further suggested that race plays an important role in the encounters between youths and the police. Because blacks more closely fit the typification of "bad" youths, they are more likely to be viewed as suspicious and more likely to be stopped, interrogated, and ultimately arrested. The greater frequency of arrests for black youths then confirms the initial typification of black youths as "bad" and dangerous (see also Anderson 1990).

Several years after the research by Piliavin and Briar, Black and Reiss (1970) conducted a similar but more extensive study. Their analysis was based on the observations of thirty-six trained observers who rode in patrol cars or walked with patrolmen on all shifts on all days of the week, for seven weeks, in Boston, Chicago, and Washington, D.C. The observers were instructed to complete a booklet of questions about each police-citizen incident. Two hundred eighty-one incidents involved a juvenile suspect. In 84 percent of these cases the demeanor of the juvenile could be classified as either "civil," "very deferential," or "antagonistic." In the majority of these cases (68 percent) the juvenile was civil; in 13 percent of the cases the juvenile was very deferential; and in 16 percent of the cases the juvenile was antagonistic. The observers also recorded whether or not the police made an arrest during the encounter. Of the civil suspects, 16 percent were arrested, while of the antagonist suspects, 22 percent were arrested. This pattern is similar to Piliavin and Briar's findings, although the difference in the arrest rate between civil and antagonistic suspects is not as dramatic. One finding was not at all anticipated: Of the deferential suspects, 22 percent were also arrested (the same percentage observed for antagonistic suspects). Black and Reiss speculated that suspects who fear they are likely to be arrested, because of the seriousness of their acts or the circumstances surrounding them, are deferential to police as a tactic, which is apparently unsuccessful.

Lundman et al. (1978) subsequently replicated Black and Reiss' finding about the counterintuitive effect of an extremely deferential demeanor on arrest probability in a study conducted in a large midwestern city. Using a methodology similar to Black and Reiss', they found that 5 percent of the civil juveniles were arrested; 22 percent of the antagonistic juveniles were arrested; and 30 percent of the very deferential juveniles were arrested.

A fairly large literature on the nature of police/citizen encounters accumulated in the 1970s and 80s (for a review, see Klinger 1994). These studies consistently supported the general assertion that demeanor is a significant determinant of police dispositions and the specific hypothesis that citizen hostility increases the likelihood of arrest. Recently, Klinger (1994) challenged the conventional wisdom on the role of demeanor in police dispositions, citing two serious flaws in previous research. First, according to Klinger, the common way of measuring demeanor is invalid. The concept of "citizen demeanor" as used in the literature refers to behavior that is legally permissible but that conveys a lack of deference or respect for the police officer. For measures of demeanor to be valid, then, they must encompass only behavior that is not against the law. Previous measures have often included, as part of "demeanor," behaviors such as physical attacks on police officers during the encounter. These behaviors are indeed disrespectful but they are also criminal. Such measures of demeanor are invalid, in other words, because they confound criminal behavior with legally permissible behavior.

A second, related problem with past research is the failure to include sufficient controls for the influence of crime on arrests. The likelihood of an arrest is obviously going to vary along with the degree of criminal involvement of the suspect. Therefore, to demonstrate the unique impact of demeanor on the decision to make an arrest, it is necessary to take criminal behavior into account. There are three dimensions of criminality that need to be considered: (1) the legal nature of what occurred prior to the police being called to the scene (i.e., the preintervention conduct of suspects); (2) the legal nature of citizen behavior toward the police during the interaction (e.g., attacks by citizens on police officers); and (3) the legal nature of citizen behavior toward other citizens during the interaction (e.g., assaults by citizens on other citizens). Klinger pointed out that the early studies of demeanor and police dispositions failed to control for any of these dimensions of criminality. Studies published in the 1980s contained limited controls for preintervention crime but no controls for crimes during the police/citizen interaction. Because of these methodological limitations, previous research fails to provide a rigorous test of the widely accepted "hostility thesis."

Klinger attempted to overcome these limitations in an observational study of police behavior in Dade County, Florida. Trained civilian observers accompanied police officers on 877 eight-hour patrol shifts. The observers collected information on demeanor, the criminal behavior of suspects, and the action taken by police (arrest versus no arrest) for 245 incidents involving interpersonal disputes. Klinger's measure of demeanor reflected hostility toward the police. It was based on the language used by citizens and their cooperation with the police (the measure explicitly excluded criminal behavior on the part of the suspect). Three levels of hostile demeanor were distinguished: civil, moderately hostile, or highly hostile. Three measures of suspect's criminal behaviors were also included as control variables: the seriousness of suspect's criminal behavior prior to the arrival of the police (no crime, minor property crime, minor violent crime or major property crime, moderate violence, or major violence); violence between citizens while the police were at the scene (no assault, unarmed assault, armed assault); and violence against the police (no attack, attack).

Klinger first examined the simple relationship between his measure of demeanor and the decision to make an arrest. Consistent with the long tradition of research in this field, he found a moderately strong, positive relationship: the greater the degree of hostility, the higher the likelihood of an arrest. However, in multivariate analyses with statistical controls for suspect's criminal behavior, the measure of demeanor was no longer significantly related to arrest decision. Klinger (1994, 489) concluded that "hostile suspects are more likely to be arrested because they are more likely to commit crimes against and in the presence of the police, not because their demeanor connotes a lack of respect for police authority."

In response to Klinger's research, Lundman (1994) reanalyzed data from a previous police/citizen encounter study that had revealed significant demeanor effects on arrests. Lundman included controls for both prior criminal behavior of suspects and criminal behaviors in the presence of the police. In addition, Lundman extended Klinger's earlier research by introducing a variety of measures of demeanor, all of which were based on spoken words (thereby avoiding any confounding of criminal behavior with demeanor). Demeanor is not a simple, unidimensional concept. It encompasses polite interaction, deferential interaction, cooperative interaction, hostile interaction, and possible mixtures of these factors. Accordingly, Lundman created multiple measures to reflect the different dimensions of demeanor.

Following the same basic analytic approach of Klinger, Lundman examined the effect of the measures of demeanor on decisions to make arrests in three kinds of police/citizen encounters: public drunkenness encounters, juvenile encounters, and traffic violation encounters. The results revealed a complex pattern. Some measures of demeanor exhibited significant effects on arrest in the multivariate analyses, while others did not. For example, a measure of hostile demeanor similar to that used by Klinger (with categories of entirely polite, somewhat impolite, and very impolite) was not significantly related to arrest for any of the encounters. In contrast, a measure of greater than average impoliteness was significantly related to arrests for public drunkenness and juvenile encounters but not for traffic violations. Lundman concluded that the conventional wisdom regarding the influence of demeanor needs to be regarded cautiously. Early studies were weak methodologically because they did not control for crime within the police/citizen encounter. Nevertheless, recent research applying more sophisticated techniques suggests that demeanor matters but its effect is more complex than originally thought.

Psychiatrists/Psychologists   The general typifications (diagnostic categories) of psychiatrists and psychologists are imbedded in the medical model, whereby people are generally classified as sick or healthy, although the specific typifications depend on the specific theory of mental illness (e.g., psychoanalytic theory, cognitive theory, or behaviorism). This section examines how these general typifications or constructions are applied in specific cases and how they influence the processing of past information (biography reconstruction), future information (selective perception), and information from presumably objective, standardized diagnostic instruments.

In the 1960s and 70s, considerable research appeared on the diagnostic procedures used to commit persons to mental hospitals and to evaluate patients within those institutions. This early work is nicely illustrated by the studies of Thomas Scheff (1964) and D. L. Rosenhan (1973). Both studies used observational techniques, and although separated by approximately one decade, they arrived at similar conclusions.

As a nonparticipant observer, Scheff studied the involuntary commitment procedures in a midwestern state. At the time of the study, this state required a psychiatric examination by two court-appointed psychiatrists in all commitment proceedings. The examining psychiatrists were asked to use these examinations and the patients' official records to make one of the following recommendations to the court: release, commit for thirty-day observation, or commit indefinitely. Because official records were often incomplete, these recommendations were based largely on the examinations.

Scheff observed twenty-six such examinations. They were conducted quickly, averaging only ten minutes each and ranging from five to seventeen minutes. Two lines of questioning were pursued. One line attempted to establish the circumstances that led to the patient's hospitalization, and the other attempted to establish the patient's orientation and capacity for abstract thinking. As to the latter, patients were rapidly asked a series of questions concerning the date, the president, and the governor and were asked to solve various arithmetic problems. For example, one examiner asked rapidly, "What year is it? What year was it seven years ago? Seventeen years before that?" and so on. Only two of the patients were able to answer the questions. Based on these types of questions, only two of the twenty-six cases were recommended for release; eighteen were recommended for commitment; and six were recommended for commitment for a thirty-day observation period, although Scheff concluded that only about eight of the twenty-six met the legal criteria for commitment.

This tendency to overdiagnose mental illness might be explained by the typifications and theories of mental illness held by most mental health professionals (the medical model of mental illness) and the organizational constraints under which they work. The medical model suggests that mental illness deteriorates rapidly without treatment, that effective treatments are available, that there are few negative consequences associated with psychiatric treatment, and that mental disorders are harmful to the patient and to others. Hence, as with physical illness, when in doubt it is safer to over-diagnose (treat a few people who need no treatment) than to underdiagnose (not treat a few people who need treatment) (Light 1982).

Once a person is defined as mentally ill, information about his or her life is frequently reorganized, and perceptions of present behavior are selectively structured to be consistent with the diagnosis. This, of course, is not a conscious effort on the part of medical personnel to justify their original diagnosis; rather it is part of the normal methods by which people construct social reality.

A classic study by D. L. Rosenhan (1973) illustrates these processes within the context of the mental hospital. Rosenhan conducted an experiment in which eight psychologically normal people gained admission to mental hospitals located in five different states. Each pseudo-patient called the hospital for an appointment, and at the appointment complained of hearing voices. Other than complaining about these symptoms and providing a false name and occupation, no other incorrect information was given. The pseudo-patients accurately described their own life situations, including their troubles and satisfactions; all eight people would be considered to have led quite normal lives. None of the pseudo-patients was detected, and all were admitted to the hospital.

Although all of the pseudo-patients led normal lives, this is not how their lives were interpreted psychologically. Their lives were interpreted consistent with their psychiatric diagnosis and status as mental patient. For example, one patient had a close relationship with his mother and a remote relationship with his father during childhood; during adolescence and adulthood the relationships reversed. His relationship with his wife was generally close and warm, with an occasional argument, and his children were rarely spanked. The following is the case summary of the patient:

> This white 30-year-old male ... manifests a long history of considerable ambivalence in close relationships, which began in early childhood. A warm relationship with his mother cools during his adolescence. A distant relationship to his father is described as becoming very intense. Affective stability is absent. His attempts to control emotionality with his wife and children are punctuated by angry outbursts and in the case of the children, spankings. And while he says that he has several good friends, one senses considerable ambivalence imbedded in those relationships also....

This early work by Scheff and Rosenhan generated considerable controversy throughout the 1970s and 80s. Critics faulted these researchers for exaggerating the ease with which commitments to mental hospitals could be obtained and questioned the continued relevance of the research to the contemporary era, an era in which mental hospitalization is relied on much less frequently than in the past (Gove 1975, 1982). As noted in Chapter 5, the number of people institutionalized for mental illness is in fact far less today than it was in the 1950s, 60s, and 70s. Nevertheless, the work of Scheff and Rosenhan still points to important cognitive processes by which psychiatrists and psychologists make decisions about illness and arrive at diagnoses through the application of the medical model. Recent work by Mark Peyrot (1995) reaffirms one of the core insights of Scheff and Rosenhan, namely, the tendency for mental health professionals to interpret ambiguous situations in terms of pathology rather than normalcy.

Peyrot examined the use of a standardized diagnostic tool, the Minnesota Multiphasic Personality Inventory (MMPI), by mental health professionals in a forensic psychiatry organization that makes recommendations on criminal justice cases, child custody cases, and workmen's compensation cases. The MMPI is a sophisticated psychological test based on a large number of questionnaire items. These items are combined into different scales which purportedly measure the major traits of the test-taker's psyche. The MMPI has been accepted by the courts as a "valid, reliable, and objective" instrument for diagnosing psychiatric conditions (Peyrot 1995, 575).

In the organization studied by Peyrot, the MMPI is administered to patients by clinical psychologists. The psychologists bring the results of the testing to "case conferences" attended by psychiatrists, who have conducted clinical interviews with the patients, and by social workers, who have interviewed the patients' families and others involved in the case. During the conferences the various professionals review the details of the case and discuss possible recommendations. The final responsibility for the case decision rests with the psychiatrist to whom the case has been assigned.

Peyrot attended these conferences and observed the ways in which the MMPI is actually used to assist in the diagnostic process. He argues that there is an important difference between the formal properties of the MMPI and its "properties-in-use." In practice, the properties of the MMPI are situational in the sense that they are interpreted in different ways depending on the nature of the case. The most telling feature of this process is that the MMPI results are selectively interpreted to confirm the clinical diagnoses of the psychiatrists.

One way in which this is done is by relaxing the formal standards for "normal limits." For each scale on the MMPI, there is a range in which scores are considered to be normal. Scores beyond these limits ostensibly indicate pathology. In practice, the normal limits are interpreted flexibly depending upon the construction of the case by the psychiatrists and psychologists. Peyrot cited the following illustration:

> *Case One*: The psychiatrist presented a case involving a man charged with carrying a concealed gun. the psychiatrist said that the gun was part of the client's "paranoid delusional system," that it was for "defense against his enemies," but when he questioned the man further about these "enemies," he became "very vague." The psychiatrist said that he was worried that the man might use the gun, and then asked for a reading of the MMPI. The psychologist reported that the "testing confirms paranoia," that there is "a peak score on 6" (the paranoia scale). The psychologist also noted that there was "moderate elevation on (the) acting out (scale)," and that this might indicate that he would use the gun (although the score was within the normal limits, no specific mention was made of this). Another psychiatrist said the man was "dangerous." The psychiatrist in charge of the case said that he thought the man would require hospitalization and medication. (Peyrot 1995, 578)*

In this case, the MMPI results for the paranoid scale were consistent with the clinical diagnosis—the patient's score was above the level regarded as normal. On the other hand, the score on the "acting out" scale, which is relevant to the judgment of dangerousness, was within the normal range. Nevertheless, the clinical psychologist noted that there was "moderate elevation" on the acting out scale, consistent with the psychiatrist's judgment concerning dangerousness. The fact that the actual score was within the normal range was not mentioned or discussed. By relaxing the "normal limit property" of the MMPI, the staff was able to interpret potentially ambiguous results as consistent with the clinical profile.

Peyrot also found that this tendency to resolve discrepancies between clinical diagnoses and MMPI scores in favor of the former is not haphazard or unsystematic. Rather, it facilitates the "discovery" of psychopathologies: "at least in the cases analyzed here, staff members seem inclined to privilege evidence of problems over evidence that no problems exist" (1995, 584). Thus, consistent with the earlier arguments of Rosenhan and Scheff, Peyrot concluded that psychiatrists are likely to be predisposed to discern symptoms of disorder and to be wary of the dangers of failing to treat disturbed individuals. This increases the likelihood that persons subject to clinical evaluation will be diagnosed as mentally ill, even when highly sophisticated diagnostic tools such as the MMPI are employed.

In sum, research suggests that the general images or typifications of deviance held by social control agents are intermeshed in general commonsense theories of such behaviors. These theories provide cues through which general typifications are applied to specific cases. Through three processes (retrospective interpretation, biography reconstruction, and selective percep-

---

*From Mark Peyrot, "Psychological Testing and Forensic Decision Making." *Social Problems* 42:4 (1995), p. 578. © 1995 by The Society for the Study of Social Problems. Reprinted by permission of the publisher.

tion), past and present behavior and formal test results are organized to reinforce or lock in initial definitions of reality (arrest and diagnostic decisions).

ORGANIZATIONAL PRODUCTS: SUICIDE STATISTICS

Constructionists argue that being labeled a deviant (delinquent, alcoholic, mentally ill) is more a function of the methods of reality construction employed by social control agents than of rule breaking. Consequently, the records or statistics of social control organizations can be understood as emergent products of these methods. These statistics tell us less about the level and distribution of norm violations among social units than about the level or distribution of organizational activities among social units.

The work of Jack D. Douglas (1967, 1971) in the 1960s and early 1970s stimulated constructionist research on the linkage between organizational routines and official suicide statistics. Douglas (1971) argued that coroners and medical examiners employ the conventional definition of suicide when making determinations about the cause of death: "the intentional taking of one's own life." To apply this definition, they use commonsense ideas or theories about the nature of the act (e.g., position of the wound), the person (e.g., depressed), and the social situation (e.g., unemployed) to infer suicidal intention. They vary considerably, however, in the amount of evidence collected, as to which dimension is emphasized, and how the data are interpreted. Consider the act itself and the immediate situation prior to the act. Was a suicide note left? If not, how much weight should be given to this? Douglas (1967) reported that in one city a death is not recorded as a suicide unless a note is present. What is the position of the wound? Was alcohol present? Was there a family quarrel? These immediate factors may be interpreted in relation to other factors, such as the personality and background of the victim. Was the person depressed? How long was he or she unemployed? Additionally, given that suicide carries a negative connotation, families frequently pressure examiners and coroners not to classify deaths as suicides.

Studies of the decision making of coroners and medical examiners thus suggest that classifying an act as a suicide is inherently problematic and depends upon the nature of the situation. As a result, the suicide rate of an area reflects to a large extent the routines by which coroners and medical examiners collect and interpret information to infer suicidal intention.

In comparing the suicide rates of one area over time or the suicide rates of various areas to one another, two types of errors are important: random and systematic. The former refers to errors in the decision-making process that do not bias suicide rates in one direction or another. Because decision-making rules are clumsy, cumbersome, and ambiguous, some nonsuicides may be classified as suicides and some suicides may be classified as nonsuicides; these errors, however, balance each other out. While they result in some wrong decisions about individual suicides, they produce valid rates in the aggregate. Research problems are generated by systematic errors, that is, errors that distort suicide rates, either over or underestimating them. These errors can vary from jurisdiction to jurisdiction so that in one jurisdiction the suicide rate is overestimated and in another it is underestimated. They are particularly troublesome when they are related to conditions hypothesized as causing suicide. If the hypothesized causal conditions are present in jurisdictions where suicides are overestimated and not present in jurisdictions where suicides are underestimated, the causal theory of suicide may appear to be valid when it is not.

To illustrate the problem, Douglas (1967) reconsidered Emile Durkheim's theory of suicide (see Chapter 2). Durkheim hypothesized that social disintegration and deregulation cause a high rate of suicide. He also assumed that Catholic countries are more integrated than Protestant countries. His theory thus implies that Catholic countries should show lower suicide rates than Protestant countries, a proposition generally supported by the official statistics on suicide. Douglas suggested that this pattern may reflect systematic measurement error. Since suicide is more negatively evaluated in the Catholic than in the Protestant religion, Catholic families make greater efforts than Protestant families to conceal suicides and to exert pressure on coroners not to classify their loved ones as suicides. Hence, fewer unexplained Catholic than Protestant deaths may be classified as suicides, thereby lowering the official suicide rate of Catholics.

Recent research by Van Poppel and Day (1996) supports Douglas' hypothesis about the effects of religion on the recording of suicides. Van Poppel and Day collected data on causes of death in the Netherlands for the years 1905–1910, a period contemporaneous with that used by Durkheim. The categories for causes of death included various types of suicide (e.g., suicide by poison, suicide by asphyxia, suicide by drowning), other common causes of death, and two rather vague categories: "sudden death" and "unspecified or ill-defined causes of death." Van Poppel and Day argued that these latter categories serve as convenient alternatives in cases where suicide might be suspected but coroners are reluctant to classify the deaths as such. Accordingly, if members of different religious groups differ in their efforts to conceal suicides, this should be reflected in differential death rates for "sudden death" and "unspecified or ill-defined causes of death."

Van Poppel and Day computed age-standardized, sex-specific death rates for the respective categories of cause of death for Catholics and Protestants. When death rates for the suicide categories were compared across religious groups, the results seemed to support Durkheim's conclusions. The combined suicide rate for Catholic males was only 47 percent of that for Protestant males, and the rate for Catholic females was only 35 percent of that for Protestant females. This pattern was reversed, however, when the ambiguous categories of "sudden death" and "unspecified or ill-defined causes of death" were examined. For "sudden death," the rate for

Catholics was almost 50 percent higher than that for Protestants; for "unspecified or ill-defined causes of death," the rate for Catholics was almost twice that for Protestants (the results were similar for males and females). Van Poppel and Day concluded that "the gap between Protestant and Catholic suicide rates in the Netherlands during the years 1905 through 1910 appear to be the result of nothing more mysterious than differences in how deaths to Catholics and deaths to Protestants were recorded" (1996, 505).

The constructionist perspective has thus drawn attention to a serious limitation of the traditional approach to the study of suicide. Traditional approaches assume that official suicide statistics are generated primarily by norm violations (suicides). Therefore, the official suicide rate can be used "as is" to test theories about the social causes of suicide. The potential importance of organizational routines is essentially ignored (see Model A of Figure 6.2). Constructionists, on the other hand, are keenly aware of the importance of organizational routines in the creation of official suicide statistics. However, constructionists tend to focus exclusively on these organizational routines. The role of norm violations is neglected (Model B of Figure 6.2). Nevertheless, some researchers have joined the two perspectives to assess the ways in which social causes, norm violations, and organizational routines operate in combination to generate official suicide rates (Model C of Figure 6.2).

An example of this integrated approach is the work by Farberow, MacKinnon, and Nelson (1977). They estimated the relative contributions of variation in real suicide rates and in the decision-making processes of coroners in explaining variation in recorded suicide rates among 411 counties in eleven states. To the extent that recorded rates reflect real rates, vari-

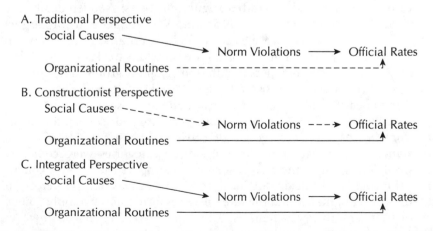

FIGURE 6.2   ALTERNATIVE PERSPECTIVES ON PROCESSES GENERATING OFFICIAL SUICIDE RATES
Note: The dotted lines signify process ignored.

ation in recorded rates should be predicted by variation in the social factors that cause suicide, such as the unemployment rate, income level, social mobility, and percent foreign born. To the extent that recorded rates reflect the decision making of coroners, variation in recorded rates should be predicted by variation in the factors that affect their decision making, such as their background, educational level, and training, and their views on how to do the job (e.g., the extent to which they consider the deceased's reputation in making their decision as to the cause of death). Farberow et al. thus compared the relative efficiency of predicting recorded suicide rates from the social factors thought to cause suicide and the factors thought to affect the decision making of coroners.

The results showed that a model including only social factors accounted for 24 percent of the variation in recorded suicide rates among counties, while one including only decision-making factors accounted for 14 percent of the variation in recorded suicide rates among counties. While both social and decision-making factors were important, social factors appeared to be twice as important as decision-making factors. These estimates are very tentative, however, and should be viewed with caution. They may change in another sample. For example, if only large counties are considered (thirty thousand or more population) the respective estimates are equal; and if only small counties are considered, the decision-making factors are twice as strong as the social ones. In small counties, the stronger social ties may sensitize medical examiners and coroners to the feelings of the survivors.

Research by Pescosolido and Mendelsohn (1986) also examined the effect of social causes and organizational routines on official suicide rates. Recall that systematic bias in reporting can make a causal theory of suicide appear valid when it is not. If such bias exists, the apparent effect of social factors on official suicide rates should get smaller or even disappear when the effect of variation in reporting practices is taken into account.

Pescosolido and Mendelsohn based their analysis on 404 "county groups" in the United States. A county group is an aggregated unit that combines adjacent counties into population groups of 250,000 persons or more. For each county group, Pescosolido and Mendelsohn computed suicide rates for eight demographic groups: women 18–24, men 18–24, women 25–44, men 25–44, women 45–64, men 45–64, women over 65, and men over 65. They also collected information on indicators of the alleged social causes of suicide (e.g., proportion of the population affiliated with different religious groups, the socioeconomic attainment of the population, percentage divorced, the unemployment rate) and organizational characteristics likely to affect the recording of suicides (e.g., percentage of the population covered by a medical examiner system, percentage of the population served by a pathologist or by a toxicologist). They first analyzed official suicide rates with only social causes included as predictors, and then included organizational routines as well. They found that the effects of the social factors did not disappear; the results were highly similar across models. Pescosolido and Mendelsohn concluded that while there is significant jurisdictional variation in the ways in which coroners and medical examiners perform their tasks, "misreporting of suicides has little discernible impact on the effects of variables commonly used to test sociological theories of suicide" (1986, 80).

What can we conclude from this series of studies? With the exception of the final study, all of the research shows that the routines and backgrounds of medical examiners and coroners influence their decision to classify a death as a suicide and thus influence the variation in official or recorded suicide rates across counties and countries and over time. At the same time the studies show that variation in recorded suicide rates do not just reflect variation in the routines; they also reflect variation in real rates that are influenced by social factors. Again, reality is complex and is best represented by an integrated theory (Figure 6.2, Model C)—one that includes both the social factors that influence the real rates and the organizational routines that influence how they are recorded.

CONSTRUCTION OF SOCIAL PROBLEMS

Forms of deviance and crime vary in their frequency and seriousness. Some are ignored and some are the focus of public attention and are thought of as *social problems*. Constructionists assume that widely recognized social problems do not emerge "naturally" from objective conditions, such as their frequency and seriousness. Rather, they must be brought to public awareness through concerted activity or *agency* on the part of individuals and organizations, who make claims about the nature of social reality. This section reviews constructionist research on the making of a social problem. It specifically examines claims-making activities for two social problems pertaining to children: the problem of missing children (child abduction) and the sexual abuse of children.

Missing Children   Joel Best (1987, 1990) applied rhetorical analysis to explain claims-making activity in the construction of the missing children problem in the 1980s. Rhetoric is the formal study of persuasion. It is concerned with how different kinds of statements are used in argumentation to convince others of a particular point of view. Best identified three common types of rhetorical statements—grounds, warrants, and conclusions—and illustrated their use in the construction of the missing children problem.

Grounds are statements that provide the basic facts for discussion of an issue. These statements define the phenomenon, illustrate it with examples, and establish numerical estimates of its prevalence. In the construction of the missing children problem, claims-makers typically offered broad and inclusive grounds statements for the definition of missing children. There were few efforts to specify the age range for identifying the population of "children" or to designate precise periods of time required to indicate that persons were in fact "missing." For example, some photos of alleged missing children depicted individuals in their twenties, and some advocacy groups maintained that children who returned home on their own after a brief absence should be regarded as missing. At the same time, the examples cited in the media unambiguously implied risk or danger. Best (1987, 105) reported that newspaper and magazine articles "routinely began with accounts of one or more atrocity tales" that served to communicate a sense of the problem's "frightening, horrifying dimensions." In addition, claims-makers used the metaphor of an "epidemic" to describe the situation; implying that the problem was widespread, growing, and capable of striking indiscriminately throughout the population.

The second general type of rhetorical statement—*warrants*—refers to a statement that justifies drawing certain conclusions from the *grounds*. Warrants are important for convincing others that "something must be done" about a situation. In the construction of the missing children problem, claims-makers appealed to several rhetorical warrants. For example, children were described as both "priceless" resources and "blameless victims." Such characterizations worked to the rhetorical advantage of claims-makers by appealing to widely held sentiments and emotions about the innocence and purity of childhood.

The third type of rhetorical statement discussed by Best is a *conclusion*, which in the case of social problems construction involves setting forth an agenda of goals. The claims-makers for the missing children problem pursued multiple goals. They emphasized the importance of promoting greater awareness of the missing children problem, enlisting the public in the search for these children, and implementing prevention measures. Their calls for action were systematically linked with the grounds statements and warrants described above. In many respects, the claims-makers for the missing children problem were highly successful. This problem attained a high level of visibility by the mid-1980s. Photographs of missing children appeared on milk cartons and grocery bags, public service announcements warning about the dangers of abduction appeared in the media, children were fingerprinted at local police stations, and commercial child identification kits were marketed (Best 1987, 102). From the constructionist perspective, what is most interesting about the missing children problem of the 1980s is not so much any change in the "objective" misfortunes of children (recall that constructionists suspend belief in reality). Rather, the episode represents an effective exercise in claims-making. Claims-makers made strategic, rhetorical choices and as a result were able to create a collective definition of a condition as problematic and in need of concerted remedial action.

Child Sexual Abuse   Katherine Beckett (1996) studied claims-making activities regarding the sexual abuse of children. Child sexual abuse is obviously a very emotional issue, and there would seem to be overwhelming consensus about its wrongfulness. After all, who is in favor of sexually abusing children? Beckett argued, however, that while virtually everyone condemns "true" cases of abuse, people hold different views about what actually constitutes abuse and how cases of abuse can be determined. The concrete meaning of sexual abuse, in other words, is open to dispute and can be contested. Beckett examined the alternative way in which this social problem has been "signified" or imbued with meaning in the media, and how this signification has changed over time.

Beckett's research was based on a content analysis of four leading news magazines: *Time, Newsweek, U.S. News and World Report,* and *People Magazine.* Using the *Reader's Guide to Periodical Literature,* Beckett identified all stories pertaining to child sexual abuse that appeared in these magazines during the 1980–1994 period, a total of 103 stories. She searched each story for displays of various "issue packages" depending on the way in which child sexual abuse was depicted. Three general types of packages were differentiated: (1) the positive pedophilia package, (2) the collective denial package, and (3) the false accusations package.

The positive pedophilia package describes the issue of child sexual abuse in terms of an "hysteria" that is a symptom of an outdated, Victorian approach to sexuality (1996, 61). This package refers to children as sexual beings who should have the liberty to live the lives they want to, including having sexual relations. It emphasizes civil rights and criticizes conventional morality, as expressed in the following claim: "Our sexual prudishness does not give the state the right to deprive children of their sexual freedom or to harass those who have unpopular sexual preferences" (1996, 61).

In contrast, the collective denial package describes the sexual abuse of children as a serious but hidden problem in society. This package emphasizes the vulnerability of children and their inability to give informed consent. Child sexual abuse is an unpleasant and painful reality, and both children and adults have been unwilling to recognize and confront this reality. As a result, cases of child sexual abuse rarely receive the attention they should in the criminal justice system.

The third issue package—the false accusations package—is directly opposed to the collective denial package. As the label suggests, the false accusations package emphasizes the illegitimacy of claims about the sexual abuse of children:

> [T]he pendulum has swung too far as panicky parents, intrusive child protective workers, over-zealous therapists, and assorted "victims" cry "abuse." Accusations are made all too easily and cannot be accepted at face value. Both children's and adults' perceptions and memories are fallible and vulnerable to suggestion, and the methods used to uncover

these are highly suspect. The consequences of being wrongly accused have destroyed many innocent people's lives. Protections must be built into the system in order to prevent the harm caused by unfounded accusations. (1996, 64)

Beckett calculated the number of times each of these issue packages was displayed in the articles in her sample for three broad time periods: 1980–84, 1985–90, and 1991–94 (see Table 6.1). The results show the changes in the "media career" of the different packages. The collective denial package was clearly the dominant characterization of child sexual abuse appearing in the 1980–84 period; 85 percent of the displays reflected the themes of this package. During this early period, the media emphasized the recent "discovery" of the hidden problem of child sexual abuse. The other two packages were also represented during this time but relatively infrequently (they each constituted 7 percent of displays). In later years, the media characterizations of child sexual abuse changed dramatically. The positive pedophilia package disappeared entirely from media accounts, while the false accusations package became much more prominent, surpassing displays of the collective denial package. This pattern is even more pronounced when the recent 1991–94 period is examined in greater detail (see Table 6.2). By 1994, false accusations comprised 85 percent of the displays of issue packages compared to 15 percent for collective denial displays.

Beckett argued that this shift in the media careers of issue packages was due in large part to the activities of sponsors. In the mid-1980s and early 1990s, two organizations emerged to advance the claims associated with the false accusations package: Victims of Child Abuse Laws (VOCAL) and the False Memory Syndrome Foundation (FMSF). The activities of these organizations helped shift attention away from the collective denial of child abuse to the harms associated with unfounded allegations. Beckett

TABLE 6.1   **DISPLAYS OF CHILD SEXUAL ABUSE ISSUE PACKAGES, MULTIYEAR INTERVALS, 1980–94**

PACKAGE	1980–84	1985–90	1991–94
Positive Pedophilia	7% (8)	0% (0)	0%
Collective Denial	85% (93)	41% (54)	42% (75)
False Accusations	7% (8)	59% (66)	58% (105)
Total Displays	100% (109)	100% (120)	100% (180)

Source: Katherine Beckett, "Culture and the Politics of Signification: The Case of Child Sexual Abuse." *Social Problems* 43:1 (1996), p. 67. © 1996 by The Society for the Study of Social Problems. Reprinted by permission of the publisher.

TABLE 6.2 ANNUAL DISPLAYS OF CHILD SEXUAL ABUSE ISSUE PACKAGES, 1991–94

PACKAGE	1991	1992	1993	1994
Positive	0%	0%	0%	0%
Pedophilia	(0)	(0)	(0)	(0)
Collective	82%	45%	27%	15%
Denial	(40)	(9)	(21)	(5)
False	18%	55%	58%	85%
Accusations	(9)	(11)	(56)	(29)
Total	100%	100%	100%	100%
Displays	(49)	(20)	(77)	(54)

Source: Katherine Beckett, "Culture and the Politics of Signification: The Case of Child Sexual Abuse." Social Problems 43:1 (1996), p. 68. © 1996 by The Society for the Study of Social Problems. Reprinted by permission of the publisher.

suggested that the sponsors of the false accusations package were successful because they skillfully linked their claims with general cultural themes, such as the importance of protecting the rights of the accused, the autonomy of the family vis-a-vis the state, and suspicions about the professionalism and competence of mental health professionals, who are often assigned responsibility for detecting hidden cases of child sexual abuse.

In sum, constructionists have devoted considerable attention to how social problems are constructed—especially to the claims-making activities associated with the construction process. Research by Joel Best reveals how rhetorical techniques were used to foster widespread public concern over the plight of missing children. The work of Katherine Beckett illustrates how a seemingly uncontroversial issue—child sexual abuse—has in fact been the subject of contests and struggles over its meaning and interpretation.

RESEARCH SUMMARY

To review, constructionist research generally focuses on two questions: What is labeled deviance? Who is labeled deviant? This section has examined research on the decision-making processes by which police and psychiatrists apply general categories of delinquency and mental illness in everyday situations, on the link between the everyday decision making of coroners and the validity of suicide statistics, and on the processes by which social problems are constructed.

SOCIAL POLICY

Discussions of social policy implicitly assume the following: (1) There is an objective world in which social problems are located; (2) the world is knowable even though such knowledge may be less than perfect and difficult to obtain; and (3) some parts of the world can be defined as problematic, although reasonable people may disagree over the criteria to be employed in making such judgments. For the most part, the structural/functional, human ecological, deterrence, and labeling perspectives make these assumptions. They assume that norm and law violations exist in the world, that social scientists using research techniques can identify violators and the rate of violations, and that at least some kinds of violations constitute a social problem.

Constructionists do not clearly accept these assumptions and in some cases explicitly deny them. With regard to the first assumption, most constructionists suspend belief in objective reality; they are concerned with people's constructions of reality, not reality in any objective sense. As to the second assumption, some constructionists deny that social scientists have any special claims to knowledge (Schneider 1985). The theories and ideas of the so-called experts are in principle no different from those of laypeople; they are themselves social constructions. As to the third assumption, some constructionists argue that social scientists should not evaluate the world, defining some conditions as desirable and others as problematic. Evaluating the world interferes with adequately describing the constructions of people. Social scientists should concentrate on the latter.

What, then, does social policy mean within a constructionist framework? Does it make sense for someone to formulate social policy to change a world, if he or she has suspended belief in what that world "really is" in the first place? What should be the role of social scientists, if their constructions do not reflect that world any more accurately than do the constructions of laypeople? To constructionists, the policy recommendations of the self-proclaimed experts are no better or worse than the policy recommendations of anyone else. Moreover, to constructionists, defining some state of society as a problem about which something should be done is itself a subjective construction. Constructionists are more interested in studying that construction than they are in the "objective" state to which it refers. They examine how methods of constructing reality (typifications and lay theories) lead to social problem constructions, and how different groups with different claims about conditions compete with one another to establish the commonly agreed-upon constructions.

The constructionist perspective encompasses a variety of subschools, not all of which fully embrace the tenets of phenomenology (e.g., Rafter 1992a). If some of the phenomenological assumptions are relaxed, constructionist research can lead to more traditional social policies. For example, labeling theorists argue that the medical model of mental illness (a construction) leads to societal reactions that stabilize mental illness (career deviance). Constructionist studies of the medical model as a social construction (its historical development and situational applications) may be useful in formulating policies to alter professional and public conceptions of mental illness (Conrad and Schneider 1992). Constructionists might also direct attention to the validity of people's construction based on the findings of sociological investigations (such as the constructions that police hold about African-American young males), and direct social policy toward eradicating distorted constructions, especially if they lead to harmful outcomes.

CRITIQUE

THEORY

Microlevel Orientation   Constructionists emphasize the role of subjective meanings and individual consciousness in the construction of social reality. As a result, they focus on microlevel processes. Critics charge that the preoccupation with microlevel phenomenon in the constructionist perspective leads to the neglect of broader structural forces that shape and order microlevel processes of reality construction (Taylor et al. 1973). For example, constructionists who study how the police construct law violations and violators in everyday situations ignore the ways in which the operations of the police may serve to advance the interests of certain classes at the expense of others.

General Propositions   Constructionists charge that standard concepts in the social sciences (such as anomie, social disorganization) do not reflect the concepts people actually use to construct their worlds. They argue that the concepts of the social sciences should be formulated in terms of people's concepts, or at the very least should be translatable into them or be compatible with them. People's contextual and situational meanings, in other words, must be captured in the concepts of researchers, and the constructionist strategy ties scholarly concepts to the unique constructions of everyday situations. Yet if the social sciences are to formulate abstract propositions and generalizations, uniform and general concepts are required for the orderly description of people's constructions and construction processes. Constructionists have not, for the most part, seriously addressed the issue of how the contextual constructions of people can be translated into general concepts conducive to scientific inquiry.

Explanation and Prediction   Because of the paucity of general concepts for describing reality, explanation understood as a deduction of specific observations from general propositions is not possible within the constructionist perspective (see Chapter 1). Additionally, in conceptualizing people as actively creating their environment, constructionists do not study causal structures or processes. To the constructionist, explanation is generally equated with "understanding." Actions are said to be understood when the researcher "knows" the actors' constructions; these constructions in turn are said to be understood when the researcher "knows" the actors' techniques of construction. This concept of explanation differs from that used by the other perspectives; and as it is not based on general and abstract concepts, it does not lead to prediction.

Subjectivism   The constructionist prescription to suspend belief in an objective reality is difficult to adhere to consistently (see Woolgar and Pawluch 1985). For example, constructionists argue that the rise and fall of social problems should be understood in terms of the activities of claims-makers and not in terms of changing, "objective" conditions. But perhaps conditions become known as social problems precisely when they worsen, and they cease to be known as problems when these conditions are ameliorated. To discount this possibility, constructionists often make an implicit appeal to the reader's commonsense knowledge that the conditions under consideration probably have not changed over time. Yet this essentially constitutes a claim about the nature of reality; the reality is unchanging, but definitions and claims change. In practice, then, constructionists tend to employ a selective subjectivism. Some phenomena are considered to be problematic and legitimate matters for constructionist inquiry, whereas other phenomena can simply be taken as given.

RESEARCH

Because of their concern with remaining faithful to the constructions of the people being studied, constructionists have largely avoided structured techniques of data collection (experiments, questionnaires, interviews, official records) that express the constructions of people in terms of the constructions of social scientists. Instead, they have emphasized direct observation, particularly participant observation, which presumably allows researchers to experience reality somewhat like that of the subjects, thereby insuring that the constructions of researchers are not too different from those of the subjects.

While useful for just this reason, participant observation has limitations. Certain positions in social control organizations require considerable training and experience; thus, the constructions of people in those positions are not accessible to most participant observers. How is the participant observer to understand the more technical constructions of judges and prosecutors? Nonparticipant observation has somewhat similar limitations, for the behavior of social control agents is frequently invisible to most observers. Agents frequently go to extremes to avoid public visibility, and when researchers are present they may alter their behavior. The major problem of field observation, particularly participant observation, is observer reliability. Without techniques for structuring observations, different observers construct reality differently. How are we to choose among these constructions? Different laypeople have different understandings and constructions of reality; hence, different researchers have different understandings and constructions of reality. If we accept this premise, what is the special province or mission of the social researcher?

7 THE CONFLICT PERSPECTIVE

THEORY

Contemporary conflict approaches to the study of deviance and crime can be traced to the work of two general social theorists—Karl Marx and, more recently Ralf Dahrendorf. Observing nineteenth-century Europe, Marx argued that conflict between social classes is the basic social process in society—the key to understanding other social processes and structures. In capitalist societies, Marx argued that there are two major economic classes (those who own the means of production—the capitalists, and those employed by them—the laborers) and that their economic interests are diametrically opposed. As labor is an element or resource in the process of production, it is in the interest of capitalists to maintain low wages, which makes them more competitive on national and international markets. On the other hand, the cost of labor to capitalists is income to laborers; thus, it is in the interest of labor to increase the cost of labor. Marx argued that in accordance with the laws of competition the ranks of labor would swell with unsuccessful capitalists, artisans, and farmers, and thus that the standard of living of laborers would decrease and social conflict would escalate.

Marx also argued that this system of economic relationships affects the political, cultural, and religious institutions of society. Capitalistic societies develop laws, religions, and science that protect the interests of capitalists. For example, in Western societies governments protect the property of capitalists, and Christianity supports the capitalist order by diverting the energies of laborers toward the hereafter rather than toward their earthly miseries. Marx referred to Western religion as the "opiate" of the people.

Ralf Dahrendorf's work (1958, 1959) is sometimes described as an adaptation of Marx to twentieth-century industrial society. Whereas Marx emphasized ownership of the means of production, Dahrendorf emphasized power as the major social division; and whereas Marx argued that power is derived from ownership of the means of production, Dahrendorf argued that in contemporary industrial society power is frequently divorced from ownership of the means of production and is based on institutional authority. Dahrendorf focused on the division between those who have and those who do not have authority in institutional structures. Economic structures are important but not preeminent. Additionally, Dahrendorf argued that authority relationships in one institution (economic) do not necessarily overlap with authority relationships in other institutions (education, religion, government). Social conflict is fractured.

Neither Marx nor Dahrendorf wrote much about deviance or crime. Marx viewed deviants, and criminals in particular, as somewhat irrelevant to the social forces that shape society and history (Taylor et al. 1973). He described criminals as parasites who use the goods and services of society without contributing to it. He did not view crime as political behavior and did not view criminals as concerned with social change, only with self-preservation. In fact, he argued that crime may retard social change. Since criminals are drawn from the ranks of labor, they weaken the forces of labor. Furthermore, high crime rates lead to increases in the size of the police force, which is used to support the capitalist social order.

EARLY APPLICATIONS TO CRIME

Conflict theorists have not tried to develop or expand Marx's or Dahrendorf's few specific ideas on crime and deviance. Rather, they have derived theories from Marx's and Dahrendorf's general concepts of social conflict. The focus of conflict theory has been almost exclusively on one form of deviance: crime. Specifically, conflict theorists have focused on the following questions:

> Why are the norms of some social groups or classes transformed into law, thus making criminals out of conflicting groups or classes?
>
> Why are some laws enforced at some times but not others, thus making criminals out of those who violate some laws at some times but not others?
>
> Why are laws enforced against certain groups and classes but not others, thus making criminals out of some law violators but not others?

Generally, conflict criminologists study the social and political processes by which crime and criminals are created, "the politics of crime." The concept most important in the study of politics, *power*, is then central to the study of crime. In respect to the above three questions, conflict criminologists argue that social power determines what norms become laws and what laws are enforced against what classes of people. Subschools of conflict theory address these questions in different ways.

One of the earliest applications of conflict theory to the study of crime emphasized cultural conflict. The cultural conflict thesis developed within the early Chicago school in the 1930s. In their studies of urban life, the Chicago researchers observed cultural differences among different ethnic immigrant groups. They conceptualized cultural diversity as a cause of deviance and crime through two processes: (1) Residents of culturally diverse areas are exposed to a social environment of normative ambiguity and conflict, which reduces social controls and thereby leads to deviance and crime (see Chapter 3). (2) As the norms of ethnic groups frequently conflict with the law, those who adhere to traditional ethnic norms frequently violate contemporary laws (Sellin 1938). The latter approach to the relationship between cultural conflict and crime provides a link between the Chicago school and the conflict criminologists.

In the 1950s George B. Vold (1958) further developed this approach to cultural conflict, arguing that criminal behavior is frequently an expression of values that clash with the law. When one group has the power to transform its values into laws, it has the power to make criminals out of those who behaviorally express conflicting values. Conscientious objectors, for example, hold values inconsistent with the behavior required during wartime. Thus, during wartime—only during wartime—conscientious objectors become criminals. Delinquents can also be conceptualized as a minority group whose values violate laws; in fact, juvenile gangs sometimes take on the characteristics (group loyalty and division of labor) of warring nations. Vold also argued that people sometimes violate the law as well as their own values in an effort to achieve higher values. For example, crimes of theft, homicide, and sabotage are sometimes committed in the name of revolution. If the revolution fails, those committing the actions are defined as criminals; if it succeeds, they become heroes, and the traditional authorities become defined as criminals. Some leaders in the U.S. civil-rights movement during the 1960s advocated open violence, deemed to be wrong in principle but necessary in the struggle for human rights.

Vold attempted to shift attention away from understanding crime as individual law violations to understanding it as group struggles. However, he took only the initial step. For the most part, he used conflict theory to understand crimes which had been traditionally ignored by criminologists—the "leftovers" (racial disturbance, industrial strife, and conscientious objection), and to understand evanescent conflicts—those that are temporary (union strike), or those where the minority group either can easily change its status (conscientious objectors) or will change its status with age (delinquents). He did not focus on the stable conflicts in industrial societies, such as those based on social class, race, or gender.

Austin Turk (1969) was one of the first to formulate a general conflict theory of crime. Following Dahrendorf, Turk focused on conflict between those who have power (authorities) to control behavior and those who do not (subjects) in social institutions. Also, like Dahrendorf, Turk did not attempt to link authority to ownership of the means of production or even to positions in the economic order; he examined authority-subject relationships within institutions with little concern for overarching or overlapping authority-subject relationships across institutions. Within this general framework, he focused on legal conflict and criminalization. Specifically, he asked the following two questions: (1) Under what conditions are authority-subject differences transformed into legal conflict? (2) Under what conditions do those who violate laws (norms of the authorities) become criminalized? In other words, under what circumstances are laws enforced?

Concerning the first question, Turk specified two major conditions under which behavioral differences between authorities and subjects result in conflict: when these behavioral differences reflect cultural differences and when the subjects are organized. (1) If behavioral differences between authorities and subjects do not reflect important value differences, conflict will be minimal; that is, people rarely struggle over abstractions or behaviors that are insignificant. (2) The concept *organized* means that the act in question is part of a general culture and/or that the subjects involved can marshal forces to resist authorities. Compare, for example, homosexuality today and in the 1950s. In the 1950s homosexuals were isolated from each other, and homosexuality as a social issue was isolated from other issues. Although a homosexual may have known a few others, few homosexuals were open, "out of the closet," about their homosexuality, and fewer still were engaged in organizational and political activities to legitimize homosexuality. Hence, in the 1950s the cultural and behavioral differences between homosexuals and heterosexuals (subjects and authorities, respectively, in Turk's terms) were not a source of conflict. Conflict started in the 1960s when homosexuals came "out of the closet," linking homosexuality with other social issues, and organized for political purposes.

As to the second question, Turk also specified two conditions that increase the probability that legal norms will be enforced: when legal norms reflect cultural norms and when subjects have little power. Concerning the first condition, laws that are culturally significant to authorities are the most prone to be enforced. Thus, the probability of becoming a criminal in the United States is higher for violating burglary than price-fixing laws. The former violates both the laws and cultural norms of authorities, while the latter violates only the laws. The police subculture is also important. Police are the first line of defense and have considerable discretion in deciding what laws to enforce and when to enforce them. Laws that are consistent with the police subculture may be strongly enforced (laws on robbery), whereas those that are inconsistent with the police subculture may be only weakly enforced (laws on civil rights). Concerning the second condition, laws are most rigorously enforced against those who have the least power to resist. Turk argued that enforcement agencies carry out their functions so as to minimize their efforts. Consequently, they scrutinize the powerless, who have few resources to resist, rather than the powerful, who have resources to purchase the best legal assistance, in many cases better than that of the enforcement agencies.

To summarize, Turk specified the conditions when group differences generate group conflict and when legal norms (laws) are enforced. We now turn to three forms of social conflicts that are pervasive in contemporary society—economic, racial, and gender—and explore their implications for law formulation and application.

ECONOMIC CONFLICT

Drawing on traditional Marxism, economic conflict theorists argue that an underlying social conflict exists between those who own and control the means of production and those who do not. Those who control economic relationships constitute a ruling class that also controls social relationships in other institutions. Political, educational, and religious authorities serve their interests. This thesis has been developed in the works of numerous criminologists since the early 1970s, such as Richard Quinney, Steven Spitzer, and Piers Beirne.

As an economic conflict theorist, Richard Quinney (1974, 1977) defined the ruling class as those who own and control the means of production (the capitalists). He argued that laws in contemporary America and generally in the Western world reflect their interests and that their interests determine when and to whom laws are applied. Laws are selectively enforced against those people who threaten their interests; but when members of the ruling class themselves violate laws, those laws are not rigorously enforced. To some extent this may be true, because the ruling class tends to violate not the laws of property that are rigorously enforced (burglary, robbery, and theft) but the laws of property that are not rigorously enforced (antitrust, stock manipulation, and environmental protection). Thus, much discrimination in law enforcement is in effect discrimination in what laws are enforced. Yet, even when members of the ruling class violate laws that are generally enforced (laws of theft and personal safety), Quinney maintained that these laws are not as rigorously enforced against them as they are against the lower class.

In addition to the government, Quinney argued that major institutions (education, religion, and mass media) support the interests of the ruling class. He was particularly concerned with the development and perpetuation of a moral order that legitimizes the capitalistic legal order and with the role of various institutions in sustaining that order. For if those who neither own nor control the means of production come to accept capitalist definitions of morality, they will pattern their behavior to conform to these definitions and thus to the interests of capitalist rather than to their own interests. Quinney criticized the mass media for disseminating capitalist definitions of crime. The mass media (newspapers, magazines, radio, movies, and television) focus on lower-class crimes and ignore the crimes of big business unless they constitute sensational events. The success of the media, according to Quinney, is evidenced by the fact that the public has come to view street crime as one of the most, if not the most, serious of the problems facing society. Quinney also criticized intellectuals, who generate and articulate this ideology, and religious leaders, who support the capitalist system by adhering to the law and advocating the rule of law and who condemn from the pulpit crimes of the lower class against the property of the ruling class. He likewise criticized social scientists (criminologists and sociologists) whose theories and research on crime (generally lower-class crime) are used by the ruling class to justify social inequality and to control the behavior of the lower class.

While Quinney's theory provides a general analysis of crime and crime control in a capitalist society, various other radical conflict theorists have outlined in more detail the social processes by which a capitalist economic structure affects the nature of crime control. Steven Spitzer (1975), for example, discussed the classes of people that constitute problems for a capitalist society, how these classes of people are created within a capitalist society, and how they are controlled (criminalized):

(1) People become social problems in a capitalist society when they impede or hinder any of the following: the mode of production (e.g., people who refuse or are unable to work); the mode of distribution (e.g., the poor who steal from the rich); the processes of socialization into the modes of production and distribution (e.g., youth who do not attend or do poorly in school); and the ideology that supports these modes of production and distribution (e.g., vocal advocates of economic reform or revolution).

(2) Problematic people are created by two inherent contradictions in the capitalist system. In advanced capitalism, competition among capitalists culminates in the failure of many capitalists, thereby increasing the ranks of the proletarian class, and in advanced capitalism the economic order becomes increasingly technological and cyclical, thereby increasing the surplus population (those who play no useful economic role). Both the proletarian class and the surplus population hinder the conditions of production and distribution. Moreover, mass education, which is needed in a technologically advanced capitalist society, sharpens the critical abilities of the sons and daughters of laborers, creating a population potentially critical of the capitalist ideology.

(3) Under what circumstances are problematic populations criminalized or controlled as criminals? Spitzer hypothesized that criminalization (law enactment and enforcement) increases as the size of the problematic population increases, as the political organization of the problematic popu-

lation increases, and as other forms of social control, such as institutions of informal social control (the family, the church, the schools) become less effective.

Spitzer thus maintained that criminalization of problematic populations is not inevitable in a capitalist society. Rather, it depends on the extent to which problematic populations are perceived as threatening, which in turn is related to their size, their degree of political organization, and the effectiveness of other forms of social control.

Another influential formulation of economic conflict theory is that of Piers Beirne (1979). Beirne argued that many contemporary conflict theorists have misinterpreted Marxian theory regarding the relationship between class interests and the legal system (law formulation and enforcement). They assume a direct and simple linkage between the interests of the capitalist ruling class and the law and that the capitalist class uses the state and the legal system as instruments to implement their interests. Studies focus on the social processes, such as lobbying and political campaign financing, by which their interests are transformed into law.

Beirne (1979) argued that while this undoubtedly occurs, it is not the norm and is not necessarily implied by Marxism. He classified Marxists into two schools: instrumentalists, who assume that the state functions as an instrument of the capitalist class; and structuralists, who assume that the capitalist class is not homogeneous and unified and that the state exercises considerable autonomy from the interests of any specific social class. Thus, the capitalist class cannot always manipulate the legal system. The state may frequently pursue policies not necessarily in the interests of the capitalist class or may even pursue interests opposed to it. (See also Lynch and Groves 1986.)

Beirne's conceptualization of structural Marxism is clearly less economically deterministic than that of many conflict theorists, who view every law as somehow reflecting the interests of the capitalist class; Beirne nevertheless argued that, while not every law reflects the immediate interests of the capitalist class, most laws reflect its long-term interests. This distinction between short- and long-term interests allows Beirne to reconcile such laws as welfare for the unemployed, antitrust laws, and corporate taxes, which do not seem to be in the immediate interests of the capitalist class, with the Marxian contention that law formulation and enforcement reflect the long-term interests of the capitalist class. This distinction and logic can sometimes be torturous. For example, the New Deal legislation of the 1930s and 40s seems to have represented the interests of labor, not capital; but structural Marxists argue that in the long term it represented the interests of capital. Without some reform legislation like that of the New Deal, a more radical economic and social revolution would have occurred. This legislation, by reforming and moderating the most exploitive economic relationships of capitalism, in actuality preserved it.

The work of the economic (radical) criminologists can be briefly summarized as follows: Law enactment and enforcement serve the interests, especially the long-term interests, of those who own and control the means of production—the capitalists; and when problematic populations are not controlled by informal institutions, like the family, they are criminalized and controlled by the state. These conflict theorists shift our attention to issues not normally studied by criminologists. They emphasize the political nature of crime. Rather than studying why people violate the legal order, they focus our attention on the legal order itself. While many sociologists may not agree with them, it is important that the legal order be studied. Specifically, it is important that we study the relationship between ownership and control of the means of production and the enactment and enforcement of criminal laws, and the extent to which other institutions and even scholarship function in the service of special interests.

RACIAL CONFLICT

Many scholars have pointed out that too much conflict theory, whether Marxian or not, is based almost exclusively on class. Ethnicity and race are also important in their own right, and not only to the extent to which they link to class. The poor are not treated equally badly; some are treated worse than others.

In one of the first general works on majority-minority relations, Blalock (1967) examined the social processes that underlie minority discrimination, which functions as a major social mechanism by which majorities control minorities. Minority discrimination is hypothesized to result from economic and political threat to majorities, which in turn is related to minority size (proportion of the population); resources (money, property, prestige, authority, education, voting rights); and mobilization (organization of resources). As minorities increase in size, resources, and mobilization they begin to threaten the political and economic interests of majorities. The majorities, in turn, frequently respond with various forms of discrimination—by restricting economic and educational opportunities and restricting political rights (disenfranchisement), which in turn reduce minority resources, and by geographical segregation, which reduces the power associated with minority size.

Twenty years later, Hawkins (1987) directly applied Blalock's analysis to law enactment and enforcement. He too pointed out that much of conflict theory, whether Marxian or not, is too class based. Race and ethnicity continue to be viewed as important only to the extent to which they correlate with class. Independently of class (and the power associated with it) do ethnicity and race matter? In other words, are the poor of all ethnic groups and races equally discriminated against? Relying on historical analysis, Hawkins concluded that the Italians and Irish experienced considerably more legal discrimination than other ethnic groups. What singled them out? Drawing somewhat on Blalock, Hawkins identified three factors: size, insularity, and isolation. (1) Compared to other ethnic groups, the Irish and Italian immigrations were very large, and large minorities are more threatening than small ones who can easily be ignored. (2) Some minorities are able to insulate themselves from the majority, either by specializing in a few occupations or by residing in urban enclaves (Asians) or rural areas (Germans and Scandinavians). These minorities can easily be ignored by authorities, whereas immigrant groups (Italians and Irish) who settle in urban areas and compete over a range of occupations cannot be ignored. (3) Minorities who are culturally or physically different from the majority are likely to be perceived as threatening. All of these factors together may explain why some ethnics in earlier periods were perceived as more threatening than others, and why nonwhites today are experienced as more threatening than white ethnics.

Moreover, Hawkins observed that this focus on class, explicit for some and implicit for others, leads to the neglect of many avenues of research and to the interpretation of some findings on race as anomalies. For example, scholars have failed to incorporate into conflict theory findings showing that black offenders of white victims receive more punishment than black offenders of black victims. This pattern has been overlooked because it is not exactly clear how the race of the victim is linked to the class of the offender and to class conflict. In addition, scholars have failed to incorporate into conflict theory findings showing that blacks who commit crimes that conform to racial stereotypes are underpunished (rape and homicide) and those that commit crimes that violate race norms are overpunished (white collar crimes), because this pattern of law enforcement is not well explained within a class-based conflict theory. Finally, scholars have failed to incorporate into conflict theory the finding that blacks tend to receive more punishment in the South than in the North, because it is not clear how this geographical pattern relates to class conflict.

SYNTHESIZING ECONOMIC AND RACIAL CONFLICT THEORIES

While these theories of group conflict are similar, they focus on different social processes and describe them in very different terms. Turk's theory emphasizes authority-subject conflicts and criminalization; Blalock's and Hawkins' emphasize racial conflict and discrimination; Quinney's emphasizes capitalist-proletarian conflicts and social control; and Spitzer's emphasizes problematic populations and criminalization. These differences are not just differences of terminology, although there is some of that; there are real differences among these theories regarding who and what are threatening to whom. As to who is threatening, the Marxists (Quinney and Spitzer) refer to economic elites; Turk refers to institutional authorities; Blalock refers to majorities; and Hawkins (1987, 1994) refers to white ethnics. As to what is threatened, the Marxists refer to economic positions, Turk refers to authority positions, and Blalock and Hawkins refer to social positions. As to who are threatening, Quinney refers to proletarian and surplus labor; Turk refers to cultural differences between authorities and subjects and to the organization of subjects; Blalock and Hawkins refer to the relative size, resources, and mobilization of minorities; and Spitzer refers to the relative size and organization of problematic populations.

Despite the bewildering array of concepts (problematic populations, surplus populations, minority populations, culturally dissimilar populations), there is a common logic that underlies these theories. Social control is a response of a ruling social category (economic elites, organizational authorities, majorities) to perceived social threat that is a function of the relative size, power, organization, and mobilization of subjected social categories—the threatening populations (see Figure 7.1).

GENDER CONFLICT

Traditionally, scholarship on gender was directed by Marxian theories in which gender conflict was subservient to class conflict. However, by the 1980s feminist scholarship moved away from traditional Marxism and emphasized gender conflict as fundamental (Edwards 1988). Scholars, such as Daly (1989, 1194) and Chesney-Lind (1988), argued that gender conflict is at least as important as class and race conflict. Most societies are organized around patriarchal principles in which females are subordinated to males, and social, economic, and political inequalities in societies are tied more to gender than to class and race. Feminist scholars have sought to document the pervasiveness of the control of females in the interests of males and thereby to provide a critique of the social arrangements through which that control is exercised. Yet, while feminist theory has moved away from class and race conflict, much of the work on gender and social control has continued to treat gender conflict as analogous to class conflict. While there are clear similarities between gender conflict and class and ethnic/racial conflict, there are some distinct differences that change the nature of social threat and social control and thus the relationships between conflict, threat, and control.

Gender conflict is over much of the same things that class and racial conflicts are over: economic resources, political power, and social status. But because the conflicting genders are not physically segregated, but indeed seem to need each other in fundamental ways, the conflict is less

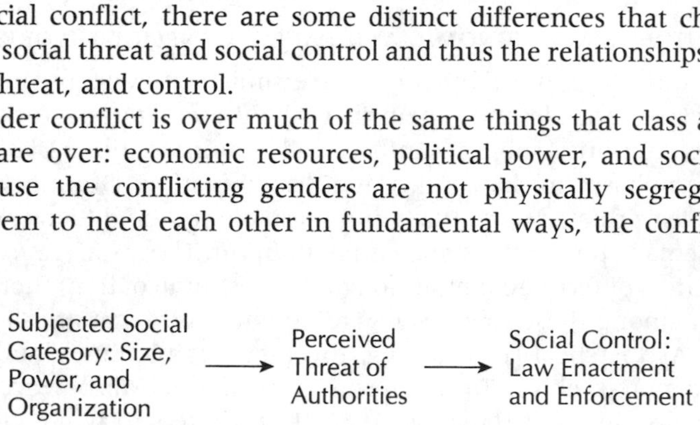

Subjected Social Category: Size, Power, and Organization $\longrightarrow$ Perceived Threat of Authorities $\longrightarrow$ Social Control: Law Enactment and Enforcement

FIGURE 7.1   SOCIAL THREAT MODEL OF SOCIAL CONTROL

physically threatening and may be less socially threatening as well—the sleeping with the enemy hypothesis.

This difference has implications for the nature of social threat. Subordinate groups that are not physically and socially isolated from super-ordinate groups, but are integrated with them in social institutions (family and work) are unlikely to be perceived as physically threatening and dangerous, especially as not dangerously criminal. This is not to suggest that females are not perceived as threatening to males. They are perceived by many males as economically, politically, and socially threatening. The magnitude of the threat may vary in direct proportion to the extent to which females deviate from conventional roles that function as vehicles of social control. While even employed married females may pose something of an economic threat, employed single females may pose both an economic and political threat; and employed, single, gay females may pose economic, political, and social threats.

These differences between gender and class conflict have implications for social threat. Concerned with physical threats (violence and crime), studies of class and racial threat have focused on the size of the disenfranchised group (the percentage of minorities, the unemployed, and the proletarian), which has no real counterpoint for gender conflict. Gender ratios are relatively invariant over political units.

Ignoring these differences between class and gender threat has led to thinking about the control of females in much the same ways as the control of the lower class and of racial and ethnic minorities. This is reflected in the large number of studies of females and the criminal justice system, although females constitute a very small portion of the those under control in that system (Rafter 1992b; Daly 1994). We do not want to discourage these studies. They are important to documenting the relationship between gender and criminal sanctioning. Yet, if we want to study gender and social control, focusing on the criminal justice system may divert us from where the action is. We agree with feminists who argue that the control of women in most contemporary societies takes place outside of formal bureaucracies of control and that when formal bureaucracies are used, the criminal justice system is the least used. When formal bureaucracies of control are used, females are controlled within the mental health system, which treats their deviance as irrational, and within the welfare system, which focuses on their family status.

In sum, because females are not physically segregated and not perceived as physically dangerous, and because they are needed by males in fundamental ways, such as sexual partners, spouses, and mothers, they are unlikely to be controlled by long term physical segregation (the criminal justice system). They are more likely to be controlled within families (see Hagan's work on gender and family control: Hagan et al. 1985, 1987); and when that is not effective some are controlled as being irresponsible by the welfare system (unmarried mothers) and some are controlled as being irrational by the mental health system.

SUMMARY

This section discussed conflict theories. Sellin (1938) and Vold (1958) might well be considered the first conflict theorists to have had a major impact on the study of deviance and crime. Generally, they argued that some crimes can be understood in terms of cultural and group conflict. Groups conflict over what is proper behavior; and some groups have the power to transform their cultural norms into laws. By the mid-1960s, conflict theories had become quite prominent and their influence extends to the present. Some theories focus on conflict generally, endeavoring to explain when group differences eventuate into open conflict and when law violators are criminalized. Some focus on economic conflict, arguing that law enactment and enforcement reflects the interests of those who own and control the means of production. Some focus on ethnic and racial conflict, arguing that law enactment and enforcement reflect the interests of ethnic and racial majorities. And some focus on gender conflict, also arguing that law enactment and enforcement reflect the interests of males. Whatever their focus, these theorists attempt to specify the conditions (e.g., group size) under which some groups are perceived as threatening by the powerful (upper class, whites, or males) and the conditions under which the powerful respond by various forms of discrimination, including the enactment and enforcement of laws that protect their interests.

RESEARCH

This section examines the general relationship between group or class interests and law formulation and enforcement.

LAW FORMULATION

The study of law formulation endeavors to explain why some rules of conduct become law—specified by the state, subject to sanction by the state, and enforced by specially authorized personnel of the state. Contrary to consensus theories, which view laws as reflecting the rules of conduct that are most widely agreed upon and intensely supported in society, conflict theories assume that power differentials between groups determine which rules of conduct become laws and which group interests become transformed into the interests of the state. This section focuses on the interests of the most powerful group in western societies (business) and how their interests are transformed in the law.

Business laws refer to laws governing the ownership, management, and transfer of property. It is instructive to begin with a discussion of the origin and development of some contemporary business laws, drawing on Jerome Hall's (1952) extensive historical research on the development of the contemporary law of theft and on the group and class interests that affected its development. Prior to the fourteenth century in Europe, it was a crime to forcibly take people's property while it was in their possession. However, there was no law governing the ownership of property entrusted to a person for transportation. It was an owner's responsibility to select trustworthy carriers. This legal arrangement was consistent with authority-subject relationships of the feudalistic social structure. Communities were mainly agricultural and somewhat self-sufficient, making the transportation of property between communities an exception to daily life. Also, the relationship between authorities and subjects (at least between authorities and their immediate subordinates) was enduring. Thus, selecting trustworthy persons as carriers was probably not the problem it is today.

With the commercialization and industrialization of the fifteenth century, this social arrangement changed. Communities became less self-sufficient, commercial trade developed between communities, and some communities emerged as trade or commercial centers; with the geographical movement of people, social relationships became less enduring. Consequently, while owners of property had a great need for trustworthy carriers, they had great difficulty finding them. This change in social conditions and the emergence of a new business class created a new interest: the protection of property while in transit.

A legal change occurred with the Carrier case in England in 1473. A person, employed to carry bales to Southampton, transported them to another area, broke the bales, and absconded with the contents. He was later caught and charged with a crime. What crime? The carrier had legally obtained possession of the goods. No law had been broken. The judge at the time argued as follows: "Breaking the bulk" ended the arrangement between the owner and carrier, and the goods legally reverted back to the possession of the owner. The carrier thus illegally acquired the goods.

In sum, the commercial revolution created a powerful new economic class with new legal interests (secure trade). It was just a matter of time before their interests were reflected in the law. This law (judicial decision) provided the foundation for contemporary laws that govern the management and transportation of property.

Another excellent example of historical research is the study of the relationship between economic interests and the origins and development of vagrancy laws. Vagrancy laws exist in nearly all states and tend to be used either to arrest "undesirables" who have violated no other laws or to force undesirables to leave the community. In a classic study, Chambliss (1964) suggested that the social conditions in England around the twelfth century, in conjunction with the interests of the landed aristocracy, explain the origin of these laws. The Black Death plague and the Crusades reduced the labor supply by 50 percent; industrialization and commercialization made urban areas more attractive to serfs; and the Crusades impoverished many of the landed aristocracy. Vagrancy laws were an effort of the landed aristocracy to control their labor supply in a time of need. In effect, the laws made it illegal to travel and to accept or to give charity, thus providing a ready and cheap supply of labor to the landed aristocracy. Incidentally, the vagrancy laws were also in the interests of the Church of England. At the time, partially because of the Crusades, the Church was in dire financial straits. With the passing of the vagrancy laws, the Church could dismiss its traditional social obligation to the poor. After some time, the labor supply increased and the administration of the laws was relaxed. By the sixteenth century the laws were revived to protect the interests of the new commercial class in being able to conduct trade in a safe and orderly manner. They were used to rid the community and countryside of undesirables, people who were potential thieves and sources of disruption. (For a critique of Chambliss and an alternative interpretation of vagrancy laws, see Adler 1989.)

During the twentieth century, various laws have been passed, presumably in the interests of labor, consumers, and the general public, that regulate business and commercial interests. Many conflict scholars have argued that these laws do nothing of the kind because they are not effectively enforced. Furthermore, because they provide the illusion that business interests are being regulated, they are in effect in the interests of business! We now examine some of the research on the enforcement of laws regulating business interests.

The enforcement of business law occurs in two stages: the selection of cases to investigate and prosecute, and the punishment of those found guilty. Compared to street crime, discovering violations is difficult. Those who have been victimized are frequently not even aware of it, violations are complex, offenders have the resources to conceal their crimes, and enforcement agencies have limited resources to discover them. For street crime, the resources of the state generally overwhelm the resources of those accused; but for business crimes it is the resources of the accused that overwhelm those of the state. Hence, most business crimes are never discovered, and of those that are discovered, most are never prosecuted. To illustrate, Coleman (1994) reported that 1,298 cases of fraud and embezzlement, each involving over $100,000, were classified as inactive in the Justice Department files in 1990 because of lack of resources to prosecute them. Coleman further noted that an antitrust case brought against Exxon by the Federal Trade Commission consumed 12 to 14 percent of the agency's antitrust budget, yet after eight years of investigations the case was dropped because of its "length and complexity."

These cases, of course, are only examples and are presented here as just that: to illustrate the extent to which laws meant to regulate the interests of business corporations are weakly enforced. More systematic research shows that these cases are reasonably representative of the enforcement of business laws. McCormick (1977) found that, from 1890 to 1969, 1,551 antitrust prosecutions were initiated under the Sherman Antitrust law. Forty-five percent were criminal cases (all could have been) and 35 percent led to criminal convictions; however, less than 2 percent (twenty-six cases) resulted in served sentences, which rarely exceeded six months with an average of approximately three months. Of these twenty-six cases, the first eleven involved union and labor defendants, and twenty-three of the twenty-six involved labor misconduct or violence. It was not until the electrical conspiracy case in 1961 that business people were imprisoned for price fixing and monopolization under the Sherman Anti-Trust Act. McCormick referred to these sentences as so light as to be viewed as a "reasonable license fee for engaging in illegal conduct." Cases such as these suggest that if any criminals are being "coddled" by the criminal justice system, it is the middle- and upper-class criminals violating laws meant to regulate business.

The extensiveness of corporate crime and the minimal level of government enforcement of the law is fully documented in a study by Marshall B. Clinard and Peter C. Yeager (1980) of the enforcement actions against the 582 largest publicly owned corporations in the United States (477 manufacturing, 18 wholesale, 66 retail, and 21 service). This is the most extensive study of corporate crime ever undertaken. During a two year period, a total of 1,365 enforcement actions were initiated against these corporations, but very few involved criminal proceedings. For example, there were 1,258 enforcement actions against the 477 manufacturing corporations, of which 66 percent resulted in a sanction; but 88.1 percent of the sanctions were administrative, 9.2 percent were civil, and only 2.7 percent were criminal. Rarely was a convicted executive imprisoned. Of the sixty-one convicted executives of parent corporations, 19 percent received probation, 10 percent a suspended sentence, 63 percent a fine, and only 8 percent were incarcerated. In nearly all of the latter cases, the sentences ranged from one to six months.

Both McCormack's historical study (1890–1969) of the enforcement of one law (Sherman Anti-Trust law) and Clinard and Yaeger's study of numerous business corporations of the late 1970s came to the same conclusion: Law violations by businesses are widespread and enforcement is minimal. Does this conclusion still hold today? While no study as extensive as Clinard and Yaeger's has been funded (funding has focused on street crimes), more limited studies of particular industries arrive at the same conclusion. Perhaps the most recent and comprehensive is the investigation of the savings and loan industry. Coleman (1994), citing reports from the General Accounting Office, found the following: The top 100 referrals for theft/fraud made to the Justice Department involved $600 million, resulted in 219 indictments, 145 convictions, $79 million in court-ordered restitution, and $4.5 million in fines; however, less than one-half million in restitution and $15,000 in fines had been collected—less than one percent of the total. Concerning the failure of twenty-six savings and loan institutions, the Justice Department received referrals recommending criminal charges against 182 people; but at the time of Coleman's research only 23 had been convicted, and of those only 15 received prison sentences. Coleman's conclusion about the lenient treatment of business law offenders is reaffirmed by the testimony of the U.S. Attorney for Southern California who appeared before Congress. The attorney testified that 60 percent of the bank fraud convictions end in probation, 10 percent receive a sentence of less than one year, and less than 5 percent receive sentences of five or more years (Calavita and Pontell 1990). It seems that while highly publicized cases (Michael Milken and Ivan Boesky) may lead to prison sentences, most cases do not receive any more punishment today than they did in the past. Why? Part of the answer is simple and suggested by conflict theory. Government agencies charged with enforcing business laws have limited resources, and business organizations have the resources to resist.

To summarize, research shows that economic interests played a major role in the historical formulation of laws regarding theft and vagrancy and that present laws enacted to regulate the behavior of economic-interest groups (such as price fixing and false advertising) are minimally enforced. Generally, corporations make whatever profits they can from violating certain laws. When the government catches up to them (if it ever does), they must cease and desist, and they frequently use some of these profits to pay a fine. Thus, considerable research supports the general proposition that "what is crime" and "who is the criminal" depend to a large extent on the power of groups who own and control the means of production.

LEVEL OF LAW ENFORCEMENT: THREAT AND NEGLECT

Conflict theory assumes that law enforcement (rates of arrest, prosecution, convictions, prison admissions, etc.) expands when the ruling class perceives its interests to be threatened. Perceived threat is thought to be associated not only with the presence of threatening acts (crime and civil disorders) but with the presence of categories of people associated with these acts (unemployed and nonwhites). As the presence of problematic acts and people increases, the ruling class strengthens the capacity of the crime control apparatus and pressures the existing crime control apparatus to expand and increase its activities. Two crime control bureaucracies have been the subject of considerable research: prisons and police.

Prisons Numerous studies have examined the emergence and development of prisons in the late eighteenth and nineteenth centuries in the West. Conflict theorists explain the development of prisons as a systematic effort on the part of authorities to control the large urban masses of immigrants and migrants of the eighteenth and nineteenth centuries and to manage the labor supply. A capitalistic system needs a ready supply of laborers who respect private property. Prison segregates those who do not respect property rights from the ranks of labor (a divide-and-conquer strategy) and instills moral and work discipline in the masses. Rusche and Kirchheimer (1939) were among the first to argue that during times of economic depression prisons absorb the unemployed, and during times of prosperity they provide a ready supply of labor. Developing this theme, contemporary conflict theorists emphasize the threatening nature of unemployment to the social relationships of production.

In studying the relationship between the unemployment and prison admission rates, crime rates must be controlled. Unemployment rates affect them. It is important to distinguish the direct effects of unemployment rates on prison admission rates from their indirect effects through crime rates. Distinct from other perspectives, conflict theory posits that it is the unemployed, themselves, not just the high crime rates that follow high unemployment, that are threatening to authorities. (See Figure 7.2.)

There is a long history of studying this relationship. Using time series from the mid-1940s to the 1970s, the early studies consistently showed a positive relationship between unemployment and imprisonment rates (see the work by Jankovic [1977] and Yeager [1979] on the United States, and the work by Greenberg [1977] on Canada). Many of these studies share one major limitation: The time series from the mid-1940s to the mid-1970s (about twenty-five to thirty years) is a relatively short period in which to examine unemployment cycles and it covers a peculiar period of time characterized by neither a major war nor an economic depression. Indeed, Jankovic (1977), using a longer series in the United States from 1929 to 1974, found that the positive relationship between unemployment and imprisonment rates does not hold during the depression and war years. His analysis highlights the fact that prisons can only absorb a small proportion of the population. In "normal" times they can absorb a significant portion of the unemployed, but when the rate of unemployment reaches epidemic proportions, such as during a depression, they can absorb only an insignificant proportion of them.

Studying a long series from 1851 to 1970 in the state of California, Berk et al. (1981) observed a positive relationship between depressions and growth in imprisonment rates; and studying a long series from 1882 to

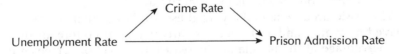

FIGURE 7.2   EFFECTS OF UNEMPLOYMENT ON PRISON ADMISSIONS RATE

1930 and from 1868 to 1936 in the state of Georgia, Tolnay and Beck (1995) and Myers (1995) detected a negative relationship between the price of cotton (a measure of prosperity) and the lynching of blacks and the imprisonment of both blacks and whites. Unfortunately, because these studies do not control for crime rates, the underlying causal processes remain unclear. A major dilemma in these time series studies seems to be whether to analyze recent series that tend to be short but include information on the most relevant variables such as crime rates; or to analyze historical series that cover long time spans but do not include information on many relevant variables.

The results from more recent studies examining data from the late 1970s and 80s seem to be even more ambiguous. For example, Galster and Scaturo (1985), in a cross-sectional analysis of all fifty U.S. states, found little empirical support for a positive effect of unemployment on imprisonment rates for any year from 1976 to 1981, although they did uncover some support of an effect for southern states. Recently, D'Alessio and Stolzenberg (1995) in a time series study found a positive and statistically significant unemployment effect on jail inmate rates that falls to insignificance when time trends are controlled.

It is clearly difficult to draw any conclusion if we examine these studies one at a time. What is needed is a summary analysis of all of them. Chiricos and Delone (1992) conducted just such an analysis (called a meta analysis) of 44 studies that yield 262 tests of the relationship between unemployment and imprisonment rates. Of those that control for crime rates, 83 percent of these relationships are positive and 55 percent are positive and statistically significant, thus supportive of conflict theory. Although the exact percentage varies by the dependent variable (admission or incarceration rates), by the research design (cross-section or time series), a mean of 55 percent is very high by social science standards.

Police   The size and functioning of the police force have also been the subject of considerable research. To a large extent the volume of crime control is limited by the processing capacity of the police department, which is a direct function of police size and police expenditures per capita. The rapid expansion of police forces during the 1960s and 70s stimulated research on the causes of this growth. Around 1980 three studies (Jacobs 1979; Jackson and Carroll 1981; Liska et al. 1981) examined the size of police departments from 1950 to 1970. While they studied the effects of various structural variables, including crime rates, population size, revenue, and income inequality, here we focus on the effects of racial threat.

The basic argument underlying these studies is that nonwhites are perceived by whites and authorities as threatening; therefore, as the nonwhite percentage of the population increases, the level of perceived threat increases. This in turn is reflected in greater support for crime control, such as increased funds for bureaucracies charged with controlling crime, such as police and prisons. In support of their argument, the early studies consistently found a substantial effect of the nonwhite percentage of the population on police size. This effect was stronger in 1970, following the civil disorders, than in 1960, and it was stronger in the South, which has had a long history of racial conflict, than in the non-South, further supporting their argument. For example, Jackson (1989) found that as the percentage of nonwhites increased from 10 to 40 percent police size increased, but as the nonwhite population increased above 40 percent, police size began to decrease. She argued that as the nonwhite population approaches 50 percent, nonwhites are no longer a minority; they are approaching a size large enough to achieve political power and authority, and nonwhite authorities are supported, not threatened, by a nonwhite majority.

Research has continued to fine-tune these findings. Chamlin (1989) argued that changes in racial composition (e.g., percent nonwhite) may be more threatening to authorities than mere levels of racial composition. He found that changes in police size from 1972 to 1982, while not affected by levels, were significantly affected by changes in both percent nonwhite and racial segregation. Jackson (1989) reported that in western and southern cities the percentage of Hispanics had more effect on police size than did the percentage of blacks; that the percentage of both Hispanics and blacks had stronger effects in large than in small cities; and that the curvilinear effect of the percentage of nonwhites (decreasing effect after 40 percent) was more evident in large than in small cities. She argued that the threat associated with the presence of minorities has decreased since the 1960s, a period marked by racial disorder, and is ameliorated by informal social control in small cities.

Liska and Chamlin (1984) extended this work on police size to the study of arrests. Clearly, the arrest rate of nonwhites is higher than that of whites. However, contrary to the threat hypothesis that an increase in the proportion of nonwhites increases people's sense of threat and thus the arrest rate of nonwhites, their findings showed that an increase in the percentage of nonwhites decreased the arrest rate of nonwhites. Liska and Chamlin suggested that this occurs for the following reason: As the percentage of nonwhites increases, the victims of nonwhite offenders also tend to be nonwhite. Nonwhite victims may be less able to define their misfortunes and victimizations as crimes deserving of police attention; crime between nonwhites may be treated as a personal matter rather than as a legal problem requiring police intervention. Hence, not only may authorities link nonwhites with the threat of crime, but authorities may also be insensitive to nonwhites' legitimate needs for protection from crime. Recently, Chamlin and Liska (1992) further extended these findings. They found that in the 1980s, an increase in the percentage of nonwhites was associated with a decrease in the property and personal arrest rates of both whites and nonwhites. They argued that a large percentage of nonwhites creates a general context or climate of neglect wherein both nonwhite and white victims experience indifference in legitimizing their complaints as crimes and mobilizing the police.

Now, how is it possible that the percentage of nonwhites increases the size of the police force but decreases control activities (arrests)? These decisions are made by different authorities. The percentage of nonwhites may be perceived as threatening by urban authorities who make decisions about budgets, but nonwhite victims may simply lack the power to influence the allocation of police resources to their cases, leading to neglect.

Perhaps the major finding across these studies is that, with a few exceptions, racial distributions of people (percent of nonwhite and residential segregation) have a more consistent effect than do economic distributions (percent poor, percent unemployed, and income inequality) on forms of crime control. To explain this, Liska (1992) proposed that the white poor are frequently viewed as respectable, while nonwhites are believed to be associated with crime. This perceived association was strengthened during the 1960s and early 1970s, the time of racial disorder in the United States, and has always been stronger in the South than in the non-South. This argument is supported by survey data, showing that the fear of crime is strongly associated with the percentage of nonwhites, controlling for the crime rate (Liska et al. 1982).

The implications for conflict theory are significant. Traditional conflict theory is couched and framed in terms of conflict between different economic classes. The crime control apparatus is thought to protect the interests of the propertied class, whose members feel threatened when conflict is accentuated by increases in income inequality, the percent unemployed, and the percent poor. In other words, crime control is thought to maintain economic relationships, particularly in times of economic crises and conflict. Racial distributions are thought to be important only to the extent to which they are linked to these economic conditions, that is, when racial minorities constitute much of the unemployed and the poor.

An alternative interpretation has been proposed by Liska et al. (1992). The strong racial composition effect may mean that the perceived threat of crime, rather than a general perceived threat to the economic order, is the catalyst to crime control. The control of street crime is what it seems to be— a response to the specific threat of crime, not a strategy to manage the economic order. Nonwhites in the contemporary United States have become culturally associated with crime; thus, an increase in the percentage of nonwhites and a decrease in racial segregation increase the day-to-day visibility of nonwhites, which in turn increases the perceived threat of crime to whites. In sum, this research suggests that in the contemporary United States, racial conflict may be more important than economic conflict in understanding crime control.

SELECTIVE ENFORCEMENT: RACE, CLASS, AND GENDER

While the previous section focuses on the general level of law enforcement, this section examines selectivity or discrimination in law enforcement. Conflict theorists state that power plays a major role in determining which people are the objects of enforcement: "... [T]hose people are arrested, tried and sentenced who can offer the fewest rewards for nonenforcement of the laws and who can be processed without creating any undue strain for the organizations which comprise the legal system" (Chambliss 1969, 84). The power to resist enforcement is linked to social class, race, and gender. Consider class. Conflict theorists argue that middle-class parents have the capacity to resist the enforcement of the law at all stages. At the arrest level, the middle-class juvenile is handled cautiously because his or her parents have the capacity to make trouble for the officer, such as initiating false arrest and slander suits. At the prosecution and court levels, the resources of the middle and upper classes are even more evident. They can afford lawyers to bargain with the prosecutor or juvenile officer over charges and over what should be done with their child, and they can also afford private detectives and expert witnesses, such as social workers and psychiatrists. They can also provide positive alternatives to legal prosecution. Rather than sending their child to an overcrowded facility and exposing him or her to hardened delinquents, middle-class parents can suggest that their child be placed in their custody. They have the resources to provide professional help (psychiatric counseling and placement in summer camps) or even to change neighborhoods and schools.

Class and Race   Research on selective law enforcement by class and race can be organized into three time periods. During the first period (early 1960s to the mid-1970s), research showed substantial racial and class disparities in the criminal justice system. At just about all decision points, the lower-class and racial minorities were substantially overrepresented, which was taken to reflect discrimination.

During the second period (mid-1970s to early 1980s) these early studies were severely criticized for weak methods, especially for not controlling for the effects of legal variables, such as prior offenses and the seriousness of the present offense. If the lower-class and racial minorities commit more offenses and more serious ones, then the fact that they are arrested, prosecuted, and imprisoned more than the middle-class and racial majorities is not evidence of racial and class discrimination in law enforcement; rather it simply reflects differences in offending by class and race. Since the mid-1970s, numerous studies have examined the effects of class and race on legal decision making while controlling for the effects of legal variables. (In other words, they have compared the arrests, prosecutions, and sentencing of lower class, middle class, and upper class, and of whites, blacks, and

Hispanics with similar types of present and past crimes.) While a few of these studies still reported race and class effects, some favoring the upper class and majority and others favoring the lower class and racial minorities, the vast majorities of studies found very little class and race effects (Hagan 1974; Hagan and Bumiller 1983; Kleck 1981). Two comprehensive reviews of the literature—Hagan and Bumiller's (1983) review of sixty studies and Kleck's (1981) review of fifty-seven studies—came to the same conclusion: Race affects criminal justice decision making because it affects the seriousness of the present offense and the number of prior offenses; once these are controlled, race has little direct effect.

While these findings across numerous studies might have ended the debate, they have actually stimulated a third stage of studies (from about the mid-1980s to today) that have examined the extent to which class and race effects, while not simple and direct, depend on place, time, and crime. That is, if minorities are oversentenced for some crimes and undersentenced for others, and if they are oversentenced in some places and undersentenced in others, then the net race effects may appear to be null, although they are substantial but variable. Recent studies have examined race effects for different crimes, times, and places.

The place studies are very interesting. There are two types of effects: (1) Place characteristics (e.g., percent poor and percent nonwhite) directly affect criminal justice decision making, and (2) they condition the effects of individual-level legal and extra-legal variables. For example, various studies have examined the extent to which the racial composition of neighborhoods or cities alters the extent to which an individual's race affects criminal justice decision making. Are blacks, for example, over or underarrested in neighborhoods or cities where the percent of blacks is low or high? Dannefer and Schutt (1982) argued that race discrimination is most likely to occur when the percentage of nonwhites is high because it is under these conditions that whites feel most threatened. White police feel particularly threatened and uncomfortable patrolling predominantly nonwhite communities. They examined two New Jersey counties, one with a high percent of nonwhites (39 percent) and one with a low percent (10 percent). Controlling for prior record and offense seriousness, they found that race affected police decision making much more than court decision making and that this effect was stronger in the county with the high percentage of nonwhites. On the other hand, Myers and Talarico (1986) reported that the effects of race on sentencing also depended on place, but that place characteristics were as likely to lead to shorter as they were to longer sentences for blacks (see also Myers 1987).

Again, what is needed is a summary analysis of all studies. On the basis of a review of thirty-eight studies, Chiricos and Crawford (1995) concluded that blacks are more likely to receive sentences of imprisonment in places where the unemployment rate and percentage black is high and in the South. Under these conditions, black offenders are more likely to be perceived as threatening and dangerous.

Finally, if there is not an overall pattern of race effects, why then are blacks and minorities so overrepresented in the prison system? Blacks constitute about 12 percent of the population but 51 percent of the state and federal prison population (Bureau of Justice Statistics 1996). Blumstein (1982) answered the above question by arguing that racial disparities in the prison population simply reflect racial disparities in the population responsible for violent and "street" crimes. Indeed, Blumstein (1982) demonstrated that about 75 percent of the racial disparity in the prison population can be traced to racial disparities in the arrest population. On the other hand, some researchers argue that even small racial and class effects should not be dismissed. Liska and Tausig (1979) showed how even small social class and racial differentials at each decision-making level can generate sizable cumulative social class and racial differentials in the prison population. They argued that if "small" differentials at all decision points regularly favor white and middle-class adolescents over black and lower-class adolescents, these differentials "multiply" through the justice system, resulting in a homogeneous black and lower-class prison population. For example, assume the following statistics: that 30 percent of blacks and 20 percent of whites are arrested over their life time (a ratio of 3:2); that 40 percent of the arrested blacks and 30 percent of the arrested whites are referred to a precourt hearing (a ratio of 4:3); that 60 percent of the referred blacks and 50 percent of the referred whites are found guilty (a ratio of 6:5); and that 70 percent of the referred blacks and 60 percent of the referred whites are institutionalized (a ratio of 7:6). As a result of these "small" differentials at each decision point, 5 percent of blacks but only 1.8 percent of whites would be institutionalized (a ratio of 5:1.8), substantially greater than the ratio at any one decision level.

In summary, conflict theorists argue that "who is the criminal" depends not only on what laws are enforced but on who has the power to resist the enforcement of the law. The power to resist is assumed to be linked to positions in the social structure, such as race and class. Research, however, has yielded inconsistent results. The findings suggest that the effect of race and class on decision making in the criminal justice system is neither simple nor direct, but contingent on other factors. Even though the effects are much smaller than originally thought, the accumulative bias of small effects over many decision-making levels can be substantial, and even small biases take on great symbolic value in a society that values "equality before the law."

Gender   To reiterate, conflict theory implies that the power to resist is linked not only to class and race, but also to gender. If females have less power than males, then conflict theory clearly implies that females should be overrepresented in the criminal justice system. Yet, even in the early research it was clear that gender effects work to the advantage of females. Females are underrepresented, not overrepresented, in the criminal justice system (for reviews, see Daly 1989; Steffensmeier et al. 1993). To a large extent, this reflects the fact that males commit more crime and more serious crime than do females. When these legal considerations are taken into account, most research shows little or no gender effect on decision making in the criminal justice process (Bishop and Frazier 1996; Daly 1989, 1994; Steffensmeier et al. 1993).

Given these results, some researchers (e.g., Chesney-Lind and Shelden 1992) have revised the gender effect hypothesis to apply only to less serious crimes, especially status offenses. They argue that patriarchal control is expressed in the harsher treatment of female juveniles over male juveniles for status offenses (truancy, incorrigibility, runaways). These offenses are ignored for males but for females they are taken to show deviance from traditional female roles. While there is some evidence in support of this hypothesis (Chesney-Lind 1988), other researchers fail to find such effects (Steffensmeier et al. 1993; Bishop and Frazier 1996; Corley et al. 1989), again yielding inconsistent findings. Consider the study of Steffensmeier et al. It is one of the largest (61,294 cases in Pennsylvania), uses recent data, includes a large number of causal variables, examines different aspects of the sentencing decision (whether or not to incarcerate, and the length of sentence), and examines sentencing for serious and nonserious crimes. For the decision to incarcerate or not, they found little gender effect for any crime, serious or not, and the small gender effect they did find favors females (underincarcerated). Of those incarcerated, they again found little gender effect on the length of sentence; for serious crimes they reported a small gender effect favoring females (males are oversentenced) and for less serious crimes, they reported a small gender effect favoring males (females are slightly oversentenced). While the latter findings seem to support the gender status hypothesis, remember that the effect is small and only occurs for length of sentence, not the decision about whether or not to incarcerate. According to Steffensmeier et al. (1993), the overall findings are clear: Sentencing is mostly affected by legal variables (seriousness of the crime and prior offenses), and the effect of gender is trivial.

Daly (1989, 1994) adopted a somewhat different tack. Rather than arguing that gender affects criminal justice decision making, she proposed that gender affects the other variables that influence the process. Specifically, she maintained that family ties are important; judges are reluctant to sentence people to prison who have strong family obligations (mothers and fathers), especially females (mothers). While her research provided some support for this, it also showed that family ties were important for both males and females and that legal variables exhibited strong effects for both females and males.

In sum, research has not supported the gender hypothesis. Gender just does not have much of an effect on legal decision making, and when it does it seems to favor females, not males. What, then, are the general implications of these findings for the conflict hypothesis that law is selectively enforced against the powerless? First, it is hard to argue that females have significantly less legal power than males. For juveniles, they share the same parents who are as likely to defend their daughters as their sons in legal proceeds. Married females usually share the same family resources as their spouses. It is hard to imagine that more family resources would be used to defend husbands and fathers than wives and mothers. Note, this is exactly what the research shows: no gender effect. If anything, it is unmarried females who may have fewer resources than other categories of males and females. Perhaps it is the marital, not maternal, status that is important. Also remember the sleeping with the enemy hypothesis. Unlike race and class, the powerful category (males) does not view the less powerful category (females) as physically threatening and, indeed, needs them in fundamental ways; males are thus unlikely to physically segregate females in jails and prisons. To the extent to which males control females, the control is likely to take place in the home and workplace; and to the extent to which control bureaucracies are used, mental health and social welfare systems are more likely to be used than jails and prisons.

SOCIAL POLICY

Conflict theorists can be divided between those who advocate reform of the present system and those who advocate radical revolution. While the call to arms among conflict scholars was loud and clear in the 1960s and 70s, since then the radicals have given way to more moderate voices.

For example, in the 1970s Quinney argued that meaningful reforms in law enactment and enforcement cannot occur within the context of a capitalistic system. If law enactment and enforcement reflect power, and if power reflects ownership and control of the means of production, then equality in law enactment and enforcement requires equality in the control and ownership of capital. Past reforms have done nothing more than strengthen the capitalist system. Quinney clearly advocated some form of socialism, with equality in both political and economic decision making and the consumption of economic goods and services. He also argued that, since the state represents the interests of the powerful, within an egalitarian society the state has no function and will disappear; hence, there will be no criminal law and consequently no crime. While much of traditional Marxism implies an inevitable transition from capitalism to socialism and eventually to communism, Quinney and other radicals of the time set forth a social action program to accelerate the "inevitable." Perhaps because of the downfall of most socialist and communist regimes in Eastern Europe and the former Soviet Union, and the movement to free markets in China, today most conflict scholars advocate liberal reform.

What is to be reformed? Remember that conflict theory focuses on inequality in law enactment and enforcement, that is, it assumes that laws reflect the interests of those who have the power to influence the enactment process and that laws are enforced against those who lack the power to resist.

Consider the enactment process. The policy implications of conflict theory are twofold. Traditionally, reformers focused on what could be done so that laws reflect the common interests, not special interests. This goal implies policies of consensus building and policies that allow this consensus to be reflected in the enactment process. To some extent, many laws do reflect common interests, such as laws about violence and street crimes. There is considerable research (Rossi et al. 1974; Wolfgang et al. 1985) showing that most people support laws for most forms of violence and most forms of property street crime. Yet the influence of special interests (business, government agencies, and racial/ethnic/religious groups) regularly finds its way into the enactment processes.

Multiculturalists, on the other hand, argue that what is needed is not consensus but an equality of power so that all groups with diverse interests have equal opportunity to have their interests heard. This implies equality of power (based on economic position and the mobilization of resources). Consider three divisions of conflict (class, race, and gender). For class, economic equality and union membership (the major vehicle in mobilizing the lower class) may have decreased over recent years; but for race and gender, economic equality and organizational mobilization, as reflected in the many minority and female advocacy groups, have substantially increased. Hence, as we might suspect, while the interests of the lower class may be less reflected in the law enactment process today than ten or fifteen years ago, the interests of minorities and females appear to be more reflected in that process today.

In addition to inequalities in access to the law enactment process, conflict theory directs attention to inequalities in law enforcement. What laws are enforced against whom? Research shows that some laws are rigorously enforced (generally those governing crime in the streets) and some are not (generally those governing crime in the suites). What can be done? President Carter, for example, initiated a policy to eliminate the regular exchange between service on government regulatory commissions and agencies and employment in the regulated businesses. He asked government employees in certain critical positions to sign a statement pledging that upon terminating government service they would not accept immediate employment in corporations that they had been charged with regulating. While only an initial step, it was one in the right direction, but it simply has not been followed up. The present relationship between regulatory agencies and the corporations they regulate is comparable to appointing people involved in organized crime to head the FBI.

Conflict theory also suggests that for those laws that are enforced, the power to resist is differentially distributed, and that laws are most rigorously enforced against those groups with the least power to resist (lower class, ethnic/racial minorities, and females). While the power to resist is certainly unequally distributed, research shows that today this power does not substantially affect the law enforcement process in the crucial decisions from arrests to sentencing. While few would deny that class, race, and gender discrimination certainly exist in some places at some times, the overall enforcement of the law is mainly affected by legal considerations (prior record and the seriousness of the present offense). There is one glaring exception: the enforcement of drug laws, especially against crack and powdered cocaine. Sentences depend not only on the amount of the cocaine involved but on the form of cocaine as well. Sentencing guidelines direct judges to multiply the quantity of powdered cocaine by 1 and the amount of crack cocaine by 100 (the 100 to 1 distinction) in determining the sentence, even though the two drugs are pharmacologically similar. While unfair on its face, this distinction has become an issue of racial discrimination because crack cocaine tends to used by blacks and powdered cocaine tends to used by whites. One federal court of appeals reported that 95 percent of crack defendants are black and 40 percent of powdered defendants are white (Tonry 1995).

These drug use laws alone have had a dramatic effect on the size and racial composition of the prison population. Drug convictions are a major cause of prison overcrowding. In the late 1970s, 6.4 percent of state and 25 percent of federal inmates were convicted of drug offenses, but by the early 1990s, these figures had increased to 25 percent and 56 percent, respectively. Drug convictions are also a major cause of the racial imbalance in the prison population. In 1986 (before the most recent War on Drugs) 8 percent of white and 7 percent of black prisoners were convicted of drug crimes; but by 1991 these figures increased to 12 percent for whites and 25 percent for blacks (Tonry 1995).

Based on conflict theory and research, what should be reformed? (1) Clearly equal access to the law enactment process is crucial in a multicultural society. If a society reflects a diversity of interests, then all interests should have access to the enactment process; yet efforts to equalize access, such as laws governing contributions to the politicians and political parties, have not been very successful. (2) Clearly, laws governing crime in the suites are not rigorously enforced. While these laws are harder to enforce (situations are complicated and defendants have considerable resources), they could be pursued more tenaciously if the agencies charged with enforcing them had adequate budgets. Yet the recent administrations have been more likely to cut than to enhance the budgets for such agencies. (3) Clearly, those laws that are enforced (laws governing street crime) should be equally enforced without regard to class, race, and gender. Most research suggests that, with the exception of drug laws, this is not where reform is most needed and focusing on enforcement diverts attention from where reform is needed: equal access to the enactment process and equal enforcement of all laws.

CRITIQUE

THEORY

Three criticisms of conflict theory are particularly noteworthy: (1) Many conflict theorists dismiss social consensus; they thus ignore the fact that many laws reflect common interests, not just the interests of the powerful. There was a clear tendency among radical conflict theorists of the 1970s to view crime as a revolutionary act—one that furthers the process of overthrowing capitalism. Yet laws on violence (homicide, assault, rape) and many property crimes (robbery, burglary, larceny, and auto theft) seem to protect the interests of almost everyone and are uniformly supported by almost everyone (Rossi et al. 1974). Indeed, many crimes affect the poor as much as the rich and may even affect the poor and racial minorities more than the rich. Hence, enforcement of laws governing the protection of life and property may be more in the interests of the poor than of the rich, who can protect themselves by residing in low-crime areas and insuring their property. This has come to be realized by many previously radical criminologists in England, who now refer to their work as "left realism" (Lea and Young 1984; Young 1987).

(2) Perhaps the major criticism of contemporary conflict theory is that it has not been sensitive to the last two decades of research; indeed, much conflict theory is not much different today than when it was developed in the 1960s and 70s. The concepts were not well-defined then and are still not well-defined today, making its propositions difficult to test empirically. Consider Quinney's major proposition: Laws are enacted and enforced that are in the interests of those who control and own the means of production. Quinney did not clearly specify what is in their interests and frequently ended up saying that all laws that are passed and enforced "must be" in their interests; otherwise those laws would not have been passed or enforced. For example, Quinney argued that the antibusiness legislation of the New Deal was "really" in the interests of owners and managers. Without these reforms, a major social revolution would have occurred. This, of course, is mere speculation; there is no evidence that such a revolution would have taken place had the reforms not occurred. It is also a post

hoc interpretation. Would Quinney have predicted the legislation prior to its enactment on the basis of what his theory deemed to be in the interests of owners and managers? At the time, the legislation was vigorously fought by owners and managers. Similar critiques by Horwitz (1977) and Jacobs (1980) have been made of the theories of Spitzer and Beirne, arguing that their theories are so vaguely formulated that it is difficult to know what evidence supports or fails to support them. Conflict theorists must define clearly what is in the interests of different social categories, such as capitalists and labor, whites and blacks, and males and females in order for researchers to observe whether there is a correspondence between these interests and power, and the law.

(3) There is still too much emphasis on class conflict over race and gender conflict and various other forms of conflict. Race conflict is frequently conceptualized as a proxy for class conflict. In traditional conflict theory the power to influence the legal process (law enactment and enforcement) is assumed to be vested in one's position in the economic structure. Race is only important to the extent to which it influences class. Thus, controlling for class should eliminate any race effect. While there is a realization today that race plays a role independently of class, there is still a tendency to treat race as secondary to class. The same is true for gender conflict. While many feminists argue that gender conflict is more important than class conflict, when examining the legal process there is a clear tendency to study gender conflict as analogous to class conflict. For example, class conflict theory asserts that laws are mostly enforced against those who have the least power to resist. Since females have less political and economic power, it follows from class conflict theory that laws should be enforced more against females than males. Yet the facts are clear: The criminal justice system is filled with males (it is hard to ignore this), and when gender is studied, at every legal decision point its effect tends to be small and it frequently favors females. We are not saying that gender conflict does not exist (it certainly does) and that females do not experience discrimination (they certainly do); rather, we are saying that the criminal justice system is not the best place to study the control of females.

RESEARCH

To a large extent, research has been undervalued by conflict theorists. Some conflict theorists take a different view of theory from that of most social scientists. Many radical economic conflict theorists and some feminists, for example, argue that the function of theory is to generate social equality and justice by raising people's consciousness of their true interests, outlining and illuminating possible futures, and generally stimulating social action. Much of their work is more ideological than theoretical and more concerned with criticizing the structure of Western societies and bringing about social change than in explaining law enactment and enforcement. The pursuit of both explanation/prediction and social justice are valuable endeavors; yet they can be antithetical. Emphasis on explanation and prediction can sometimes impede social action; and emphasis on social action can sometimes impede explanation and prediction. The work of radical conflict theorists sometimes suffers from the latter. As they are frequently less concerned with empirically testing their theory than with convincing others of its validity and of the need for social action, they frequently ignore counter-evidence or construe it to fit their theory.

Consider the studies on law enforcement and the power to resist, as reflected in class and race. This body of research is extensive and rigorous. It does not present only illustrative cases (upper-class juveniles who have successfully resisted enforcement of the law and lower-class juveniles who have not successfully resisted) but uses large random samples to examine the relationship between power (social class or race) and law enforcement. Since the mid-1980s the findings have been relatively clear: Legal variables are much more important than extralegal variables (class and race) in the enforcement of the law. Yet, while this research now seems to be acknowledged—sometimes begrudgingly—it has not found its way into conflict theory. What does such research mean for the proposition that the law is enforced against those with the least power to resist? This reluctance to reformulate conflict theory has probably stifled work on how racial and class effects depend on specific times and circumstances and on how even small class and race effects over many decision points can accumulate into large race and class differences in the rise of the prison population.

Finally, the studies of law enactment and enforcement are more illustrative than theory-testing. They are organized and designed to illustrate rather than to test conflict theory. For example, many of the case studies of the enforcement of laws governing crime in the suites (cited in the research section) illustrate how businesses use their power to influence the enactment of the law, but these studies do not systematically test hypotheses about the processes by which business interests are reflected in the enactment and administration of the law. Rigorous tests require the systematic observation of a large number of cases (such as the work of Clinard and Yaeger 1980, and more recently Calavita and Pontell 1990)—not just one or two cases selected to illustrate a theoretical proposition.

SOCIAL POLICY

The implications of conflict theory are twofold: Either reduce the fundamental inequalities in society, which are the bases of inequalities of political access, or reform the process of political access so that social inequalities are not easily translated into inequalities of access. There has been little inclination to deal with fundamental social inequalities; indeed, present government policies are probably increasing, not decreasing them. While there is considerable talk about controlling access and equality before the law, there has been relatively little action of late. Consider law enactment. After most national political campaigns there is generally considerable public concern and outcry about their cost and how the money was raised. Most people seem to fully understand that with financial contributions comes access, and the greater the contribution the greater the access. That is why people and corporations contribute. After the election there are investigations and new laws passed to control the process of campaign funding, but each succeeding election leads to higher levels of contributions. The laws are either filled with loopholes or weakly enforced. In other cases meritorious laws are on the books but are just not enforced. Consider crime in the suites. As noted, offenders of these laws are not pursued conscientiously and sanctioned. Everyone knows what to do. The policy implications are clear: Properly fund the enforcement agencies. Yet, recent federal administrations have cut the budgets of many such funding agencies. Finally, some laws that are enforced, particularly those regulating street crimes, may be selectively enforced. While conflict theory asserts that laws are enforced against those who have the least power to resist, research shows that at least in regard to class, race, and gender, the power to resist plays a secondary role to legal considerations. Nevertheless, we should remember that in a country whose citizens profess a commitment to "equality before the law," even a small level of discrimination takes on great symbolic value and threatens to undermine the legitimacy of the legal and social order.

8

EPILOGUE: THE PAST, THE PRESENT, AND THE FUTURE

Previous chapters have examined six theoretical perspectives in the study of crime and deviance: structural/functional, human ecological, rational choice/deterrence, labeling, constructionist, and conflict. These perspectives offer distinctive explanations of crime and deviance, reflecting the unique concepts associated with the various perspectives and their underlying assumptions about the nature of society (whether it is essentially orderly or disorderly) and the nature of the link between the individual and society (whether individuals are passive reactors to the social environment or active agents constructing their environments). In this final chapter, we consider issues that cut across the dominant theoretical perspectives.

The first section of the chapter considers the life histories of theoretical perspectives. While all of the major perspectives have inspired theorizing and research for extended periods of time, certain perspectives tend to dominate the field at particular historical moments and then fade in popularity, often to reemerge as leading approaches in subsequent years.

The second of these issues is theoretical integration. To many scholars, the multitude of seemingly unrelated and competitive theories in the study of deviance makes the field seem fragmented, if not in disarray. In response to this state of affairs, several prominent voices have called for efforts to explicitly join theories together by means of theoretical integration. What exactly is meant by theoretical integration is rarely made clear. The chapter explores the meaning of this phrase and some of its implications for the study of crime and deviance.

The chapter concludes with a few comments about future directions in the study of crime and deviance. Predicting the future is an inherently hazardous, if not an impossible, task. Nevertheless, it is possible to speculate about broad social changes that are likely to influence theorizing and research on crime and deviance in the years ahead.

THE RISE AND FALL OF THEORETICAL PERSPECTIVES

Perspectives of crime and deviance rise and fall over time. This cycle does not just reflect the degree of empirical support but also the temper of the times. Scholars are human beings and members of societies. Their choices of and interests in what to study and how to study it also reflect the times, such as social conditions and broad cultural themes. For example, the general acceptance of biology as a fundamental science during the turn of the century gave rise to a receptive atmosphere for biological theories of human behavior, especially deviance and crime, which later fell into disrepute. Again, today's advances in biology, such as in genetics, are providing a fertile ground for biological theories of human behavior, especially crime and deviance.

Today's postmodernism movement also reminds us that scholars are not simply embedded in an overarching society; they are also members of a class, race, and gender. Postmodernists examine how class-race-gender influence decisions of what to study and how to study it. They note that much of today's scholarship reflects the interests, concerns, and decisions of middle- and upper-class white males, and they ask how scholarship would be different if these decisions were made by lower-class persons, nonwhites, and females.

Finally, what to study and how to study it depend on what is politically feasible. Some projects are not supported or funded at a particular time either because they challenge popular beliefs and values or because they challenge the authority of economic or political elites. For example, it is unlikely that projects studying the negative consequences of religions would be given high priority today given the political strength of religious groups. Similarly, it is unlikely that research studying how the lifestyles of rape victims may facilitate victimization would be supported by granting agencies, given widespread acceptance of the view that women have the right to live their lives the way they want to. On the other hand, since the 1980s the federal government has provided considerable funding to study legal punishment as a deterrent for crime. Such funding priorities encourage scholars to pursue some questions and to neglect others, thus influencing the rise and fall of perspectives. We now review the temper of the times from the beginning of the twentieth century to today and discuss how the general social context has influenced the rise and fall of theoretical perspectives.

From the turn of the twentieth century to the 1920s, the country experienced considerable industrialization, urbanization, and immigration. These were turbulent times. The reorganization of work around urban factories and the expansion of cities as a result of the immigration from eastern and southern Europe led to considerable urban turmoil. These social trends influenced scholarship for the next thirty to forty years, until World War II. They shaped American sociology around the study of the urban life, and they directed attention to how these trends disorganize urban life, leading to crime and deviance. The social disorganization perspective dominated the study of crime and deviance from 1920 to 1940. It is no accident that the theory developed in a university located in a city that most reflected these trends: Chicago.

With the end of World War II, the United States was ready for stability and rebuilding. So was sociology and social science, more generally. The focus of scholarly attention shifted to perspectives that emphasize integration and stability. Structural/functionalism, the major perspective of the time, examined how well-integrated and stable societies function; that is, how social structure (patterns of stable or persistent behavior) contributes to agreed-upon cultural goals. Crime and deviance were explained as the outcome of flaws in the integration of culture (e.g., economic goals) and social structure (e.g., economic opportunities). Merton's anomie theory exemplified this perspective.

By the mid-1960s the stability and consensus of the postwar years had come to an end. The sons and daughters of the war generation had come of age and had begun to question the values upon which the postwar stability had been built. The mid-1960s and 1970s were marked more by change than stability and more by conflict than consensus, reflected in Vietnam protests on university campuses, the racial turmoil (riots) in the streets, and the growing influence of the feminist movement.

In academia this change in the temper of the times was reflected in the rise of perspectives that study change and conflict. When times are stable and consensus is achieved, social norms offer clear reference points for judging deviance, and laws provide clear reference points for judging crime; but in changing and unstable times, the social norms (and laws) are also unclear, changing, and questioned. The study of deviance as norm violations becomes problematic. We are forced to ask, deviance from what norms and from whose norms? During this period of time the definitional perspectives of deviance rose to prominence to explain how norms emerge and are applied in specific situations (social constructionism), how laws are formulated and enforced (social conflict), and the consequences of the application of norms and the enforcement of laws (labeling).

By the 1980s times had again changed. Perhaps as a reaction to the liberalism of the 1960s and 70s, the country became more conservative, witnessed in the back-to-basics movements in schools and in the renewed emphasis on traditional values in public discourse. These concerns were clearly expressed in the political campaigns and administrations of Presidents Reagan (1980–84 and 1984–88) and Bush (1988–92); and of particular interest to this book, they were expressed in the popular support for more punishment of those who violate basic values as expressed in laws on street crime.

The shift in the public mood was reflected in the rise of the deterrence perspective, which focuses on the role of punishment in controlling crime, during the 1980s. This is a striking instance where the political agenda directed the scholarship by providing substantial funding for one kind of research rather than others, in this case, research on the role of legal punishment in controlling crime.

Times are again changing, but without some historical perspective it is hard to delineate present trends. Yet, a few trends that are important to the study of crime and deviance seem clear. Employment is being reorganized away from northern and midwestern urban factories (which are relocating to southern rural areas and to third world countries) toward service industries located in the suburbs—the processes of deindustrialization. Those who can are following work to the new factories of the less urbanized South and to the service industries in the suburbs, leaving a disadvantaged urban population. And immigration (legal and illegal) to cities in the Southwest and South has contributed to the growth of disadvantaged urban populations.

Given these circumstances, it is not surprising that there has been a resurgence of interest in the social disorganization theory. Although the contemporary processes—deindustrialization and deurbanization—seem to be the exact opposite of those that stimulated the rise of this theory in the 1920s to 40s—industrialization and urbanization—their consequences seem to be the same: social disorganization.

In sum, we suggest that the rise and fall of theoretical perspectives is not merely the result of the supporting evidence; it also reflects the temper of the times. While we emphasize the rise of one perspective during one era, other perspectives do not just fade away. Work continues on many of them. At times scholars work on two, three, or four of these perspectives. Perhaps a good way to think about the situation is that work on some perspectives occupies the foreground and work on others occupies the background during particular eras, but the foreground and background continually change.

Because work on multiple theoretical perspectives continues to be active, some in the foreground and some in the background, many scholars have called for theoretical integration: an effort to somehow pull these theories together, rather than shift from one to the other as the times change and fight over which one is best. We turn now to this issue—an important one for theorizing and research today.

THEORETICAL INTEGRATION
―――――――――――――○―――――――――――――

Interest in theoretical integration has grown rather steadily over the course of the past several decades, as reflected in sessions on this topic at annual professional meetings and special conferences devoted exclusively to it (Akers 1994; Messner et al. 1989). In this section, we explore in detail the nature of theoretical integration as an intellectual enterprise. The meaning and rationale for theoretical integration are considered first. Then, different strategies and directions for integration are reviewed. The section concludes with a discussion of general criteria for evaluating the success of integrated explanations of crime and deviance.

THE MEANING OF AND RATIONALE FOR THEORETICAL INTEGRATION

To understand the meaning of the concept *integration* the dictionary is a useful place to start. Webster defines the infinitive verb form "to integrate" as "to bring parts together into a unified whole." While the phrase "unified whole" is not itself perfectly clear, especially in regard to theory, it tends to mean a relationship or order among parts. Hence, according to Webster, to integrate theories is to formulate relationships among them.

Why might scholars desire to pursue such an activity? There is perhaps an intuitively appealing aura surrounding the notion of *theoretical integration* that derives from the very terms in the phrase. The central role of theory in the scientific enterprise can hardly be challenged. As Randall Collins (1986, 1345) reminds us, "the essence of science is precisely theory." Moreover, a good scientific theory is one that integrates or unifies empirical findings. It offers "a systematically unified account of quite diverse phenomena" (Hempel 1966, 75). Given the positive meanings attached to both *theory* and *integration*, the desirability of theoretical integration might appear to be self-evident.

It is important to differentiate, however, between *theorizing*, an activity that organizes empirical findings within a general abstract framework, and *theoretical integration*, an activity that creates linkages among different theories. Theoretical integration is best viewed as one means of theorizing. In other words, it is one strategy for developing better explanations. The key question to raise when considering the rationale for theoretical integration is thus whether or not it is, in fact, a more useful strategy for developing good explanations than are other strategies.

The case for theoretical integration in the field of crime and deviance has been made mainly with reference to the most prevalent alternative strategy, that of theory competition. Theory competition has been depicted quite favorably in the literature on the philosophy of science (e.g., Hempel 1966, 25–28; Stinchombe 1968, 27–28). According to the classical model of the scientific process, theoretical development proceeds by verifying theories, which involves the evaluation of hypotheses derived from a theory. The acceptability of a theory increases as it successfully survives more and more tests. However, because the number of possible tests is virtually infinite, it is often useful to develop "crucial tests." Crucial tests can be conducted when the implications of one theory contradict those of another. For example, perhaps theory A implies "p" and theory B implies "not p." Logic demands that both "p" and "not p" cannot be true at the same time. The value of crucial tests, therefore, lies in their efficiency and economy: Their results simultaneously lend credibility to one theory while raising doubts about another (Stinchombe 1968, 27–28).

The strategy of using crucial tests to evaluate competing theories has informed a large number of studies in the literature on crime and deviance. Consider, for example, research by Jensen and Brownfield (1983). They examined parental attachment and drug use in an effort to assess Hirschi's social control theory in comparison with social learning theory (discussed in Chapter 3). Hirschi's theory stipulates that attachment to others (especially parents) creates bonds to the conventional order and thereby inhibits deviant behavior. Given the logic of Hirschi's argument, attachment to parents should always reduce children's drug use. Whether or not the parents themselves use drugs should have no bearing on the inhibiting effect of attachment. Social learning theory, in contrast, emphasizes the importance of role models. Accordingly, social learning theory implies that the effects of attachment should vary depending on the drug use of parents, who are likely to be significant role models. Attachment should reduce drug use only for children who are attached to nonusing parents. Attachment to parents who use drugs themselves should not inhibit children's drug use; it might even increase it. Note the contradictory nature of these predictions: Attachment either reduces children's drug use for all children regardless of parents' behavior, or it does not. The findings of the crucial test will thus lend credibility to one of the theories while simultaneously challenging the other. In Jensen and Brownfield's study, the inhibiting effect of parental attachment depended on parental drug use, thereby supporting social learning theory and raising questions about Hirschi's control theory.

Critics of theory competition charge that while this strategy appears to be very attractive in principle, it has serious limitations in practice. Perhaps the most prominent critic of theory competition in the field of crime and deviance is Delbert Elliott (Elliott 1985; Elliott et al. 1985; Elliott et al. 1979). Elliott advances several criticisms of theory competition. First, the major theories rarely permit the derivation of unambiguous, truly distinctive hypotheses. Different theories typically predict similar outcomes, and a given set of empirical findings can often be reconciled with various theories. For example, the prediction that high unemployment leads to high levels of crime is consistent with anomie theory (blocked access to the legitimate means for success leads to anomie), and rational choice/deterrence theory (unemployed persons have less to lose and more to gain from crime). Hence, devising tests that are truly "crucial" is not very easy in practice.

Second, Elliott contends that the results of allegedly crucial tests are seldom definitive. This is due in part to methodological problems, such as the difficulties in developing adequate measures of key concepts. Inconsistent findings could mean that a given theory is invalid, but they could also reflect inadequate measurement of concepts that are highly abstract and inherently difficult to measure.

Finally, in Elliott's view, the explanatory power associated with theories that manage to survive the so-called crucial tests tends to be extremely weak. The primary reason for the poor performance of these theories is that they typically involve a "single explanatory variable" (Elliott 1985, 127). Hence, insofar as the causes of crime and deviance are multiple in nature (which seems difficult to dispute), it will be necessary to combine different theories to capture the entire range of relevant causal variables. The theory competition strategy discourages this kind of activity by forcing unproductive choices among theories. For these reasons, Elliott concludes that the "competitive hypothesis approach has often seemed to inhibit theory development rather than to enhance it" (1985, 126).

While some might quarrel with aspects of Elliott's characterization of theory competition (Liska et al. 1989), it is difficult to disagree with his general assertion that traditional theories have had only limited success in explaining crime and deviance. Thus, it seems only prudent to consider new points of departure, including efforts at theoretical integration.

TYPES OF INTEGRATION

Some years ago Hirschi (1979) suggested that strategies of integration in the study of deviance and crime can be classified as one of three types: up-and-down or deductive integration, side-by-side or parallel integration, and end-to-end or sequential integration. Each type is defined by a principle that links one or more theories together. Up-and-down integration refers to identifying a higher level of abstraction or generality that encompasses much of the constituent theories. Side-by-side (horizontal) integration refers to partitioning the subject matter of crime and deviance into cases that are explained by different theories. End-to-end (sequential) integration refers to specifying the temporal order between causal variables, so that the dependent variables of some theories constitute the independent variables of others. These three types of integration can be applied equally well to micro-level, macro-level, or cross-level integration, thereby yielding a nine-cell typology defined by the principles of theoretical integration and by the levels of analysis (Table 8.1).

TABLE 8.1   TYPES OF INTEGRATION

		LEVEL OF ANALYSIS		
		MICRO	*MACRO*	*CROSS-LEVEL*
PRINCIPLE	Side-by-Side			
OF LINKAGE	End-to-End			
(INTEGRATION)	Up-and-Down			

Side-by-Side (Horizontal) Integration   Depending on how it is done, this type of integration may seem to be the easiest, or it may not even be considered theoretical integration at all. The most common form of side-by-side integration is to partition cases of deviance and crime by the theories that best explain them. By as early as the 1940s it had become clear to criminologists that crime and criminals are heterogeneous phenomena. Embezzlement may have little in common with homicide, and upper-class white female criminals may have little in common with lower-class African American male criminals. However, to avoid ending up with as many theories as there are cases, general criteria (principles) must be developed for partitioning deviance and crime. Should characteristics of deviants, such as class, race, and gender be used; should types of crime and deviance, such as drug use, homicide, and alcoholism be used; or should both characteristics of deviants and deviance be used?

Constructing schemes for classifying deviance and deviants into general types (typologies) is one strategy for implementing side-by-side integration. Over the course of the past fifty years or so, numerous typologies have been formulated that organize the subject matter of deviance into types of deviant behaviors and types of deviants. In some typologies these types simply reflect commonly used categories (burglary, homicide, prostitution), while in others, more sophisticated distinctions are employed (e.g., Farr and Gibbons 1990). Although typologies continue to serve as the principal basis for organizing textbooks on crime and deviance, the construction of typologies has been criticized for being more concerned with technical considerations than with theory development. Typologies have been judged mainly on the basis of the clarity, parsimony, mutual exclusivity, and inclusivity of the types. Unfortunately, the relevance of these typologies for theory development has been considered rather infrequently. For typology construction and theory construction to go hand in hand, the types must be theoretically relevant. If they are not, the typologies will be little more than theoretically sterile classification systems, and the exercise of typology construction will not contribute to meaningful side-by-side theoretical integration.

To partition the subject matter of deviance in a theoretically informed way, the partitioning principle should identify the conditions under which a theory applies. The logic of some theories seems more applicable to some types of deviants and deviance than to others. For example, rational decision-making theory may not be applicable to most homicides, especially homicides between intimates. On the other hand, it may be very applicable to corporate crime. Consider also deterrence and labeling theories. Deterrence theory argues that as punishment increases, deviance decreases; labeling theory argues that as labeling increases, deviance increases. The two terms, punishment and labeling, can easily be equated because most forms of punishment also label, and most forms of deviant labeling also punish. Can these two theories be integrated or are they inherently inconsistent? Tittle (1975) argued that each theory applies in different conditions, and depending on these conditions, punishment (labeling) will either increase or decrease the probability of future deviance. For example, convicting a woman for prostitution is more likely to produce a deviant career than convicting a woman for shoplifting. Being publicly labeled as a prostitute opens opportunities to continue the practice while closing opportunities for conventional relationships. In contrast, being convicted for shoplifting probably limits opportunities for continuing the practice while not necessarily closing opportunities for conventional employment.

   End-to-End (Sequential) Integration   To reiterate, end-to-end integration refers to using a dependent variable in one theory as an independent variable in another, and an independent variable in one theory as a dependent variable in another. This type of integration is most applicable when causal conditions can be ordered on a continuum of immediate to remote causes (Jessor and Jessor 1973). "Immediate" causes refer to those causal conditions that act quickly, and more or less directly, on deviance and crime. The effects are not mediated by other specified conditions. At the individual level of analysis, we tend to think of perceptions and beliefs as immediate causes of behavior. "Remote" causes refer to those causal conditions that act indirectly, or through other conditions, on deviance and crime. For example, at the individual level of analysis social status or religious affiliation are often regarded as remote causes of behavior, operating through beliefs and attitudes.

   Some theories focus on immediate causes, generally psychological states or day-to-day social experiences. Differential association theory, for example, places its emphasis on morals (definitions of right and wrong) and how these are learned in day-to-day experiences with peers. The extent to which these experiences are embedded in patterns of culture and social structure that characterize some but not other social units is of minimal concern. Other theories focus on remote causes. Some study complex patterns of social interaction that characterize small-scale social units, such as family power structures, or those that characterize large scale social units, such as industrialization. Some study the demographic conditions that characterize small-scale units, such as household density, or those that characterize large-scale social units, such as population change. These conditions affect deviance and crime by altering the beliefs, perceptions, and day-to-day experiences that directly affect deviance and crime. Social disorganization theory, for example, purports that population heterogeneity and population change, as indirect causes of social disorganization, affect deviance and crime by reducing the strength of day-to-day conventional ties that control motives to deviate.

One of the difficulties with end-to-end integrations is that they frequently do not really integrate the different theories in any meaningful sense. In particular, such approaches often fail to consider differences in basic assumptions associated with the constituent theories (Hirschi 1979). For example, if one theory (differential association) assumes that motives are important in understanding deviance, whereas another theory (social control) assumes that such motives are unimportant, these theories can be truly integrated only if these assumptions are reconciled. If contradictory assumptions are not reconciled, or if they are simply ignored, the extent to which the theories have in fact been integrated is open to question.

Up-and-Down Integration Up-and-down integration, or deductive integration, is the classic form of theoretical integration. It is accomplished by identifying a level of abstraction or generality that will incorporate some of the parts of two or more theories within it. This can be done by recognizing that theory A contains more abstract or general assumptions than theory B and, therefore, that key parts of theory B can be incorporated within the structure of theory A. Or it can be done by abstracting more general assumptions from theories A and B, allowing parts of both theories to be incorporated in a new theory C. We call the former method theoretical reduction and the latter method theoretical synthesis.

Figure 8.1 illustrates how theoretical reduction might occur in the study of deviance. Theory X is the more general theory. It implies two direct causes of deviance (conditions D and F), and through these conditions it implies links between conditions A and C and deviance. Theory Y is a simpler theory, including just two propositions. Condition F leads directly to

General Theory X   Specific Theory Y

A ⟶ C   B ⟶ F
C ⟶ D   F ⟶ Deviance
C ⟶ F
D ⟶ Deviance
F ⟶ Deviance

Figure 8.1   Deductive Integration

deviance, and condition B leads to deviance indirectly because it leads to condition F, which leads in turn to deviance. Because the more general theory X also contains the prediction that condition F leads directly to deviance, it would be useful to integrate the simpler theory Y into the more general theory X. However, Y predicts that condition B leads to deviance, which cannot be derived from the general theory X because condition B is not a part of the theory. To deduce the proposition that condition B causes deviance from theory X, we must equate the concept of condition B with a concept in theory X (such as condition C). For example, if B refers to unemployment and C refers to status change, we can argue that unemployment is a special case of status change. Then, the prediction in theory Y that condition C leads to condition F also implies that condition B leads to condition F (substitute B for C in the third proposition). Now the proposition that B causes deviance can also be deduced from theory X. Since both propositions about deviance in theory Y are also part of the more general theory X, theory Y can be reduced to (incorporated within) theory X.

With the possible exception of economics, this type of integration is rarely attempted in the social sciences. In one attempt at deductive integration, Burgess and Akers (1966; see also Gibbs 1972) tried to subsume Sutherland's differential association theory within social learning theory. They equated concepts contained in differential association theory with those contained in the premises of learning theory and argued that the learning that takes place in interaction in primary groups (contact with definitions favorable and unfavorable to deviant behavior) is really just a special case of operant conditioning.

Many scholars in the social sciences view deduction as a form of theoretical imperialism because the theory being deduced loses its individual identity. The phrase *theoretical reduction* has a very negative connotation among many social scientists. For example, Burgess and Akers' (1966) attempt to subsume Sutherland's differential association theory under behaviorist principles has been characterized as a "revisionist takeover" that is a "travesty of Sutherland's position" (Taylor et al. 1973, 131–132).

Cross-Level Integration   Cross-level integration (integrating micro and macro theories) is sometimes thought to be both the most difficult and perhaps the most necessary type of theoretical integration. It is assumed to present unique problems. Some of these can be illustrated with reference to the three principles of integration. Consider side-by-side micro/macro integration. Are there some types of deviants or deviance that are better suited to micro or macro explanations? Historically, numerous scholars have tried to show that some types of deviance are individual in nature and others are social in nature. Criminal behaviors that are rare and seemingly difficult to understand (for example, exhibitionism) have been thought to be best explained by psychological theories at the individual level of analysis. The experiences that lead to the immediate or causal psychological states are assumed to be the products of unique personal biographies not clearly tied to the patterns of culture and structure that characterize large and small-scale social units. On the other hand, criminal behaviors that are common and seemingly understandable (e.g., burglary), particularly when committed in groups and supported by a subculture, are thought to be best explained at the macro level. The experiences that lead to them are thought to be shared by many and to be tied to the culture and structural patterns of large scale social units.

The problems and simplistic nature of this historical micro-macro partition were made evident by Durkheim's analysis of suicide—a rare act of deviance seemingly difficult to understand. He showed that suicide variation among macro units is also linked to the cultural and structural patterns of these units. Hence, what was thought to be a purely psychological phenomenon turned out to be a social phenomenon as well. Generally, it is not clear that side-by-side integration of macro- and micro-level theories is possible or even desirable.

On the other hand, end-to-end integration of micro- and macro-level theories seems quite possible and desirable. (We have already discussed this integration in terms of remote and immediate causes.) A typical form of such integration is contextual analysis, in which concepts used in macro-level theory (e.g., neighborhood disorganization, racial composition of a city, and income inequality) are included in micro research. For example, people may be characterized by their own attitudes and race and by the average attitude and racial composition of their social units, such as their school, neighborhood, and city. In many cases the contextual conditions cause the individual conditions, and thus may be thought of as remote causes in an end-to-end integration. For example, neighborhood disorganization may affect psychological disorganization, leading to crime and deviance; thus, psychological disorganization may be conceptualized as mediating the effect of neighborhood disorganization on crime.

Contextual analysis, used extensively in many areas of research, has not been used much in the study of deviance and crime. Even fewer studies have examined the causal link between contextual and individual conditions in an end-to-end integration. Recently, however, interest in contextual analysis has been increasing, and several studies have looked at the effects of neighborhood contexts on crime and delinquent behavior (Elliott et al. 1996; Gottfredson et al. 1991; Peoples and Loeber 1994; Sampson 1986a).

PATHS TO THEORETICAL INTEGRATION

Conceptual Integration Some scholars have argued that if theoretical integration is too difficult, one might start with conceptual integration. To conceptually integrate theories, the theorist equates concepts in different theories, arguing that while the words and terms are different, the theoretical meanings and operations of measurement are similar (see Pearson and Weiner 1985). Akers, for example, argued that the concepts of many theories (social bonding, strain) can be equated with the concepts of social learning. The concept *belief* in bonding theory is similar to the concept *definitions* in social learning, and the concept *blocked opportunities* in strain theory is similar to the concept *differential reinforcement* in social learning theory.

The purpose of conceptual integration is not always clear. Is it an end in itself or a means to some form of theoretical integration? As an end in itself, its value is quite limited. It would seem to apply to those theories that use different concepts and measures to represent the same things and that make similar predictions. For example, if theory A states that X increases deviance and if theory B states that Y increases deviance, and if the meanings of X and Y are similar, then conceptually integrating A and B yields conceptual parsimony. But if theory A states that Y increases deviance and theory B states that X decreases deviance, then conceptually integrating X and Y makes no sense and yields inconsistent predictions. However, in an area of study such as deviance and crime, where there are probably more terms, words, and concepts than meaningful distinctions, there is considerable opportunity for fruitful conceptual integration.

"Small" or "Middle Range" Integration   Part of the problem of theoretical integration is that theories are perceived as general theories rather than as parts of an emerging theory. Hence, scholars feel that all the concepts and propositions must be combined. This has made the task of integration seem monumental. Yet the concepts and propositions of most theories are only loosely linked. We can easily borrow ideas (concepts and propositions) from different theories and explore how they fit. Some propositions of different theories may be incompatible because they are tightly linked to incompatible assumptions. Other propositions, however, may not be so tightly linked to such assumptions, and some propositions of different theories may be deduced from a common set of assumptions, even if they were originally derived from incompatible assumptions.

One classic example of middle-range or small integration is Cloward and Ohlin's (1964) revision of Merton's anomie theory. They borrowed from differential association theory the idea that knowledge of illegitimate means must be learned and that opportunities to learn them are differentially available. This idea, traditionally embedded in the general assumptions of Sutherland's differential association theory, is not necessarily incompatible with assumptions of Merton's anomie theory, although many of the assumptions of the general ecology perspective, in which Sutherland's theory was originally embedded, are incompatible with many of the assumptions of the structural functional perspective, in which

Merton's theory was originally embedded. Indeed, the idea that illegitimate opportunities are differentially available seems eminently compatible with the idea that legitimate opportunities are differentially available.

EVALUATING CONCEPTUAL AND THEORETICAL INTEGRATION

As stated at the outset of this chapter, social science embraces the goal of integrating or unifying empirical findings under a set of abstract constructs and relational principles. The most efficient means to that goal is clearly more ambiguous and controversial than the agreed-upon goal. We have briefly reviewed some of the requisites and problems inherent in alternative methods for integrating existing theoretical perspectives. We have also identified another strategy for theoretical development, theory competition. It is difficult to determine the best strategy.

Whatever strategy is adopted, the end product must, of course, be assessed with reference to the general criteria of theory evaluation. Theoretical growth has often been interpreted in terms of increasing empirical support (Wagner and Berger 1985). We wish to emphasize, however, an additional criterion that is particularly relevant in the assessment of integrated theories: logical coherence. Many contemporary efforts that purport to pursue the goal of theoretical integration might be better described as attempts at prediction. Variables from two or more theories are included in the same analysis, but there is little concern with relating the various concepts to one another. Instead, attention focuses on the extent to which adding variables to the analysis increases predictive power. In this spirit, much contemporary research combines concepts from differential association theory, control theory, anomie theory, and deterrence theory into empirical models to predict all types of crime and deviance.

The problem with this strategy, as we have commented earlier, is that it does not deal with incompatibilities in basic assumptions or premises of these theories (cf. Hirsch 1979). Theorists must either be able to show how seemingly contradictory premises can in fact be reconciled, or they must explicitly acknowledge their selection of certain premises in favor of others in those instances where genuine contradictions exist. In short, theoretical growth is not likely to be promoted by integrated theories unless theorists seriously attend to the logical structure of their arguments.

FUTURE DIRECTIONS

We noted above that the life histories of theoretical perspectives on crime and deviance reflect the larger social context. Theories emerge and gain popularity when they are compatible with widely shared social experiences (i.e., when they "make sense" to academics and the general public) (Lilly et al. 1989, 11). Similarly, theories fall out of favor when they no longer resonate with widespread perceptions of social reality. The precise direction of theorizing on crime and deviance in the future is impossible to predict, but it will surely be just as dependent on the larger social context as in the past. We conclude this chapter by speculating briefly on the implications for the study of crime and deviance of a social phenomenon that has been the subject of considerable interest during the transition from the twentieth to the twenty-first century: globalization.

Although scholars disagree over the precise meaning of globalization (see Mittelman 1996), Waters (1995) has formulated a useful definition that captures the spirit of many approaches to the study of this topic: Globalization is "a social process in which the constraints of geography on social and cultural arrangements recede and in which people become increasingly aware that they are receding" (1995, 3). Globalization thus entails a greater capacity for people to establish social relationships and to interact over greater and greater distances. Some of the more important manifestations of globalization include the penetration of capitalist economic markets into virtually all areas of the globe; the formation of multinational and transnational organizations, and a concomitant weakening of the authority of traditional nation-states; the expanding territories over which people travel for business and leisure; and the instantaneous and widespread diffusion of ideas and information via mass media of communication and computer networks.

How might globalization affect the study of crime and deviance? Perhaps globalization will reproduce social conditions similar to those of earlier times, thereby stimulating a resurgence of interest in those theoretical perspectives that originally focused on such conditions. For example, if globalization facilitates the rapid diffusion of social innovations from one part of the world to another, it may accelerate the processes of general social change everywhere. Perspectives that deal with consequences of rapid social change for the normative order, such as anomie theory, might thus "make sense" in the explanation of deviant behavior. Another social development that has been associated with globalization is enhanced ethnic consciousness. Technological advances in transportation and communications allow ethnic groups (especially ethnic minorities) to establish and strengthen ethnic identities without regard to national borders. Such increased ethnic consciousness might lead to cultural and normative conflicts. These are the kinds of social conditions that were at the center of much theorizing in the classical social disorganization perspective during the early years of the twentieth century, and they may be highly relevant to the early years of the twenty-first century as well.

Another possibility is that globalization might generate new forms of social relationships that inspire the formulation of novel theoretical perspectives. Consider, for example, the Internet, which has been labeled by some as the "first true 'cyberspace'" (Shields 1996, 1). The Internet has permitted the formation of "simulated communities" (Waters 1995, 150) where people engage in regular, on-going social interaction without ever being in the physical presence of one another. These simulated communities raise interesting questions for the study of deviance. Is the Internet, as suggested by some, a "'free space' unfettered by moral codes" (Shields 1996, 1)? If not, what kinds of moral codes and norms are emerging to govern the interactions in the simulated (or "virtual") communities on the Internet? What kinds of deviance will accompany these norms? How will these norms be enforced and by whom? What forms of social control will emerge? Will existing theoretical perspectives be able to explain the norm violations in simulated communities, or will new concepts and theories need to be invented? Whatever the answer to these questions, it seems certain that the study of crime and deviance will be an exciting and challenging enterprise in the years ahead.

REFERENCES

Adler, Freda, and William S. Laufer, eds. 1995. *The Legacy of Anomie Theory*. New Brunswick, NJ: Transaction.

Adler, Jeffrey S. 1989. "A Historical Analysis of the Law of Vagrancy." *Criminology* 27:209–229.

Ageton, Suzanne S., and Delbert S. Elliott. 1974. "The Effects of Legal Processing on Self-Concept." *Social Problems* 22:87–100.

Agnew, Robert. 1985. "Social Control Theory and Delinquency: A Longitudinal Test." *Criminology* 23:47–61.

———. 1992. "Foundation for a General Strain Theory of Crime and Delinquency." *Criminology* 30:47–87.

Akers, Ronald L. 1985. *Deviant Behavior: A Social Learning Approach*, 3rd ed. Belmont, CA: Wadsworth.

———. 1994. *Criminological Theories: Introduction and Evaluation*. Los Angeles, CA: Roxbury.

Anderson, Elijah. 1978. *A Place on the Corner*. Chicago, IL: University of Chicago Press.

———. 1990. *Streetwise: Race, Class, and Change in an Urban Community*. Chicago, IL: University of Chicago Press.

Andrews, D. A., and J. Stephen Wormith. 1989. "Personality and Crime: Knowledge Destruction and Construction in Criminology." *Justice Quarterly* 6:289–309.

Arnold, Robert. 1964. "Mobilization for Youth: Patchwork or Solution?" *Dissent* 11:347–354.

Austin, James, and Barry Krisberg. 1981. "Wider, Stronger, and Different Nets: The Dialectics of Criminal Justice Reform." *Journal of Research in Crime and Delinquency* 18:165–196.

Bailey, William C. 1990. "Murder, Capital Punishment, and Television: Execution Publicity and Homicide Rates." *American Sociological Review* 55:628–633.

Bailey, William C., and Ruth D. Peterson. 1989. "Murder and Capital Punishment: A Monthly Time-Series Analysis of Execution Publicity." *American Sociological Review* 54:722–743.

Bartol, Curt R. 1995. *Criminal Behavior: A Psychosocial Approach*, 5th ed. Englewood Cliffs, NJ: Prentice Hall.

Bayley, David H. 1994. *Police for the Future*. New York: Oxford University Press.

Beccaria, Cesare Bonesana. 1963. *On Crimes and Punishments*. Indianapolis, IN: Bobbs-Merrill.

Beck, Allen J., and Bernard E. Shipley. 1989. *Recidivism of Prisoners Released in 1983*. Washington, DC: U.S. Department of Justice, Bureau of Justice Statistics.

Beck, Allen, Darrell Gillard, Lawrence Greenfeld, Caroline Harlow, Thomas Hester, Louis Jankowski, Tracy Snell, James Stephan, and Danielle Morton. 1993. *Survey of State Prison Inmates, 1991*. Washington, DC: U.S. Department of Justice, Bureau of Justice Statistics.

Becker, Gary S. 1968. "Crime and Punishment: An Economic Approach." *Journal of Political Economy* 76:169–217.

Becker, Howard S. 1963. *Outsiders: Studies in the Sociology of Deviance*. New York: Free Press.

Beckett, Katherine. 1996. "Culture and the Politics of Signification: The Case of Child Sexual Abuse." *Social Problems* 43:57–76.

Beirne, Piers. 1979. "Empiricism and the Critique of Marxism on Law and Crime." *Social Problems* 26:373–385.

Bentham, Jeremy. 1843. *An Introduction to the Principles of Morals and Legislation*. Works 1. Oxford: Clarendon Press [1907 ed.]

Berk, Richard A., Alec Campbell, Ruth Klap, and Bruce Western. 1992. "The Deterrent Effect of Arrest in Incidents of Domestic Violence: A Bayesian Analysis of Four Field Experiments." *American Sociological Review* 57:698–708.

Berk, Richard A., David Rauma, Sheldon L. Messinger, and Thomas F. Cooley. 1981. "A Test of the Stability of Punishment Hypothesis: The Case of California, 1851–1970." *American Sociological Review* 46:805–829.

Bernard, Thomas J. 1984. "Control Criticisms of Strain Theories." *Journal of Research in Crime and Delinquency* 21:373–379.

Bernard, Thomas J. 1995. "Merton versus Hirschi: Who Is Faithful to Durkheim's Heritage?" Pp. 81–90 in *The Legacy of Anomie Theory*, edited by Freda Adler and William S. Laufer. New Brunswick, NJ: Transaction.

Best, Joel. 1987. "Rhetoric in Claims-Making: Constructing the Missing Children Problem." *Social Problems* 34:101–121.

———. 1989. *Images of Issues: Typifying Contemporary Social Problems*. New York: Aldine de Gruyter.

———. 1990. *Threatened Children: Rhetoric and Concern about Child Victims*. Chicago, IL: University of Chicago Press.

Bishop, Donna M., and Charles E. Frazier. 1996. "Race Effects in Juvenile Justice Decision-Making: Findings of a Statewide Analysis." *Journal of Criminal Law and Criminology* 86:392–414.

Black, Donald J., and Albert J. Reiss Jr. 1970. "Police Control of Juveniles." *American Sociological Review* 32:699–715.

Blalock, Hubert M. 1967. *Toward a Theory of Minority-Group Relations*. New York: Wiley.

Blau, Judith R., and Peter M. Blau. 1982. "The Cost of Inequality: Metropolitan Structure and Violent Crime." *American Sociological Review* 47:114–129.

Blumer, Herbert. 1971. "Social Problems as Collective Behavior." *Social Problems* 18:298–306.

Blumstein, Alfred. 1982. "On the Racial Disproportionality of the United States Prison Population." *Journal of Criminal Law and Criminology* 73:1259–1281.

———. 1988. "Prison Populations: A System Out of Control." Pp. 231–266 in *Crime and Justice: A Review of Research*, vol. 10, edited by Michael Tonry and Norval Morris. Chicago, IL: University of Chicago Press.

Bordua, David J. 1959. "Juvenile Delinquency and Anomie: An Attempt at Replication." *Social Problems* 6:230–238.

Bowditch, Christine. 1993. "Getting Rid of Troublemakers: High School Disciplinary Procedures and the Production of Dropouts." *Social Problems* 40:493–509.

Braithwaite, John. 1981. "The Myth of Social Class and Delinquency Reconsidered." *American Sociological Review* 46:36–57.

———. 1989. *Crime, Shame, and Reintegration*. Cambridge, MA: Cambridge University Press.

———. 1995. "Reintegrative Shaming, Republicanism, and Policy." Pp. 191–205 in *Crime and Public Policy: Putting Theory to Work*, edited by Hugh D. Barlow. Boulder, CO: Westview Press.

Breault, K. D. 1986. "Suicide in America: A Test of Durkheim's Theory of Religious and Family Integration, 1933–1980." *American Journal of Sociology* 92:628–656.

Brown, Don W. 1978. "Arrest Rates and Crime Rates: When Does a Tipping Effect Occur?" *Social Forces* 57:671–682.

Brown, Waln K., Timothy P. Miller, Richard L. Jenkins, and Warren A. Rhodes. 1991. "The Human Costs of 'Giving the Kid Another

Chance.'" *International Journal of Offender Therapy and Comparative Criminology* 35:296–302.

Buikhuisen, Wouter, and P. H. Dijksterhuis. 1971. "Delinquency and Stigmatization." *British Journal of Criminology* 11, 186.

Bureau of Justice Statistics. 1990. *Justice Expenditures and Employment, 1988.* Washington, DC: U.S. Department of Justice.

Bureau of Justice Statistics. 1995. *Correctional Populations in the United States, 1994.* Washington, DC: U.S. Department of Justice.

Bureau of Justice Statistics Bulletin. 1996. *Prison and Jail Inmates at Midyear, 1996.* U.S. Department of Justice. Washington, DC: U.S. Government Printing Office.

Burgess, Ernest. 1925. "The Growth of the City." Pp. 47–62 in *The City*, edited by Robert E. Park and Ernest Burgess. Chicago, IL: University of Chicago Press.

Burgess, Robert L., and Ronald L. Akers. 1966. "A Differential Association-Reinforcement Theory of Criminal Behavior." *Social Problems* 14:128–147.

Bursik, Robert J., Jr. 1988. "Social Disorganization and Theories of Crime and Delinquency: Problems and Prospects." *Criminology* 26:519–551.

———. 1989. "Political Decisionmaking and Ecological Models of Delinquency: Conflict and Consensus." Pp. 105–117 in *Theoretical Integration in the Study of Crime and Delinquency: Problems and Prospects*, edited by Steven F. Messner, Marvin D. Krohn, and Allen E. Liska. Albany, NY: State University of New York Press.

Bursik, Robert J., Jr., and Harold G. Grasmick. 1993. *Neighborhoods and Crime: The Dimensions of Effective Community Control.* New York: Lexington Books.

Burton, Velmer S., Jr., and Francis T. Cullen. 1992. "The Empirical Status of Strain Theories." *Journal of Crime and Justice* 15:1–30.

Calavita, Kitty, and Henry N. Pontell. 1990. "'Heads I Win, Tails You Lose': Deregulation, Crime, and Crises in the Savings and Loan Industry." *Crime and Delinquency* 36:309–341.

Chambliss, William J. 1964. "A Sociological Analysis of the Law of Vagrancy." *Social Problems* 12:67–77.

———. 1969. *Crime and the Legal Process.* New York: McGraw-Hill.

Chamlin, Mitchell B. 1989. "A Macro Social Analysis of Change in Police Force Size, 1972–1982." *Sociological Quarterly* 30:615–624.

———. 1991. "A Longitudinal Analysis of the Arrest-Crime Relationship: A Further Examination of the Tipping Effect." *Justice Quarterly* 8:187–199.

Chamlin, Mitchell B., and Allen E. Liska. 1992. "Social Structure and Crime Control Revisited: The Declining Significance of Group Threat." Pp. 105–112 in *Social Threat and Social Control*, edited by Allen E. Liska. Albany, NY: SUNY Press.

Chapman, Jeffrey I., Werner Hirsch, and Sidney Sonenblum. 1975. "Crime Prevention, the Police Production Function and Budgeting." *Public Finance* 30:197–215.

Chesney-Lind, Meda. 1988. "Girls in Jail." *Crime and Delinquency* 34:150–168.

Chesney-Lind, Meda, and Randall G. Shelden. 1992. *Girls, Delinquency, and Juvenile Justice*. Pacific Grove, CA: Brooks/Cole.

Chilton, Roland J. 1964. "Continuity in Delinquency Area Research: A Comparison of Studies for Baltimore, Detroit, and Indianapolis." *American Sociological Review* 29:71–83.

Chiricos, Theodore G., and Charles Crawford. 1995. "Race and Imprisonment: A Contextual Assessment of the Evidence." Pp. 281–309 in *Ethnicity, Race and Crime*, edited by Darnell F. Hawkins. Albany, NY: SUNY Press.

Chiricos, Theodore G., and Miriam A. DeLone. 1992. "Labor Surplus and Punishment: A Review and Assessment of Theory and Evidence." *Social Problems* 39:421–446.

Cicourel, Aaron V. 1968. *The Social Organization of Juvenile Justice*. New York: Wiley.

Clark, J., and L. L. Tifft. 1966. "Polygraph and Interview Validation of Self-Reported Deviant Behavior." *American Sociological Review* 31:516–23.

Clarke, Ronald V., and Patricia M. Mayhew. 1980. *Designing Out Crime*. London, UK: HMSO.

Clarren, Sumner N., and Alfred I. Schwartz. 1976. "Measuring a Program's Impact: A Cautionary Note." Pp. 121–134 in *Sample Surveys of the Victims of Crime*, edited by Wesley G. Skogan. Cambridge, MA: Ballinger.

Clinard, Marshall, and Daniel J. Abbott. 1973. *Crime in Developing Countries*. New York: Wiley.

Clinard, Marshall B., and Peter C. Yeager. 1980. *Corporate Crime*. New York: Free Press.

Cloward, Richard, and Lloyd Ohlin. 1964. *Delinquency and Opportunity*. New York: Free Press.

Cohen, Albert K. 1955. *Delinquent Boys: The Culture of the Gang*. Glencoe, IL: Free Press.

Cohen, Bernard P. 1989. *Developing Sociological Knowledge: Theory and Method*, 2nd ed. Chicago, IL: Nelson-Hall.

Cohen, Deborah Vidaver. 1995. "Ethics and Crime in Business Firms: Organizational Culture and the Impact of Anomie." Pp. 183–206 in *The Legacy of Anomie Theory*, edited by Freda Adler and William S. Laufer. New Brunswick, NJ: Transaction.

Cohen, Lawrence E., and Kenneth C. Land. 1984. "Discrepancies between Crime Reports and Crime Surveys." *Criminology* 22:499–530.

Cohen, Lawrence E., and Marcus Felson. 1979. "Social Change and Crime

Rate Trends: A Routine Activities Approach." *American Sociological Review* 44:588–608.

Cole, Stephen. 1975. "The Growth of Scientific Knowledge." Pp. 175–220 in *The Idea of Social Structure: Papers in Honor of Robert K. Merton,* edited by Lewis A. Coser. New York: Harcourt Brace Jovanovich.

Coleman, James William. 1994. *The Criminal Elite.* New York: St. Martin's Press.

Collins, Randall. 1986. "Is 1980's Sociology in the Doldrums?" *American Journal of Sociology* 91:1336–1355.

Coltrane, Scott, and Neal Hickman. 1992. "The Rhetoric of Rights and Needs: Moral Discourse in the Reform of Child Custody and Child Support Laws." *Social Problems* 39:400–420.

Conrad, Peter, and Joseph W. Schneider. 1992. *Deviance and Medicalization: From Badness to Sickness.* Philadelphia, PA: Temple University Press.

Cook, Philip J. 1980. "Research in Criminal Deterrence: Laying the Groundwork for the Second Decade." Pp. 211–268 in *Crime and Justice: An Annual Review of Research,* vol. 2, edited by Norval Morris and Michael Tonry. Chicago, IL: University of Chicago Press.

———. 1986. "The Demand and Supply of Criminal Opportunities." Pp. 1–25 in *Crime and Justice: An Annual Review of Research,* vol. 17, edited by Michael Tonry and Norval Morris. Chicago, IL: University of Chicago Press.

Corley, Charles J., Stephen Cernkovich, and Peggy Giordano. 1989. "Sex and the Likelihood of Sanction." *Journal of Criminal Law and Criminology* 80:540–556.

Cornish, Derek B., and Ronald V. Clarke, eds. 1986. *The Reasoning Criminal: Rational Choice Perspectives on Offending.* New York: Springer-Verlag.

Crutchfield, Robert D., Michael R. Geerken, and Walter R. Gove. 1982. "Crime Rate and Social Integration: The Impact of Metropolitan Mobility." *Criminology* 20:467–478.

Cullen, Francis T. 1983. *Rethinking Crime and Deviance Theory: The Emergence of a Structuring Tradition.* Totowa, NJ: Rowman and Allanheld.

D'Alessio, Steward J., and Lisa Stolzenberg. 1995. "Unemployment and the Incarceration of Pretrial Defendants." *American Sociological Review* 60:350–359.

Dahrendorf, Ralf. 1958. "Out of Utopia: Toward a Reorientation of Sociological Analysis." *American Journal of Sociology* 64:115–127.

———. 1959. *Class and Class Conflict in Industrial Society.* Stanford, CA: Stanford University Press.

Daly, Kathleen. 1989. "Neither Conflict nor Labeling nor Paternalism Will Suffice: Intersections of Race, Ethnicity, Gender, and Family in Criminal Court Decisions." *Crime and Delinquency* 35:136–168.

———. 1994. *Gender, Crime, and Punishment.* New Haven, CT: Yale University Press.

Danigelis, Nick, and Whitney Pope. 1979. "Durkheim's Theory of Suicide As Applied to the Family: An Empirical Test." *Social Forces* 57:1081–1106.

Dannefer, Dale, and Russell K. Schutt. 1982. "Race and Juvenile Justice Processing in Court and Police Agencies." *American Journal of Sociology* 87:1113–1132.

Darwin, Charles. 1859. *On the Origin of Species by Means of Natural Selection.* London, UK: John Murray.

———. 1871. *The Descent of Man and Selection in Relation to Sex.* New York: D. Appleton Co.

Davis, Anne E., Simon Dinitz, and Benjamin Pasamanick. 1972. "The Prevention of Hospitalization in Schizophrenia: Five Years after an Experimental Program." *American Journal of Orthopsychiatry* 12:375–388.

Decker, Scott, Richard Wright, and Robert Logie. 1993. "Perceptual Deterrence among Active Burglars: A Research Note." *Criminology* 31:135–147.

Dentler, Robert A., and Kai T. Erikson. 1959. "The Functions of Deviance in Groups." *Social Problems* 7:98–102.

Dixon, Jo, Cynthia Gordon, and Tasnim Khomusi. 1995. "Sexual Symmetry in Psychiatric Diagnosis." *Social Problems* 42:429–448.

Douglas, Jack D. 1967. *The Social Meanings of Suicide.* Princeton, NJ: Princeton University Press.

———. 1971. *American Social Order.* New York: Free Press.

Durkheim, Emile. [1893] 1964. *The Division of Labor in Society.* New York: Free Press.

———. [1897] 1966. *Suicide: A Sociological Study.* New York: Free Press.

Edwards, Anne. 1988. *Regulation and Repression.* Winchester, MA: Allen and Unwin, Inc.

Elliott, Delbert S. 1985. "The Assumption That Theories Can Be Combined with Increased Explanatory Power: Theoretical Integrations." Pp. 123–149 in *Theoretical Methods in Criminology*, edited by Robert E. Meier. Beverly Hills, CA: Sage.

Elliott, Delbert S., and Suzanne S. Ageton. 1980. "Reconciling Race and Class Differences in Self-Report and Official Estimates of Delinquency." *American Sociological Review* 45:95–110.

Elliott, Delbert S., Suzanne S. Ageton, and R. J. Cantor. 1979. "An Integrated Theoretical Perspective on Delinquent Behavior." *Journal of Research in Crime and Delinquency* 16:3–27.

Elliott, Delbert S., David Huizinga, and Suzanne Ageton. 1985. *Explaining Delinquency and Drug Use.* Beverly Hills, CA: Sage.

Elliott, Delbert S., William J. Wilson, David Huizinga, Robert J. Sampson, Amanda Elliott, and Bruce Rankin. 1996. "The Effects of Neighborhood Disadvantage on Adolescent Development." *Journal of Research in Crime and Delinquency* 33:389–426.

Ellis, Lee. 1990. "Introduction: The Nature of the Biosocial Perspective." Pp. 3–17 in *Crime in Biological, Social, and Moral Contexts*, edited by Lee Ellis. New York: Praeger.

Erikson, Kai. 1966. *Wayward Puritans: A Study in the Sociology of Deviance*. New York: John Wiley and Sons.

Eysenck, Hans J. 1989. "Personality and Criminality: A Dispositional Analysis." Pp. 89–110 in *Advances in Criminological Theory*, vol. 1, edited by William S. Laufer and Freda Adler. New Brunswick, NJ: Transaction.

Farberow, Norman L., Douglas R. MacKinnon, and Franklyn L. Nelson. 1977. "Suicide: Who's Counting?" *Public Health Reports* 92:223–232.

Faris, Robert E. L. 1967. *Chicago Sociology, 1920–1932*. San Francisco, CA: Chandler.

Faris, Robert E. L., and H. Warren Dunham. 1939. *Mental Disorders in Urban Areas*. Chicago, IL: University of Chicago Press.

Farnworth, Margaret, and Michael J. Lieber. 1989. "Strain Theory Revisited: Economic Goals, Educational Means, and Delinquency." *American Sociological Review* 54:263–274.

Farr, Kathryn, and Don C. Gibbons. 1990. "Observations on the Development of Crime Categories." *International Journal of Offender Therapy and Comparative Criminology* 34:223–237.

Federal Bureau of Investigation. [various years]. *Crime in the United States*. Washington, DC: U.S. Government Printing Office.

Felson, Marcus, and Ronald V. Clarke. 1995. "Routine Precautions, Criminology, and Crime Prevention." Pp. 179–190 in *Crime and Public Policy: Putting Theory to Work*, edited by Hugh D. Barlow. Boulder, CO: Westview Press.

Fishbein, Diana H. 1990. "Biological Perspectives in Criminology." *Criminology* 28:27–72.

Foster, Jack D., Simon Dinitz, and Walter C. Reckless. 1972. "Perceptions of Stigma Following Public Intervention for Delinquent Behavior." *Social Problems* 20:202–209.

Garfinkle, Harold. 1956. "Conditions of Successful Degradation Ceremonies." *American Journal of Sociology* 61:420–424.

———. 1967. *Studies in Ethnomethodology*. Englewood Cliffs, NJ: Prentice Hall.

Galster, George C., and Laura A. Scaturo. 1985. "The U.S. Criminal Justice System: Unemployment and the Severity of Imprisonment." *Journal of Research in Crime and Delinquency* 27:163–189.

Geerken, Michael R., and Walter R. Gove. 1977. "Deterrence, Overload, and Incapacitation: An Empirical Evaluation." *Social Forces* 56:424–447.

Gibbons, Don C. and Marvin D. Krohn. 1991. *Delinquent Behavior*, 5th ed. Englewood Cliffs, NJ: Prentice Hall.

Gibbs, Jack P. 1969. "Marital Status and Suicide in the United States: A Special Test of the Status Integration Theory." *American Journal of Sociology* 74:521–533.

———. 1975. *Crime, Punishment, and Deterrence.* New York: Elsmere.

———. 1972. *Sociological Theory Construction.* Hinsdale, IL: Dryden.

Gibbs, Jack P., and Walter T. Martin. 1964. *Status Integration and Suicide: A Sociological Study.* Eugene, OR: University of Oregon Books.

Gill, Virginia Teas, and Douglas W. Maynard. 1995. "On 'Labeling' in Actual Interaction: Delivering and Receiving Diagnoses of Developmental Disabilities." *Social Problems* 42:11–37.

Goffman, Erving. 1961. *Asylums: Essays on the Social Situation of Mental Patients and Other Inmates.* Garden City, NY: Doubleday.

Goldman, Marion S. 1987. "Prostitution, Economic Exchange, and the Unconscious." Pp. 187–209 in *Advances in Psychoanalytic Sociology*, edited by J. Rabow, Gerald M. Platt, and Marion S. Goldman. Malabar, FL: Krieger.

Goldstein, Jeffrey H. 1986. *Aggression and Crimes of Violence*, 2nd ed. New York: Oxford University Press.

Goode, Erich, ed. 1996. *Social Deviance.* Boston, MA: Allyn and Bacon.

Gorman, D. M., and Helen Raskin White. 1995. "You Can Choose Your Friends, but Do They Choose Your Crime? Implications of Differential Association Theories for Crime Prevention Policies." Pp. 131–155 in *Crime and Public Policy: Putting Theory to Work*, edited by Hugh D. Barlow. Boulder, CO: Westview Press.

Gottfredson, Denise, Richard J. McNeil, and Gary D. Gottfredson. 1991. "Social Area Influences on Delinquency: A Multilevel Analysis." *Journal of Research in Crime and Delinquency* 28:197–226.

Gottfredson, Michael, and Travis Hirschi. 1990. *A General Theory of Crime.* Palo Alto, CA: Stanford University Press.

Gould, Leroy. 1969. "Who Defines Delinquency? A Comparison of Self-Reported and Officially-Reported Indexes of Delinquency for Three Racial Groups." *Social Problems* 16:325–335.

Gouldner, Alvin W. 1970. *The Coming Crisis of Western Sociology.* New York: Basic Books.

Gove, Walter R. 1982. "Labelling Theory's Explanation of Mental Illness: An Update of Recent Evidence." *Deviant Behavior* 3:307–327.

Gove, Walter R., ed. 1975. *The Labelling of Deviance: An Evaluation of a Perspective.* New York: Wiley.

Grasmick, Harold G., and Robert J. Bursik Jr. 1990. "Conscience, Significant Others, and Rational Choice: Extending the Deterrence Model." *Law and Society Review* 24:837–861.

Grasmick, Harold G., Robert J. Bursik Jr., and Bruce J. Arneklev. 1993. "Reduction in Drunk Driving as a Response to Increased Threats of Shame, Embarrassment, and Legal Sanctions." *Criminology* 31:41–67.

Grasmick, Harold G., John Hagan, Brenda Sims Blackwell, and Bruce J. Arneklev. 1996. "Risk Preferences and Patriarchy: Extending Power-Control Theory." *Social Forces* 75:177–199.

Greenberg, David F. 1977. "The Dynamics of Oscillatory Punishment Processes." *Journal of Criminal Law and Criminology* 68:643–651.

Greenberg, David F., Ronald C. Kessler, and Charles H. Logan. 1979. "A Panel Model of Crime Rates and Arrest Rates." *American Sociological Review* 44:843–850.

Greenwood, Peter W., and Allan Abrahams. 1982. *Selective Incapacitation: Report Prepared for the National Institute of Justice.* Santa Monica, CA: Rand Corporation.

Greenwood, Peter W. and Susan Turner. 1987. *Selective Incapacitation Revisited: Why the High-Rate Offenders are Hard to Predict.* Santa Monica, CA: Rand Corporation.

Hagan, John. 1974. "Extra-legal Attributes in Criminal Sentencing: An Assessment of a Sociological Viewpoint." *Law and Society Review* 8:357–383.

Hagan, John, and Kristin Bumiller. 1983. "Making Sense of Sentencing: A Review and Critique of Sentencing Research." Pp. 1–54 in *Research on Sentencing: The Search for Reform,* vol. 2, edited by Alfred Blumstein, Jacqueline Cohen, Susan E. Martin, and Michael H. Tonry. Washington, DC: National Academy Press.

Hagan, John, A. R. Gillis, and John H. Simpson. 1985. "The Class Structure of Delinquency: Toward a Power-Control Theory of Common Delinquent Behavior." *American Journal of Sociology* 90:1151–1178.

Hagan, John, A. R. Gillis, and John H. Simpson. 1990. "Clarifying and Extending Power-Control Theory." *American Journal of Sociology* 95:1024–1037.

Hagan, John, John H. Simpson, and A. R. Gillis. 1987. "Class in the Household: A Power-Control Theory of Gender and Delinquency." *American Journal of Sociology* 92:788–816.

Hall, Jerome. 1952. *Theft, Law and Society.* Indianapolis, IN: Bobbs-Merrill.

Hardt, Robert H., and Sandra Peterson-Hardt. 1977. "Self-Reporting of Delinquency." *Journal of Research in Crime and Delinquency* 14:247–261.

Harris, Anthony R. 1975. "Imprisonment and Expected Value of Criminal Choice: A Specification and Test of Aspects of the Labeling Perspective." *American Sociological Review* 40:71–87.

———. 1976. "Race, Commitment to Deviance, and Spoiled Identity." *American Sociological Review* 41:432–442.

Hawkins, Darnell F. 1987. "Beyond Anomalies: Re-thinking the Conflict Perspective on Race and Criminal Punishment." *Social Forces* 65:719–745.

Hawkins, Darnell F. 1994. "Ethnicity: The Forgotten Dimension of American Social Control". Pp. 99–116 in *Inequality, Crime, and Social Control,* edited by George S. Bridges and Martha A. Myers. Boulder, CO: Westview Press.

Hawkins, Richard, and Gary Tiedeman. 1975. *The Creation of Deviance.* Columbus, OH: Charles E. Merrill.

Hawley, Amos. 1950. *Human Ecology: A Theory of Community Structure.* New York: Ronald Press.

Heitgard, Janet L., and Robert J. Bursik Jr. 1987. "Extracommunity Dynamics and the Ecology of Delinquency." *American Journal of Sociology* 92:775–787.

Hempel, Carl. 1966. *Philosophy of Natural Science.* Englewood Cliffs, NJ: Prentice Hall.

Hilgartner, Stephen, and Charles L. Bosk. 1988. "The Rise and Fall of Social Problems: A Public Arenas Model." *American Journal of Sociology* 94:53–78.

Hindelang, Michael J. 1978. "Race and Involvement in Common Law Personal Crimes." *American Sociological Review* 43:93–109.

Hindelang, Michael J., Travis Hirschi, and Joseph G. Weis. 1981. *Measuring Delinquency.* Berkeley, CA: University of California Press.

Hirschi, Travis. 1969. *Causes of Delinquency.* Berkeley, CA: University of California Press.

———. 1979. "Separate and Unequal Is Better." *Journal of Research in Crime and Delinquency* 16:34–37.

Horney, Julie, and Ineke Haen Marshall. 1992. "Risk Perceptions among Serious Offenders: The Role of Crime and Punishment." *Criminology* 30:575–592.

Horwitz, Allan. 1977. "An Exchange of Marxian Theories of Deviance and Social Control: A Critique of Spitzer." *Social Problems* 24:362–363.

Hughes, Everett C. 1958. *Men and Their Work.* New York: Free Press.

Inciardi, James A., ed. 1991. *The Drug Legalization Debate.* Newbury Park, CA: Sage.

Jackson, Pamela I. 1989. *Minority Group Threat, Crime, and Policing.* New York: Praeger.

Jackson, Pamela I., and Leo Carroll. 1981. "Race and the War on Crime: The Sociopolitical Determinants of Municipal Expenditures in 90 Non-Southern U.S. Cities." *American Sociological Review* 46:290–305.

Jacobs, David. 1979. "Inequality and Police Strength: Conflict Theory and Coercive Control in Metropolitan Areas." *American Sociological Review* 44:913–925.

———. 1980. "Marxism and the Critique of Empiricism: A Comment on Beirne." *Social Problems* 27:467–470.

Jankovic, Ivan. 1977. "Labor Market and Imprisonment." *Crime and Social Justice* 8:17–37.

Jeffrey, C. Ray. 1990. *Criminology: An Interdisciplinary Approach*. Englewood Cliffs, NJ: Prentice Hall.

Jensen, Gary F. 1972a. "Delinquency and Adolescent Self-Conceptions: A Study of the Personal Relevance of Infraction." *Social Problems* 20:84–102.

———. 1972b. "Parents, Peers, and Delinquent Action: A Test of the Differential Association Perspective." *American Journal of Sociology* 78:562–575.

———. 1995. "Salvaging Structure through Strain: A Theoretical and Empirical Critique." Pp. 139–158 in *The Legacy of Anomie Theory*, edited by Freda Adler and William S. Laufer. New Brunswick, NJ: Transaction.

Jensen, Gary F., and David Brownfield. 1983. "Parents and Drugs: Specifying the Consequences of Attachment." *Criminology* 21:543–554.

Jensen, Gary F., and Kevin Thompson. 1990. "What's Class Got to Do with It? A Further Examination of Power-Control Theory." *American Journal of Sociology* 95:1009–1023.

Jessor, R., and S. Jessor. 1973. "The Perceived Environment in Behavioral Science: Some Conceptual Issues and Some Illustrative Data." *American Behavioral Scientist* 16:801–828.

Katz, Alfred H., and Eugene I. Bender. 1990. *Helping One Another: Self-Help Groups in a Changing World*. Oakland, CA: Third Party Publishing Co.

Katz, Jack. 1988. *The Seductions of Crime: Moral and Sensual Attractions in Doing Evil*. New York: Basic Books.

Kelly, Delos H. 1996. *Deviant Behavior: A Text-Reader in the Sociology of Deviance*, 5th ed. New York: St. Martin's Press.

Kitsuse, John I., and Malcolm Spector. 1973. "Toward a Sociology of Social Problems: Social Conditions, Value-Judgments, and Social Problems." *Social Problems* 20:407–419.

Kleck, Gary. 1981. "Racial Discrimination in Sentencing: A Critical Evaluation of the Evidence with Additional Evidence on the Death Penalty." *American Sociological Review* 43:783–805.

Klein, Malcolm W. 1976. "Issues and Realities in Police Diversion Programs." *Crime and Delinquency* 22:421–427.

Klinger, David A. 1994. "Demeanor or Crime? Why 'Hostile' Citizens Are More Likely to Be Arrested." *Criminology* 32:475–493.

Kobbervig, Wayne, James Inverarity, and Pat Lauderdale. 1982. "Deterrence and the Death Penalty: A Comment on Phillips." *American Journal of Sociology* 88:161–164.

Kobrin, Solomon. 1959. "The Chicago Area Projects—A Twenty-Five Year Assessment." *Annals of the American Academy of Political and Social Sciences* 322:20–29.

Kornhauser, Ruth R. 1978. *Social Sources of Delinquency: An Appraisal of Analytic Models*. Chicago, IL: University of Chicago Press.

Kposowa, Augustine J., K. D. Breault, and Gopal K. Singh. 1995. "White Male Suicide in the United States: A Multivariate Individual-Level Analysis." *Social Forces* 74:315–323.

Krahn, Harvey, Timothy F. Hartnagel, and John W. Gartrell. 1986. "Income Inequality and Homicide Rates: Cross-National Data and Criminological Theories." *Criminology* 24:269–295.

Lander, Bernard. 1954. *Towards an Understanding of Juvenile Delinquency.* New York: Columbia University Press.

Lea, John. 1992. "The Analysis of Crime." Pp. 69–94 in *Rethinking Criminology: The Realist Debate,* edited by Jock Young and Roger Matthews. London, UK: Sage Publications.

Lea, John, and Jock Young. 1984. *What Is to Be Done about Law and Order?* Harmondsworth, UK: Penguin.

Lehmann, Jennifer M. 1995. "Durkheim's Theory of Deviance and Suicide: A Feminist Reconsideration." *American Journal of Sociology* 4:904–930.

Lemert, Edwin M. 1951. *Social Pathology.* New York: McGraw-Hill.

———. 1967. *Human Deviance, Social Problems and Social Control.* Englewood Cliffs, NJ: Prentice Hall.

———. 1981. "Diversion in Juvenile Justice: What Hath Been Brought." *Journal of Research in Crime and Delinquency* 18:34–46.

Light, Donald W. 1982. "Learning to Label: The Social Construction of Psychiatrists. Pp. 33–47 in *Deviance and Mental Illness,* edited by Walter R. Gove. Beverly Hills, CA: Sage.

Lilly, J. Robert, Francis T. Cullen, and Richard A. Ball. 1989. *Criminological Theory: Context and Consequences.* Newbury Park, CA: Sage.

Link, Bruce G. 1987. "Understanding Labeling Effects in the Area of Mental Disorders: An Assessment of the Effects of Expectations of Rejection." *American Sociological Review* 52:96–112.

Link, Bruce G., and Francis T. Cullen. 1983. "Reconsidering the Social Rejection of Ex-Mental Patients: Levels of Attitudinal Response." *American Journal of Community Psychology* 11:261–273.

———. 1990. "The Labeling Theory of Mental Disorder: A Review of the Evidence." Pp. 75–105 in *Research in Community and Mental Health,* vol. 6, edited by James R. Greenley. Greenwich, CT: JAI Press.

Link, Bruce G., Francis T. Cullen, James Frank, and John F. Wozniak. 1987. "The Social Rejection of Former Mental Patients: Understanding Why Labels Matter." *American Journal of Sociology* 92:1461–1500.

Link, Bruce G., Francis T. Cullen, Elmer Struening, Patrick E. Shrout, and Bruce P. Dohrenwend. 1989. "A Modified Labeling Theory Approach to Mental Disorders: An Empirical Assessment." *American Sociological Review* 54:400–423.

Liska, Allen E. 1971. "Aspirations, Expectations, and Delinquency: Stress and Additive Models." *Sociological Quarterly* 12:99–107.

Liska, Allen E. 1973. "Causal Structures Underlying the Relationship between Delinquent Involvement and Delinquent Peers." *Sociology and Social Research* 58:23–26.

———. 1992. "Introduction to the Study of Social Control." Pp. 1–33 in *Social Threat and Social Control*, edited by Allen E. Liska. Albany, NY: State University of New York Press.

Liska, Allen E., and Paul E. Bellair. 1995. "Violent-Crime Rates and Racial Composition: Convergence over Time." *American Journal of Sociology* 101:578–611.

Liska, Allen E., and Mitchell B. Chamlin. 1984. "Social Structure and Crime Control among Macrosocial Units." *American Journal of Sociology* 90:383–395.

Liska, Allen E., and Mark Tausig. 1979. "Theoretical Interpretations of Social Class and Racial Differentials in Legal Decision-Making for Juveniles." *Sociological Quarterly* 20:197–207.

Liska, Allen E., and Barbara Warner. 1991. "Functions of Crime: A Paradoxical Process." *American Journal of Sociology* 96:1441–1463.

Liska, Allen E., Marvin D. Krohn, and Steven F. Messner. 1989. "Strategies and Requisites for Theoretical Integration in the Study of Crime and Deviance." Pp. 1–19 in *Theoretical Integration in the Study of Crime and Deviance*, edited by Steven F. Messner, Marvin D. Krohn, and Allen E. Liska. Albany, NY: State University of New York Press.

Liska, Allen E., Joseph J. Lawrence, and Michael Benson. 1981. "Perspectives on the Legal Order: The Capacity for Social Control." *American Journal of Sociology* 87:412–426.

Liska, Allen E., Joseph J. Lawrence, and Andrew Sanchirico. 1982. "Fear of Crime as a Social Fact." *Social Forces* 60:760–771.

Liska, Allen E., Andrew Sanchirico, and Mark Reed. 1988. "Fear of Crime and Constrained Behavior: Specifying and Estimating a Reciprocal Effects Model." *Social Forces* 66:827–837.

Little, Craig. 1995. *Deviance and Control: Theory, Research, and Policy*, 3rd ed. Itasca, IL: F. E. Peacock.

Logan, Charles H. 1972. "General Deterrence Effects of Imprisonment." *Social Forces* 51:63–72.

Lundman, Richard J. 1976. "Will Diversion Reduce Recidivism?" *Crime and Delinquency* 22:428–437.

———. 1984. *Prevention and Control of Juvenile Delinquency*. New York: Oxford University Press.

———. 1994. "Demeanor or Crime? The Midwest City Police-Citizen Encounters Study." *Criminology* 32:631–653.

Lundman, Richard J., Paul T. McFarlane, and Frank R. Scarpitti. 1976. "Delinquency Prevention: A Description and Assessment of Projects Reported in the Professional Literature." *Crime and Delinquency* 22:297–308.

Lundman, Richard J., Richard J. Sykes, and John P. Clark. 1978. "Police Control of Juveniles: A Replication." *Journal of Research in Crime and Delinquency*. 15:74–91.

Lynch, Michael J., and W. Byron Groves. 1986. *A Primer in Radical Criminology*. New York: Harrow and Heston.

McCord, William, and Joan McCord. 1960. *Origins of Alcoholism*. Stanford, CT: Stanford University Press.

McCormick, Albert E., Jr. 1977. "Rule Enforcement and Moral Indignation: Some Observations on the Effects of Criminal Antitrust Convictions upon Societal Reaction Processes." *Social Problems* 25:30–39.

Maguire, Kathleen, and Ann L. Pastore, eds. 1995. *Sourcebook of Criminal Justice Statistics 1994*. U.S. Department of Justice, Bureau of Justice Statistics. Washington, DC: USGPO.

———. 1996. *Sourcebook of Criminal Justice Statistics 1995*. U.S. Department of Justice, Bureau of Justice Statistics. Washington, DC: USGPO.

Makkai, Toni, and John Braithwaite. 1994. "Reintegrative Shaming and Compliance with Regulatory Standards." *Criminology* 32:361–383.

Manderscheid, R. W., and M. A. Sonnerschein. 1994. *Mental Health, United States, 1992*. Rockville, MD: Center for Mental Health Services.

Mankoff, Milton. 1971. "Societal Reaction and Career Deviance: A Critical Analysis." *Sociological Quarterly* 12:204–218.

Marvell, Thomas B., and Carlisle E. Moody. 1996. "Specification Problems, Police Levels, and Crime Rates." *Criminology* 34:609–646.

Marx, Karl. 1964. *Selected Writings in Sociology and Social Philosophy*, edited by T. B. Bottomore and M. Rubel. New York: McGraw-Hill.

Matsueda, Ross L. 1982. "Testing Control Theory and Differential Association." *American Sociological Review* 47:489–504.

———. 1989. "The Dynamics of Moral Beliefs and Minor Deviance." *Social Forces* 68:428–457.

Matsueda, Ross L., and Karen Heimer. 1987. "Race, Family Structure, and Delinquency: A Test of Differential Association and Social Control Theories." *American Sociological Review* 52:826–840.

Matthews, Victor M. 1968. "Differential Identification: An Empirical Note." *Social Problems* 15:376–383.

Matza, David. 1964. *Delinquency and Drift*. New York: Wiley.

———. 1969. *Becoming Deviant*. Englewood Cliffs, NJ: Prentice Hall.

Mechanic, David. 1969. *Mental Health and Social Policy*. Englewood Cliffs, NJ: Prentice Hall.

Menard, Scott. 1995. "A Developmental Test of Mertonian Anomie Theory." *Journal of Research in Crime and Delinquency* 32:136–174.

Merton, Robert K. 1938. "Social Structure and Anomie." *American Sociological Review* 3:672–682.

Merton, Robert K. 1968. *Social Theory and Social Structure*. New York: Free Press.

———. 1971. "Epilogue: Social Problems and Sociological Theory." Pp. 793–845 in *Contemporary Social Problems*, 3rd ed., edited by Robert K. Merton and Robert Nisbet. New York: Harcourt Brace Jovanovich.

Messner, Steven F. 1988. "Merton's 'Social Structure and Anomie': The Road Not Taken." *Deviant Behavior* 9:33–53.

Messner, Steven F., and Judith R. Blau. 1987. "Routine Leisure Activities and Rates of Crime: A Macro-Level Analysis." *Social Forces* 65:1035–1052.

Messner, Steven F., and Reid M. Golden. 1992. "Racial Inequality and Racially Disaggregated Homicide Rates: An Assessment of Alternative Theoretical Explanations." *Criminology* 30:421–447.

Messner, Steven F., and Richard Rosenfeld. 1997. *Crime and the American Dream*, 2nd ed. Belmont, CA: Wadsworth.

Messner, Steven F., and Kenneth Tardiff. 1986. "Economic Inequality and Levels of Homicide: An Analysis of Urban Neighborhoods." *Criminology* 24:297–317.

Messner, Steven F., Marvin D. Krohn, and Allen E. Liska, eds. 1989. *Theoretical Integration in the Study of Crime and Delinquency: Problems and Prospects*. Albany, NY: State University of New York Press.

Michalowski, Raymond J., and Ronald C. Kramer. 1987. "The Space between Laws: The Problem of Corporate Crime in a Transnational Context." *Social Problems* 34:34–53.

Minor, W. William, and Joseph Harry. 1982. "Deterrent and Experiential Effects in Perceptual Research: A Replication and Extension." *Journal of Research in Crime and Delinquency* 19:190–203.

Mittelman, James H., ed. 1996. *Globalization: Critical Reflections*. Boulder, CO: Lynne Rienner Publishers.

Morrissey, Joseph P. 1982. "Deinstitutionalizing the Mentally Ill: Process, Outcomes, and New Directions." Pp. 147–176 in *Deviance and Mental Illness*, edited by Walter R. Gove. Beverly Hills, CA: Sage.

Morrissey, Joseph P., M. J. Witkin, and H. E. Bethel. 1986. *Trends by State in the Capacity and Volume of Inpatient Services, State and County Mental Hospitals, U.S., 1976–1980*. Rockville, MD: Center for Mental Health Services.

Myers, Martha A. 1987. *The Social Contexts of Criminal Sentencing*. New York: Springer-Verlag.

———. 1995. "Gender and Southern Punishment after the Civil War." *Criminology* 33:17–46.

Myers, Martha A., and Susette Talarico. 1986. "Urban Justice, Rural Injustice: Urbanization and Its Effect on Sentencing." *Criminology* 24:367-391.

Nagin, Daniel S., and Raymond Paternoster. 1994. "Personal Capital and Social Control: The Deterrence Implications of a Theory of Individual Differences in Criminal Offending." *Criminology* 32:581–606.

Nye, F. Ivan. 1958. *Family Relationships and Delinquent Behavior*. New York: Wiley.

O'Brien, Robert M. 1995. "Crime and Victimization Data." Pp. 57–81 in *Criminology: A Contemporary Handbook*, edited by Joseph F. Sheley. Belmont, CA: Wadsworth.

Osgood, D. Wayne, and Hart F. Weichselbaum. 1984. "Juvenile Diversion: Where Practice Mistakes Theory." *Journal of Research in Crime and Delinquency* 21:35–56.

Parsons, Talcott. 1970. "Equality and Inequality in Modern Society, or Social Stratification Revisited." Pp. 13–72 in *Social Stratification: Research and Theory for the 1970s*, edited by Edward O. Laumann. Indianapolis, IN: Bobbs–Merrill Company.

Pasamanick, Benjamin, Frank R. Scarpetti, and Simon Dinitz. 1967. *Schizophrenics in the Community: An Experimental Study in the Prevention of Hospitalization*. New York: Meredith.

Passas, Nikos. 1990. "Anomie and Corporate Deviance." *Contemporary Crises* 14:157–178.

Paternoster, Raymond. 1987. "The Deterrent Effect of Perceived Severity of Punishment: A Review of the Evidence and Issues." *Justice Quarterly* 4:173–217.

Paternoster, Raymond, and Leeann Iovanni. 1989. "The Labeling Perspective and Delinquency: An Elaboration of the Theory and an Assessment of the Evidence." *Justice Quarterly* 6:359–394.

Pearson, Frank S., and Neil Alan Weiner. 1985. "Toward an Integration of Criminological Theories." *Criminology* 76:116–150.

Peoples, Faith, and Rolf Loeber. 1994. "Do Individual Factors and Neighborhood Context Explain Ethnic Differences in Juvenile Delinquency?" *Journal of Quantitative Criminology* 10:141–157.

Pescosolido, Bernice A., and Robert Mendelsohn. 1986. "Social Causation or Social Construction of Suicide? An Investigation into the Social Organization of Official Rates." *American Sociological Review* 51:80–101.

Pescosolido, Bernice A., and Sharon Georgianna. 1989. "Durkheim, Suicide, and Religion: Toward a Network Theory of Suicide." *American Sociological Review* 54:33–48.

Petersilia, Joan, and Peter W. Greenwood. 1978. "Mandatory Prison Sentences: Their Projected Effects on Crime and Prison Populations." *Journal of Criminal Law and Criminology* 69:604–615.

Peyrot, Mark. 1995. "Psychological Testing and Forensic Decision Making: The Properties-in-Use of the MMPI." *Social Problems* 42:574–586.

Pfohl, Stephen J. 1985. *Images of Deviance and Social Control: A Sociological History*. New York: McGraw-Hill.

Phillips, David P. 1980. "The Deterrent Effect of Capital Punishment: New Evidence on an Old Controversy." *American Journal of Sociology* 86:139–148.

———. 1982a. "The Fluctuation of Homicide after Publicized Executions: Reply to Kobbervig, Inverarity, and Lauderdale." *American Journal of Sociology* 88:165–167.

———. 1982b. "Deterrence and the Death Penalty: A Reply to Zeisel." *American Journal of Sociology* 88:170–172.

Phillips, Derek. 1963. "Rejection: A Possible Consequence of Seeking Help for Mental Disorders." *American Sociological Review* 28:963–972.

Piliavin, Irving, and Scott Briar. 1964. "Police Encounters with Juveniles." *American Journal of Sociology* 70:206–214.

Piliavin, Irving, Rosemary Gartner, Craig Thornton, and Ross L. Matsueda. 1986. "Crime, Deterrence, and Rational Choice." *American Sociological Review* 51:101–119.

Piven, Frances Fox, and Richard A. Cloward. 1971. *Regulating the Poor: The Functions of Public Welfare*. New York: Vintage Books.

Pope, Whitney. 1976. *Durkheim's Suicide: A Classic Reanalyzed*. Chicago, IL: University of Chicago Press.

Poppel, Frans van, and Lincoln H. Day. 1996. "A Test of Durkheim's Theory of Suicide—Without Committing the 'Ecological Fallacy.'" *American Sociological Review* 61:500–507.

Quinney, Richard. 1970. *The Social Reality of Crime*. Boston, MA: Little, Brown.

———. 1974. *Critique of Legal Order*. Boston, MA: Little, Brown.

———. 1975. *Analysis and Critique of Crime in America*. Boston MA: Little, Brown.

———. 1977. *Class, State, and Crime*. New York: David McKay.

Rafter, Nicole Hahan. 1992a. "Claims-Making and Socio-Cultural Context in the First U.S. Eugenics Campaign." *Social Problems* 39:17–34.

———. 1992b. "Criminal Anthropology in the United States." *Criminology* 30:525–545.

Reckless, Walter C. 1961. "A New Theory of Delinquency and Crime." *Federal Probation* 25:42–46.

Reckless, Walter C., and Simon Dinitz. 1967. "Pioneering with Self-Concept as a Vulnerability Factor in Delinquency." *Journal of Criminal Law, Criminology, and Police Science* 58:515–523.

Reiss, Albert J., Jr. 1951. "Delinquency as the Failure of Personal and Social Controls." *American Sociological Review* 16:196–207.

Reiss, Albert J., and Lewis Rhodes. 1964. "An Empirical Test of Differential Association Theory." *Journal of Research in Crime and Delinquency* 1:5–18.

Reissman, Frank, and David Carroll. 1995. *Redefining Self-Help: Policy and Practice*. San Francisco, CA: Jossey-Bass.

Roncek, Dennis W., and Pamela A. Maier. 1991. "Bars, Blocks, and Crime Rates Revisited: Linking the Theory of Routine Activities to the Empiricism of 'Hot Spots.'" *Criminology* 29:725–753.

Rosenfeld, Richard, and Steven F. Messner. 1991. "The Social Sources of Homicide in Different Types of Societies." *Sociological Forum* 6:51–70.

Rosenhan, David L. 1973. "On Being Sane in Insane Places." *Science* 179:250–258.

Ross, H. Laurence. 1984. "Social Control through Deterrence: Drinking and Driving Laws." Pp. 21–35 in *Annual Review of Sociology*, vol. 10, edited by Ralph H. Turner and James F. Short. Palo Alto, CA: Annual Review.

———. 1992. *Confronting Drunk Driving: Social Policy for Saving Lives*. New Haven, CT: Yale University Press.

Rossi, Pater H., Emily Waite, Christine E. Bose, and Richard E. Berk. 1974. "The Seriousness of Crimes: Normative Structure and Individual Differences." *American Sociological Review* 39:224–237.

Rowe, David C., and D. Wayne Osgood. 1984. "Heredity and Sociological Theories of Delinquency: A Reconsideration." *American Sociological Review* 49:526–540.

Rubin, Paul H. 1978. "The Economics of Crime." *Atlantic Economic Review* 28:38–43.

Rusche, Georg, and Otto Kirchheimer. 1939. *Punishment and Social Structure*. New York: Russell and Russell.

Sacks, Harvey. 1972. "An Initial Investigation of Usability of Conversational Data for Doing Sociology." Pp. 31–74 in *Studies in Social Interaction*, edited by David Sudnow. New York: Free Press.

Saltzman, Linda, Raymond Paternoster, Gordon P. Waldo, and Theodore G. Chiricos. 1982. "Deterrent and Experiential Effects: The Problem of Causal Order in Perceptual Deterrence Research." *Journal of Research in Crime and Delinquency* 19:172–189.

Sampson, Robert J. 1986a. "Effects of Socioeconomic Context on Official Reaction to Juvenile Delinquency." *American Sociological Review* 51:876–885.

———. 1986b. "Crime in Cities: The Effects of Formal and Informal Social Control." Pp. 271–311 in *Communities and Crime*, edited by Albert J. Reiss Jr. and Michael Tonry. Chicago, IL: University of Chicago Press.

Sampson, Robert J., and W. Byron Groves. 1989. "Community Structure and Crime: Testing Social-Disorganization Theory." *American Journal of Sociology* 94:774–802.

Sampson, Robert J., and John H. Laub. 1993. *Crime in the Making: Pathways and Turning Points through Life*. Cambridge, MA: Harvard University Press.

Sandstrom, Kent L. 1990. "Confronting Deadly Disease: The Drama of

Identity Construction among Gay Men with Aids." *Journal of Contemporary Ethnography* 19:271–294.

Scheff, Thomas J. 1964. "The Societal Reaction to Deviance: Ascriptive Elements in the Psychiatric Screening of Mental Patients in a Midwestern State." *Social Problems* 11:401–413.

———. 1984. *Being Mentally Ill.* Chicago, IL: Aldine.

Schlossman, Steven, Gail Zellman, and Richard Shavelson, with Michael Sedlak and Jane Cobb. 1984. *Delinquency Prevention in South Chicago: A Fifty-Year Assessment of the Chicago Area Project.* Santa Monica, CA: Rand.

Schneider, Joseph W. 1985. "Social Problems Theory: The Constructionist View." *Annual Review of Sociology* 11:209–229.

Schur, Edwin M. 1971. *Labeling Deviant Behavior.* New York: Harper and Row.

———. 1973. *Radical Non-Intervention: Rethinking the Delinquency Problem.* Englewood Cliffs, NJ: Prentice Hall.

———. 1979. *Interpreting Deviance: A Sociological Introduction.* New York: Harper and Row.

Schur, Edwin M., and Hugo Adam Bedau. 1974. *Victimless Crimes: Two Sides of a Controversy.* Englewood Cliffs, NJ: Prentice Hall.

Schutz, Alfred. 1966. *Collected Papers III: Studies in Phenomenological Philosophy,* edited by I. Schutz. The Hague: Martins Nijhoff.

Schwartz, Barry. 1994. *The Costs of Living: How Market Freedom Erodes the Best Things in Life.* New York: W. W. Norton.

Schwartz, Richard D., and Jerome H. Skolnick. 1962. "Two Studies of Legal Stigma." *Social Problems* 10:133–143.

Scott, Marvin B., and Stanford M. Lyman. 1968. "Accounts." *American Sociological Review* 33:46–62.

Scully, Diana, and Joseph Marolla. 1984. "Convicted Rapists' Vocabulary of Motives: Excuses and Justifications." *Social Problems* 31:530–544.

Sellin, Thorsten. 1938. *Cultural Conflict and Crime.* New York: Social Science Research Council.

———. 1955. *The Royal Commission on Capital Punishment, 1949–53.* Report of the Great Britain Parliament. London, UK: HMSO.

———. 1961. "Capital Punishment." *Federal Probation* 25:3–11.

Shah, Saleem A., and Loren H. Roth. 1974. "Biological and Physiological Factors in Criminology." Pp. 101–174 in *Handbook of Criminology,* edited by Daniel Glaser. Chicago: Rand McNally.

Shaw, Clifford R. 1930. *The Jack-Roller: A Delinquent Boy's Own Story.* Chicago, IL: University of Chicago Press.

———. 1931. *The Natural History of a Delinquent Career.* Chicago, IL: University of Chicago Press.

Shaw, Clifford R., and Henry D. McKay. 1931. *Social Factors in Delinquency.* Chicago, IL: University of Chicago Press.

———. 1942. *Juvenile Delinquency in Urban Areas.* Chicago, IL: University of Chicago Press.

Shaw, Clifford R., Henry D. McKay, and James F. McDonald. 1938. *Brothers in Crime*. Chicago, IL: University of Chicago Press.

Shaw, Clifford R., Frederick M. Zorbaugh, Henry D. McKay, and Leonard S. Cottrell. 1929. *Delinquency Areas*. Chicago, IL: University of Chicago Press.

Shelley, Louise I. 1981. *Crime and Modernization: The Impact of Industrialization and Urbanization on Crime*. Carbondale and Edwardsville, IL: Southern Illinois University Press.

Sherman, Lawrence W., and Richard A. Berk. 1984. "Deterrence Effects of Arrest for Domestic Assault." *American Sociological Review* 49:261–271.

Sherman, Lawrence W., Janell D. Schmidt, Dennis P. Rogan, Patrick R. Gartin, Ellen G. Cohn, Dean J. Collins, and Anthony R. Bacich. 1991. "From Initial Deterrence to Long-Term Escalation: Short-Custody Arrest for Poverty Ghetto Domestic Violence." *Criminology* 29:821–849.

Shields, Rob. 1996. "Introduction: Virtual Spaces, Real Histories and Living Bodies." Pp. 1–10 in *Cultures of Internet: Virtual Spaces, Real Histories and Living Bodies*, edited by Rob Shields. London: Sage Publications Ltd.

Shihadeh, Edward S., and Nicole Flynn. 1996. "Segregation and Crime: The Effect of Black Social Isolation on the Rates of Black Urban Violence." *Social Forces* 74:1325–1353.

Short, James F. 1957. "Differential Association and Delinquency." *Social Problems* 4:233–239.

———. 1958. "Differential Associations with Delinquent Friends and Delinquent Behavior." *Pacific Sociological Review* 1:20–25.

Siegel, Larry J. 1995. *Criminology*, 5th ed. Minneapolis/St. Paul, MN: West Publishing Co.

Simpson, Miles E., and George H. Conklin. 1989. "Socioeconomic Development, Suicide, and Religion: A Test of Durkheim's Theory of Religion and Suicide." *Social Forces* 67:945–964.

Skogan, Wesley G. 1990. *Disorder and Decline: Crime and the Spiral of Decay in American Neighborhoods*. Berkeley, CA: University of California Press.

Smith, Douglas A., and Raymond Paternoster. 1990. "Formal Processing and Future Delinquency: Deviance Amplification as Selection Artifact." *Law and Society Review* 24:1109–1131.

Spitzer, Steven. 1975. "Towards a Marxism Theory of Deviance." *Social Problems* 22:638–651.

Stack, Steven. 1980. "The Effects of Marital Dissolution on Suicide." *Journal of Marriage and the Family* 42:83–92.

———. 1987. "Publicized Executions and Homicide, 1950–1980." *American Sociological Review* 52:532–540.

Stafford, Mark C., and Jack P. Gibbs. 1985. "A Major Problem with the Theory of Status Integration and Suicide." *Social Forces* 63:643–661.

———. 1988. "Change in the Relation between Marital Integration and Suicide Rates." *Social Forces* 66:1060–1079.

Stanfield, Robert. 1966. "The Interaction of Family Variables and Gang Variables in the Aetiology of Delinquency." *Social Problems* 13:411–417.

Stark, Rodney. 1987. "Deviant Places: A Theory of the Ecology of Crime." *Criminology* 25:893–909.

Steffensmeier, Darrell, John Kramer, and Cathy Streifel. 1993. "Gender and Imprisonment Decisions." *Criminology* 31:411–446.

Stinchombe, Arthur. 1968. *Constructing Social Theories.* New York: Harcourt, Brace and World.

Sutherland, Edwin. 1939. *Criminology.* Philadelphia, PA: Lippincott.

Sutherland, Edwin, and Donald Cressey. 1970. *Principles of Criminology.* New York: Lippincott.

Sykes, Gresham M., and David Matza. 1957. "Techniques of Neutralization: A Theory of Delinquency." *American Sociological Review* 22:664–670.

Szasz, Thomas S. 1960. "The Myth of Mental Illness." *American Psychologist* 15:113–118.

———. 1970. *Ideology and Insanity: Essays on the Psychiatric Dehumanization of Man.* Garden City, NY: Anchor Books.

Taylor, Ian, Paul Walton, and Jock Young. 1973. *The New Criminology.* New York: Harper and Row.

Tedeschi, James T., and Richard B. Felson. 1994. *Violence, Aggression, and Coercive Action.* Washington, DC: American Psychological Association.

Thoits, Peggy A. 1985. "Self-Labeling Processes in Mental Illness: The Role of Emotional Deviance." *American Journal of Sociology* 91:221–249.

Thornberry, Terence P. 1973. "Race, Socio-Economic Status and Sentencing in the Juvenile Justice System." *Journal of Criminal Law, Criminology and Police Science* 64:90–98.

Tittle, Charles R. 1975. "Deterrents or Labeling?" *Social Forces* 53:399–410.

Tittle, Charles R., and Allan R. Rowe. 1974. "Certainty of Arrest and Crime Rates: A Further Test of the Deterrence Hypothesis." *Social Forces* 52:455–462.

Toby, Jackson. 1957. "Social Disorganization and Stake in Conformity: Complementary Factors in the Predatory Behavior of Hoodlums." *Journal of Criminal Law, Criminology, and Police Science* 48:12–17.

Tolnay, Stewart E., and E. M. Beck. 1995. *A Festival of Violence.* Urbana, IL: University Illinois Press.

Tonry, Michael. 1995. *Malign Neglect—Race, Crime and Punishment in America.* New York: Oxford University Press.

Townsend, J. Marshall. 1976. "Self-Concept and the Institutionalization of Mental Patients: An Overview and Critique." *Journal of Health and Social Behavior* 17:263–271.

Troyer, Ronald J. 1992. "Some Consequences of Contextual Constructionism." *Social Problems* 39:35–37.

Turk, Austin T. 1969. *Criminality and Legal Order*. Chicago, IL: Rand McNally.

Turner, Jonathan H. 1978. *The Structure of Sociological Theory*, rev. ed. Homewood, IL: Dorsey Press.

Turner, Jonathan H., ed. 1989. *Theory Building in Sociology: Assessing Theoretical Cumulation*. Newbury Park, CA: Sage.

Van den Haag, Ernest. 1975. *Punishing Criminals: Concerning a Very Old and Painful Question*. New York: Basic Books.

Van Dine, Stephan, John P. Conrad, and Simon Dinitz. 1977. "The Incapacitation of the Dangerous Offender: A Statistical Experiment." *Journal of Research in Crime and Delinquency* 14:22–35.

———. 1978. "Response to Our Critics." *Journal of Research in Crime and Delinquency* 15:135–139.

Van Poppel, Frans, and Lincoln H. Day. 1996. "A Test of Durkheim's Theory of Suicide—Without Committing the Ecological Fallacy." *American Sociological Review* 61:500–507.

Vaughn, Diane. 1983. *Controlling Unlawful Organizational Behavior: Social Structure and Corporate Misconduct*. Chicago, IL: University of Chicago Press.

Voas, Robert B., and John H. Lacey. 1990. "Drunk Driving Enforcement, Adjudication, and Sanctions in the United States." Pp. 116–158 in *Drinking and Driving: Advances in Prevention and Research*, edited by R. Jean Wilson and Robert E. Mann. New York: Guilford Press.

Vold, George B. 1958. *Theoretical Criminology*. New York: Oxford University Press.

Voss, Harwin. 1964. "Differential Association and Delinquent Behavior." *Social Problems* 12:78–85.

Wagner, David, and Joseph Berger. 1985. "Do Sociological Theories Grow?" *American Journal of Sociology* 90:697–728.

Walters, Glenn D. 1992. "A Meta-Analysis of the Gene-Crime Relationship." *Criminology* 30:595–613.

Warner, Barbara, and Glenn L. Pierce. 1993. "Reexamining Social Disorganization Theory Using Calls to the Police as a Measure of Crime." *Criminology* 31:493–517.

Warr, Mark, and Mark Stafford. 1991. "The Influence of Delinquent Peers: What They Think or What They Do?" *Criminology* 29:851–866.

Waters, Malcolm. 1995. *Globalization*. London, UK: Routledge.

Wegner, Eldon L. 1990. "Deinstitutionalization and Community-Based Care for the Chronically Mentally Ill." Pp. 295–324 in *Research in Community and Mental Health*, vol. 6, edited by James R. Greenley. Greenwich, CT: JAI Press.

Weinberg, S. Kirson. 1976. "Shaw-McKay Theories of Delinquency in

Cross-Cultural Context." Pp. 167–185 in *Delinquency, Crime and Society*, edited by James F. Short Jr. Chicago, IL: University of Chicago Press.

Weinstein, Raymond M. 1990. "Mental Hospitals and the Institutionalization of Patients." Pp. 273–294 in *Research in Community and Mental Health*, vol. 6, edited by James R. Greenley. Greenwich, CT: JAI Press.

Williams, Kirk R., and Richard Hawkins. 1986. "Perceptual Research on General Deterrence: A Critical Review." *Law and Society Review*. 20:545-572.

———. 1989. "The Meaning of Arrest for Wife Assault." *Criminology* 27:163–181.

Wilson, James Q. 1975. *Thinking About Crime*. New York: Basic Books.

Wilson, James Q., and Richard J. Herrnstein. 1985. *Crime and Human Nature*. New York: Simon and Schuster.

Wilson, William J. 1987. *The Truly Disadvantaged: The Inner City, the Underclass, and Public Policy*. Chicago, IL: University of Chicago Press.

Winfree, L. Thomas, and Howard Abadinsky. 1996. *Understanding Crime: Theory and Practice*. Chicago, IL: Nelson-Hall.

Wing, J. K. 1962. "Institutionalism in Mental Hospitals." *British Journal of Social and Clinical Psychology* 1:38–51.

Wirth, Louis. 1938. "Urbanism as a Way of Life." *American Journal of Sociology* 40:1–24.

Witkin, Herman A., Sarnoff A. Mednick, Fini Schulsinger, Eskild Bakkestrom, Karl O. Christiansen, Donald R. Goodenough, Kurt Hirschhorn, Clause Lundsteen, David R. Owne, John Phillip, Donald B. Rubin, and Martha Stocking. 1977. "XYY and XXY Men: Criminality and Aggression." Pp. 165–187 in *Biosocial Bases of Criminal Behavior*, edited by Sarnoff Mednick and Karl O. Christiansen. New York: Gardner Press.

Wolfgang, Marvin D. 1960. "Cesare Lombroso." Pp. 232–291 in *Pioneers in Criminology*, edited by Herman Mannheim. Chicago, IL: Quadrangle Books.

Wolfgang, Marvin D., R. M. Figlio, P. E. Tracy, and S. I. Singer. 1985. *The National Survey of Crime Severity*. Washington, DC: U.S. Department of Justice.

Woolgar, Steve, and Dorothy Pawluch. 1985. "Ontological Gerrymandering: The Anatomy of Social Problems Explanations." *Social Problems* 32:214–227.

Yeager, Mathew G. 1979. "Unemployment and Imprisonment." *Journal of Criminal Law and Criminology* 70:586–588.

Young, Jock. 1987. "The Tasks Facing a Realist Criminology." *Contemporary Crises* 11:337–356.

Yu, Jiang, and Allen E. Liska. 1993. "The Certainty of Punishment: A Reference Group Effect and Its Functional Form." *Criminology* 31:447–464.

Zeisel, Hans. 1982. "Comment on the Deterrent Effect of Capital Punishment." *American Journal of Sociology* 88:167–169.

Zhang, Lening, and Steven F. Messner. 1994. "The Severity of Official Punishment for Delinquency and Change in Interpersonal Relations in Chinese Society." *Journal of Research in Crime and Delinquency* 31:416–433.

Zhang, Lening, Dengke Zhou, Steven F. Messner, Allen E. Liska, Marvin D. Krohn, Jianhong Liu, and Zhou Lu. 1996. "Crime Prevention in a Communitarian Society: Bang-jiao and Tiao-jie in the People's Republic of China." *Justice Quarterly* 13:199–222.

Zimmerman, Don H. 1978. "Ethnomethodology." *American Sociologist* 13:6–14.

Zimring, Franklin E., and Gordon J. Hawkins. 1973. *Deterrence.* Chicago, IL: University of Chicago Press.

———. 1995. *Incapacitation.* New York: Oxford University Press.

INDEX

NAME INDEX

Abadinsky, Howard, 81
Abbott, Daniel J., 69
Adler, Freda, 35, 36
Adler, Jeffrey S., 192
Ageton, Suzanne S., 23, 128
Agnew, Robert, 36–37, 76
Akers, Ronald L., 63–64, 73, 214, 220, 222
Anderson, Elijah, 61, 159
Andrews, D. A., 13
Arnold, Robert, 50
Austin, James, 140

Bailey, William C., 97
Bartol, Curt R., 7, 8, 9, 12
Bayley, David H., 112
Beccaria, Cesare Bonesana, 88
Beck, Allen J., 129
Beck, E. M., 196
Becker, Howard S., 14, 118, 119, 120, 124, 143
Beckett, Katherine, 172–74
Bedau, Hugo Adam, 138
Beirne, Piers, 183, 185, 207
Bellair, Paul E., 48
Bender, Eugene I., 83
Bentham, Jeremy, 88
Berger, Joseph, 223
Berk, Richard A., 130–31, 195–96
Bernard, Thomas J., 36, 52
Best, Joel, 18, 155, 170–71, 174
Bishop, Donna M., 202
Black, Donald J., 159
Blalock, Hubert M., 186, 187, 188
Blau, Judith R., 45–46, 69, 71

Blau, Peter M., 45–46, 69
Blumer, Herbert, 154
Blumstein, Alfred, 105, 201
Bordua, David J., 69
Bosk, Charles L., 155–56
Bowditch, Christine, 127
Braithwaite, John, 23, 123–24, 132
Breault, K. D., 41
Briar, Scott, 157–58, 159
Brown, Don W., 93
Brown, Waln K., 130
Brownfield, David, 215
Buikhuisen, Wouter, 126–27
Bumiller, Kristin, 200
Burgess, Ernest, 56–58, 83
Burgess, Robert L., 63, 220
Bursik, Robert J., Jr., 60, 70, 80, 83, 84, 88
Burton, Velmer S., Jr., 36, 44
Bush, George, 213

Calavita, Kitty, 208
Carroll, David, 83
Carroll, Leo, 196
Carter, Jimmy, 204–5
Chambliss, William J., 191–92, 199
Chamlin, Mitchell B., 93, 197–98
Chapman, Jeffrey I., 104
Chesney-Lind, Meda, 188, 202
Chilton, Roland J., 69
Chiricos, Theodore G., 196, 200–201
Cicourel, Aaron V., 18, 157–58
Clarren, Sumner N., 21
Clark, J., 23
Clarke, Ronald V., 81, 86, 89

Subject Index

—O—